JN077482

KYOTO AREA STUDIES ON ASIA

CENTER FOR SOUTHEAST ASIAN STUDIES, KYOTO UNIVERSITY

VOLUME 26

Conceptualizing the Malay World

KYOTO AREA STUDIES ON ASIA

CENTER FOR SOUTHEAST ASIAN STUDIES, KYOTO UNIVERSITY

KYOTO AREA STUDIES ON ASIA

CENTER FOR SOUTHEAST ASIAN STUDIES, KYOTO UNIVERSITY

KYOTO AREA STUDIES ON ASIA

CENTER FOR SOUTHEAST ASIAN STUDIES, KYOTO UNIVERSITY

VOLUME 26

Conceptualizing the Malay World

Colonialism and Pan-Malay Identity in Malaya

By

SODA Naoki

Kyoto University Press

First published in 2020 jointly by:

Kyoto University Press
69 Yoshida Konoe-cho
Sakyo-ku, Kyoto 606-8315, Japan
Telephone: +81-75-761-6182
Fax: +81-75-761-6190
Email: sales@kyoto-up.or.jp
Web: http://www.kyoto-up.or.jp

Trans Pacific Press
PO Box 164, Balwyn North
Victoria 3104, Australia
Telephone: +61-(0)3-9859-1112
Fax: +61-(0)3-8611-7989
Email: tpp.mail@gmail.com
Web: http://www.transpacificpress.com

Edited by Karl Smith, Melbourne, Australia.
Designed and set by Sarah Tuke, Melbourne, Australia.

Distributors

Australia and New Zealand
James Bennett Pty Ltd
Locked Bag 537
Frenchs Forest NSW 2086
Australia
Telephone: +61-(0)2-8988-5000
Fax: +61-(0)2-8988-5031
Email: info@bennett.com.au
Web: www.bennett.com.au

USA and Canada
Independent Publishers Group (IPG)
814 N. Franklin Street
Chicago, IL 60610
USA
Telephone inquiries: +1-312-337-0747
Order placement: 800-888-4741
  (domestic only)
Fax: +1-312-337-5985
Email: frontdesk@ipgbook.com
Web: http://www.ipgbook.com

Asia and the Pacific (except Japan)
Kinokuniya Company Ltd.
Head office:
3-7-10 Shimomeguro
Meguro-ku
Tokyo 153-8504
Japan
Telephone: +81-(0)3-6910-0531
Fax: +81-(0)3-6420-1362
Email: bkimp@kinokuniya.co.jp
Web: www.kinokuniya.co.jp
Asia-Pacific office:
Kinokuniya Book Stores of Singapore
Pte., Ltd.
391B Orchard Road #13-06/07/08
Ngee Ann City Tower B
Singapore 238874
Telephone: +65-6276-5558
Fax: +65-6276-5570
Email: SSO@kinokuniya.co.jp

ISSN   1445–9663 (Kyoto Area Studies on Asia)
ISBN   978–1–925608–37–0

About the Author

SODA Naoki is Professor at the Institute of Global Studies, Tokyo University of Foreign Studies. He received his doctorate in area studies from Kyoto University. His research interests are modern Southeast Asian history and Malaysian history and politics.

Contents

Tables

Photos

Abbreviations

AMCJA   All-Malaya Council of Joint Action
API   Angkatan Pemuda Insaf (Movement of Aware Youth)
APM   Akademi Pengajian Melayu (Academy of Malay Studies)
ATMA   Institut Alam dan Tamadun Melayu (Institute of the Malay World and Civilisation)
AWAS   Angkatan Wanita Sedar (Movement of Aware Women)

BPUPKI   Badan Penyelidik Usaha Persiapan Kemerdekaan Indonesia (Committee for the Investigation of Preparatory Efforts for Indonesian Independence)

DMDI   Dunia Melayu Dunia Islam (The Malay and Islamic World)

GAPENA   Gabungan Persatuan Penulis Nasional Malaysia (Federation of National Writers' Associations of Malaysia)

KMM   Kesatuan Melayu Muda (Young Malay Union)
KRIS   Kekuatan Rakyat Istimewa (Special Strength of the People) or Kesatuan Rakyat Indonesia Semenanjung (Union of the Peninsular Indonesian People)

MABBIM   Majlis Bahasa Brunei Darussalam-Indonesia-Malaysia (Language Council of Brunei Darussalam-Indonesia-Malaysia)
MBIM   Majlis Bahasa Indonesia-Malaysia (Language Council of Indonesia-Malaysia)
MCA   Malayan/Malaysian Chinese Association
MCKK   Malay College, Kuala Kangsar
MCP   Malayan Communist Party
MIC   Malayan/Malaysian Indian Congress
MPAJA   Malayan People's Anti-Japanese Army

MPR	Majelis Permusyawaratan Rakyat (People's Consultative Assembly)
MVI	Malayan Volunteer Infantry
MWTC	Malay Women's Training College
NEP	New Economic Policy
PAS	Persatuan Islam Se-Malaya (Pan-Malayan Islamic Party), Parti Islam SeMalaya/SeMalaysia (Pan-Malayan/Pan-Malaysian Islamic Party)
Partindo	Partai Indonesia (Indonesian Party)
PKI	Partai Komunis Indonesia (Communist Party of Indonesia)
PKMM	Partai Kebangsaan Melayu Malaya (Malay Nationalist Party of Malaya)
PMIP	Pan-Malayan/Pan-Malaysian Islamic Party
PNI	Partai Nasional Indonesia (Indonesian National Party)
PPKI	Panitia Persiapan Kemerdekaan Indonesia (Committee for the Preparation of Indonesian Independence)
PRB	Partai Rakyat Brunei (Brunei People's Party)
PRM	Partai Rakyat Malaya/Malaysia (People's Party of Malaya/Malaysia)
PUTERA	Pusat Tenaga Rakyat (Centre of People's Power)
SF	Socialist Front
SITC	Sultan Idris Training College
TKR	Tentara Keamanan Rakyat (People's Security Army)
TNI	Tentara Nasional Indonesia (Indonesian National Armed Forces)
UMNO	United Malays National Organisation

Maps

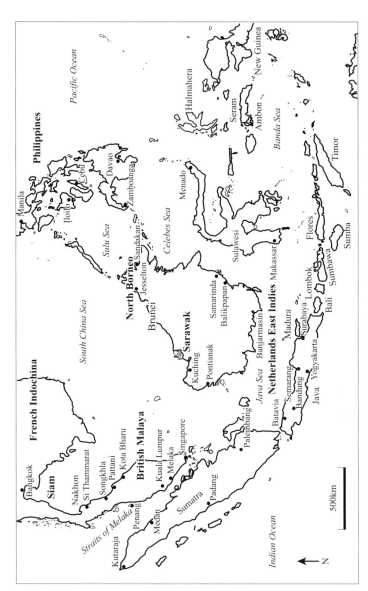

Map 1: The Malay world around 1930

Map 2: British Malaya around 1930

Acknowledgements

This book is a revised version of my doctoral dissertation entitled "Indigenizing Colonial Knowledge: The Formation of Pan-Malay Identity in British Malaya." Twelve years have passed since the dissertation was accepted by the Graduate School of Asian and African Area Studies, Kyoto University, in 2008. The completion of this study is the culmination of a very long journey supported by numerous individuals and institutions although I am unable to name all of them here.

I am greatly indebted to my academic supervisors during my study at Kyoto University. First of all, I am deeply grateful to Kato Tsuyoshi for his invaluable assistance and support as supervisor of my doctoral dissertation. He not only gave me careful guidance as an inspiring and encouraging mentor but also has stimulated me intellectually as an enthusiastic and creative researcher with a broad and deep appreciation of the Malay-Indonesian world. Through his ceaseless quest for knowledge and understanding, he has shown me the passion that a scholar should possess towards research. My special thanks also go to my Master's supervisor, the late Tsuchiya Kenji. He inspired me to study nationalism in Southeast Asia, always setting a rare example as an area studies scholar. His untimely passing was a great loss to Southeast Asian Studies, but he bequeathed an intellectual legacy that continues to inspire the following generations of scholars and students. I also owe a great debt to Kimura Masaaki, who helped to shape my interest in Asian history and politics when I was an undergraduate student at the Faculty of Law. I learned a lot from his lectures and seminars, which always showed the breadth and depth of his scholarship.

In Kyoto I benefited tremendously from the advice and assistance of many people. My sincere thanks are due to Tamada Yoshifumi, Koizumi Junko and Ishikawa Noboru, who offered careful and critical comments on the draft of my dissertation from which I profited immensely. For insightful suggestions on my research, I am especially grateful to Shiraishi Takashi, Patricio N. Abinales, Caroline S. Hau and the late Donna J. Amoroso. I also learned much from two of the pioneering figures in area studies on the Malay world: Tsubouchi Yoshihiro and Tachimoto Narifumi. I also greatly benefited from the discussion with my fellow students, particularly Sadayoshi Yasushi, Nagatsu Kazufumi, Goh Pek Chen, Lai Quee Foong, Okamoto Masaaki, Onimaru Takeshi, the late Mizutani Yasuhiro and Kawano Motoko as well as Nagai Fumio and Yokoyama Takeshi. Faizah Safina Bakrin, Muhammad Izham Ismail and Jalilah Abdul Jalil helped me read and transliterate Jawi texts.

While I conducted research at the National Museum of Ethnology in Osaka between 2001 and 2002, Matsubara Masatake, Oshikawa Fumiko and Abe Ken'ichi were always generous with advice and encouragement. Since I started to teach Malaysian studies at the Tokyo University of Foreign Studies in 2002, my former and current colleagues in the Malay Language Program, Shoho Isamu, Nomoto Hiroki, Dollah Ali, Saiful Bahari Ahmad and last but not least Faridah Mohamed, have been very helpful and understanding. I would also like to note my appreciation to Ikehata Setsuho, Saito Teruko, Ogawa Hidefumi, Aoyama Toru, Tosa Keiko, Miyata Toshiyuki, Furihata Masashi and Kikuchi Yoko.

My research in Malaysia was made possible by generous support from many individuals and institutions. During my study at the Faculty of Social Sciences and Humanities, Universiti Kebangsaan Malaysia, from 1996 to 1999, Shamsul Amri Baharuddin and the late Mohamed Yusoff Ismail always gave me warm encouragement and helpful support. For advice and assistance, I am also grateful to Sharifah Zaleha Syed Hassan, Sabihah Osman, Oong Hak Ching, Ding Choo Ming and James T. Collins. I would also like to thank Wan Zawawi Ibrahim, Abdullah Sipat, Azlan Ibrahim and their families for their kind help and hospitality. I also enjoyed the company and support of my friends, Athi Sivan Mariappan, Chin Yee Whah, Ruslan Uthai, Nobuta Toshihiro and Suzuki Yoichi. While I conducted research at the School of Social Sciences, Universiti Sains Malaysia, from 2006 to 2007, Khoo Boo Teik always offered me tremendous intellectual and personal support. I would also like to acknowledge my appreciation to Abdul Rahman Haji Ismail, Abu Talib Ahmad, the late Cheah Boon Kheng, Chin Yee Whah, Hara Fujio, Francis Loh Kok Wah, Tan Kim Hong, Tan Pek Leng and Toh Kin Woon for their great support during my stay in Penang. When I spent several months as a visiting researcher at the Institute of Malaysian and International Studies, Universiti Kebangsaan Malaysia, between 2013 and 2014, I was helped in many ways by Azizah Kassim, Abdul Rahman Embong, Rashila Ramli, Sumit K. Mandal and Helen Ting. My sincere gratitude also goes to Muhammad Haji Salleh and his family, Anthony Milner, Ariffin Omar, Abdul Latiff Abu Bakar and Colin Nicholas for their valuable assistance and encouragement.

This research was supported by grants from Japan Society for the Promotion of Science (JSPS KAKENHI Grant Numbers: JP25300017 and JP15K01866), Fuji Xerox Co., Ltd. Setsutaro Kobayashi Memorial Fund, the Konosuke Matsushita Memorial Foundation and the Japan Foundation, for which I am very grateful. I also wish to thank the staff of Arkib Negara Malaysia and the libraries of Kyoto University, National Museum of Ethnology, Tokyo University of Foreign Studies, Universiti Kebangsaan Malaysia, Universiti Sains Malaysia, Universiti Malaya, Universiti Pendidikan Sultan Idris, the National University of Singapore and the Institute of Southeast Asian Studies.

The publication of this book was made possible through a "Grant-in-Aid for Publication of Scientific Research Results" by Japan Society for the Promotion of Science (JSPS KAKENHI Grant Number: JP19HP5241). I am greatly indebted to Hayami Yoko, Shitara Narumi, Julius Bautista and Nakanishi Yoshihiro of Center for Southeast Asian Studies, Kyoto University, Suzuki Tetsuya of Kyoto University Press and Sugimoto Yoshio of Trans Pacific Press for their forbearance and support throughout the time it has taken me to complete the manuscript for publication. I am also very grateful to Paul H. Kratoska and anonymous reviewers for their valuable comments on the manuscript of this book. I must also thank Karl Smith for his scrupulous editing of my manuscript.

Needless to say, none of the individuals and institutions mentioned above are responsible for any errors or shortcomings in this volume.

An earlier version of Chapter 4 was published as "The Malay World in Textbook: The Transmission of Colonial Knowledge in British Malaya," *Southeast Asian Studies* 39(2) (September 2001): 188–234. Chapters 6 and 7 appeared earlier as "The Transformation of Pan-Malayism in Post-war Malay(si)a" in *Islam and Cultural Diversity in Southeast Asia, Vol. 2: Perspectives from Indonesia, Malaysia, the Philippines, Thailand, and Cambodia*, edited by Tokoro Ikuya and Tomizawa Hisao, pp. 115–145, Fuchu: Research Institute for Languages and Cultures of Asia and Africa, Tokyo University of Foreign Studies, 2018. Permission to publish revised versions here is gratefully acknowledged.

My greatest appreciation goes to my parents, Kenji and Keiko, for their unfailing support and encouragement. My father constantly helped me to develop my curiosity in my childhood and has inspired my interest in the world beyond my country. My mother was very generous and supportive and always encouraged me to do what I liked. Sadly, she is no longer around to see this book. My heartfelt gratitude also goes to my sister Yukiko and her family, who have always been very helpful and hospitable.

My final and deepest gratitude goes to my wife Yuko for her patience, cooperation, encouragement and support – intellectual and moral – throughout the writing process. Without her generous help and assistance, this book would never have been completed. I am also indebted to my children, Kohei and Aoi, the source of my happiness and inspiration.

1 Introduction

Objectives and scope of the study

Concepts of race and ethnicity rank highly among the legacies that British colonialism left to post-colonial states such as Malaysia. We cannot, however, assume that the local populace unquestioningly adopted the colonizer's racial and ethnic classifications. Not until social concepts of race and ethnicity had permeated through fields as varied as school education, mass media, public administration and legislation, would these concepts be popularized. This study examines the interrelations between the indigenization of "colonial knowledge," by which I mean "the colonizer's knowledge of the colonized," and the quest for a pan-Malay identity in Malaya, which is currently called Peninsular Malaysia. In what way, to what extent and for what purpose did the colonized accept, modify and adapt the colonizer's worldview?

Education played a vital role in knowledge transmission and identity construction in British Malaya. This research focuses primarily on Malay-medium education in Malaya. More specifically, it explores the transmission of knowledge at a central training college for male Malay-school teachers, namely the Sultan Idris Training College (SITC). Following investigations on the formal curriculum, extra-curricular activities and dormitory life at the SITC, it focuses on the teaching of history and geography based on authorized textbooks. One of these textbooks was written by a British scholar-administrator, R.J. Wilkinson (1867–1941), in English in 1908; two by another British scholar-officer, R.O. Winstedt (1878–1966), in Malay in 1918; and one by a Malay history teacher, Abdul Hadi Haji Hasan (1900–1937) in Malay in 1925, 1926 and 1929 (3 vols.).

Despite the significance of colonial education, we cannot assume that the Malays unquestioningly absorbed the new framework of knowledge brought by British colonialists. Malays could also transform and reconstitute the modern concept of "Malayness," which means the condition of being

Malay or the set of characteristics that are used to define Malay. We must understand why and how colonial education substantially contributed to bringing about an "unintended result" for the colonizer, that is, the growth of ethno-national feeling among the colonized. For this purpose, this research presents an intensive case study of the construction of Malay identity by an SITC-graduated Malay nationalist, Ibrahim Haji Yaacob (1911–1979). As President of the first left-wing Malay organization named Kesatuan Melayu Muda (KMM) (Young Malay Union), established in 1938, Ibrahim formulated an idea of a pan-Malay/Indonesian nation called *Melayu Raya* (Greater Malay [nation]) or *Indonesia Raya* (Greater Indonesia).[1] He received Malay vernacular education both at a primary school and later at the SITC. Because of this educational background, Ibrahim's personal intellectual history is an ideal case for investigating the indigenization of colonial knowledge. The single most important figure in this study is therefore Ibrahim.

One may ask what is to be achieved from exploring Ibrahim's "pan-Malayism." By "pan-Malayism" I mean an ideology espousing a Malay solidarity that transcends existing political boundaries in the Malay Archipelago. We can also call it "pan-Malay nationalism" if it is connected to the belief that the people of Malay stock in the Archipelago should form a "nation," which means a community of people who not only have a sense of belonging, a belief that they share a history, language, culture or religion, or common principles, but also seek to attain or maintain political independence, autonomy or hegemony. It is true that he did not realize his desire to build *Melayu Raya* or *Indonesia Raya*, a proposed potential nation, or what Rustam A. Sani and Shamsul A.B. call a "nation-of-intent"[2] (Rustam 1986 [1976]; 2008; Shamsul 1996c). Undoubtedly, Ibrahim and other leftist Malay nationalists were unsuccessful in the real politics of Malaya. Though they played a key role in the Malay youth movement in Malaya in the late 1930s and early 1940s, Ibrahim fled to Indonesia just after World War II, and his fellow activists failed in their political struggle against the traditional Malay ruling class.[3] Yet, his advocacy of *Melayu Raya* can be considered as a catalyst for the postwar development of pan-Malayism in Malaya. Furthermore, a case study of Ibrahim's conceptualization of a pan-Malay nation provides a clue for understanding the broader definition of Malayness, the officialization of the concept of *bumiputera* (lit. sons of the soil) and the authorization of the *bumiputera* policy in Malaysia. As Anthony Milner suggests, Ibrahim's concept of

Melayu Raya may have been relevant to the definition of Malayness and *bumiputeraness* in the course of nation-building in Malaysia (Milner 1992).

The present research also briefly examines the debates over the Malaysia proposal in the 1960s between Malaya's Prime Minister Tunku Abdul Rahman (1903–1990) and his two Malay opponents and Ibrahim's former comrades, namely, Burhanuddin Al-Helmy (1911–1969) and Ahmad Boestamam (1920–1983), in their final attempt to realize their vision of *Melayu Raya / Indonesia Raya*. Despite their resistance to Tunku's Malaysia plan, even the slimmest possibility of creating a pan-Malay/Indonesian nation had disappeared by the late 1960s. After a critical confrontation with Indonesia and conflict over the Philippines' claim to Sabah in the early and mid-1960s, major opposition to Malaysia was suppressed both inside and outside the country.

Finally, this study will conclude that while British colonizers brought new forms of knowledge to Malays, there seems to have been significant reinterpretation, transformation, and appropriation in the process of the indigenization of colonial knowledge. This indicates that the formation of pan-Malay identity in Malaya was the result of the interaction between external and internal powers and knowledge.

Some limitations in my approach to the research topic should be addressed. First, this research concentrates on the impact of British colonialism on the formation of pan-Malay identity in British Malaya, but it does not deny the significance of other currents of thought. There is little doubt that pan-Malay nationalists inherited an intellectual legacy from Malay kingship and local traditions even though most of them were not conservative traditionalists.[4] It is also obvious that contemporary nationalism in Asia, particularly Indonesian nationalism, significantly impacted on the formulation of pan-Malayism in Malaya.[5] Islamic reformism, too, contributed to the growing sense of unity between Malaya and the Netherlands East Indies or Indonesia.[6] Japanese occupation during World War II undoubtedly also played a part in the making of Malay identity.[7] However, while fully acknowledging the influence of these diverse currents of thought, this study focuses on British colonialism on the assumption that it exercised a very powerful intellectual hegemony over the local population in Malaya.

Second, there is a risk of overemphasizing the role of formal school education in the transmission of knowledge and identity formation. Knowledge can be acquired from an immeasurably wide range of oral, written and visual sources. To make this study feasible, however, it concentrates on formal school education, in particular the teaching of the history and geography of the Malay world at a teaching college for Malay-school teachers.

Finally, while the present study focuses on Malay-medium education, other types of school education for the Malays, such as English-medium education and Islamic religious education, were no less important in knowledge transplantation and identity construction. Even among Malay leftists, there are a substantial number of English-educated leaders such as Ahmad Boestamam and Ishak Haji Muhammad as well as those who were educated at religious schools like Burhanuddin Al-Helmy.

In view of these limitations, this study claims only to reveal some particular, but crucial aspects of the interplay between the transmission of knowledge and the search for Malay identity in colonial Malaya. Still, it is hoped that the present research provides a fresh perspective on the question of the transmission and appropriation of knowledge.

Sources and methods

This study is a historical analysis of the interrelations between colonial education and political thought, largely based on written materials. The main primary sources consist of published and unpublished official records, private papers, and books, essays and speeches by the main figures mentioned above. Principally because most of the persons concerned have passed away, I conducted only a limited number of interviews. Still, the oral sources helped to clarify the insiders' views.

Varying sources and methods reflect the shifting focus of the study. To outline colonial education policy for the Malays in British Malaya, the study consults official records, in particular, annual reports and other official reports on education for the Federated Malay States. For a socio-historical inquiry into student life at the SITC, especially useful are official documents such as regulations for the SITC and a memorandum on the college as well as the memoirs of former teachers and students. To examine the transmission of knowledge on the history and geography of the Malay world, the study includes a comparative textual analysis of four textbooks: Wilkinson's *A History of the Peninsular Malays* (1908), Winstedt's *Kitab Tawarikh Melayu* (1918) and *Ilmu Alam Melayu* (1918), and Abdul Hadi's three volumes of *Sejarah Alam Melayu* (1925, 1926, 1929). While books and unpublished private papers[8] written by Ibrahim Haji Yaacob are used to reconstruct his life and times, the main sources for an investigation into his conceptions of Malayness are his articles in Malay newspapers and periodicals, such as *Majlis*, *Warta Negeri*, *Warta Ahad* and *Warta Jenaka*, and his books *Melihat Tanah Air* (1941), *Sedjarah dan Perdjuangan di Malaya* (1951), *Nusa dan Bangsa Melayu* (1951) and *Sekitar Malaya Merdeka* (1957). Finally, contesting ideas of Malayness during the time of the Malaysia controversy are reconstructed mainly by examining official records of parliamentary debates in the Dewan Rakyat (House of Representatives).

Review of previous studies

It is widely acknowledged that British colonialism played a key role in producing social categories in Malaysia such as race, ethnic group and nation as well as creating dominant images of each group. Syed Hussein Alatas' pioneering work argues that "the myth of the lazy native" derives its origin largely from the colonial image of the local people (Alatas 1977). "Colonialism, or on a bigger scale, imperialism," Alatas writes, "was not only an extension of sovereignty and control by one nation and its government over another, but it was also a control of the mind of the conquered or subordinated" (Alatas 1977: 17). Charles Hirschman contends that "modern 'race relations' in Peninsular Malaysia, in the sense of impenetrable group boundaries, were a by-product of British colonialism of the late nineteenth and early twentieth centuries" (Hirschman 1986: 330). Hirschman traces the historical creation of racial/ethnic classifications to the censuses of colonial Malaya and post-independence Malaysia (Hirschman 1987). Shamsul A.B. sheds light on colonial knowledge and identity formation in Malaysia (Shamsul 1996a; 1996b; 1996c; 1999; 2004). Other scholars have also shown that colonial rule had a significant impact on the creation of ethnic and national identities in Malay(si)a and Singapore (Nair 1999; Fernandez 1999; Iguchi 2001; Ooi 2003; Aljunied 2009).

While acknowledging the strong impact of British colonialism on identity formation in Malaysia, we should neither presuppose that British colonialists were of one mind about the needs of the colonial state, nor assume that the local populace uncritically accepted anything that the colonial authorities provided. A.J. Stockwell warns against perceiving the ethnic compartmentalization in British Malaya merely in the simplistic terms of divide-and-rule. Instead, he suggests, we should understand British perceptions of the local populace in the context of their practical experience in an alien environment (Stockwell 1982). Furthermore, as Shamsul puts it, "there was a two-way traffic in the appropriation exercise during the colonial period, not only the colonialists were appropriating what the locals have to offer but the locals too were selecting, appropriating and internalising what the colonialists offered them (both through coercion and other methods)" (Shamsul 1996a: 14). Still, more in-depth case studies should be conducted on the internalization and utilization of introduced knowledge in the formation of Malay identity in British Malaya. This study is an attempt to tackle the task.

William R. Roff's *The Origins of Malay Nationalism* (Roff 1994 [1967]) and Anthony Milner's *The Invention of Politics in Colonial Malaya* (Milner 2002 [1995]) are two fundamentally important studies of colonial Malay society and politics. They represent two major approaches to prewar Malay identity politics. Roff's work traces the social roots of new Malay leadership groups and their political thinking. He found that, during the first few decades of the twentieth century, three new contending groups emerged in Malay society. The first were Arabic-educated religious reformists who conducted trade and Islamic education in major port cities. The second consisted of the largely Malay-educated intelligentsia of plebeian, peasant origin who embraced pan-Malay/Indonesian nationalism. The third comprised the English-educated administrators of the traditional elite class who founded Malay state associations. In this way, Roff focuses on the class and educational background of the new Malay leaders.

This socio-historical approach to the growth of ethnic and national feelings among Malays in British Malaya is shared with modification by other well-known studies, for instance, Firdaus Haji Abdullah's book on radical Malay politics (Firdaus 1985), Khoo Kay Kim's work on the transformation of Malay society and politics (Khoo Kay Kim 1991) and Rustam A. Sani's study on social roots of the Malay left (Rustam 2008). These studies help us to understand the social context in which new political thinking and movement developed.

Milner's study investigates the ways in which political discourse developed in colonial Malaya. He criticizes Roff's work as a "retrospective" analysis that seeks to identify unifying elements and processes in prewar Malay society. Milner describes his own strategy, in contrast, as "prospective." "In seeking to identify transition as well as continuity," Milner writes, "I look forward rather than backward into the colonial period. From a prospective rather than a retrospective angle of vision, it is easier to perceive the uncertainties, the ruptures and the tensions in any social situation" (Milner 2002 [1995]: 4). From this prospective approach, he conducts a textual analysis of the selected writings of Malays, examining not only the arguments offered but also "the vocabulary, the rhetoric, the idioms and the conventions employed" (Milner 2002 [1995]: 5). According to Milner, while three contending ideological orientations arose in Malay political thinking, that is, the sultanate or *kerajaan,* the Islamic congregation or *umat* and the Malay race or *bangsa*, a three-cornered ideological battle unexpectedly brought about the "invention" of a discourse of politics and the expansion of the public sphere in the colonial Malay community. In his recent comprehensive study on the history of Malayness, Milner also emphasizes the "localization" of the concept of the "Malay race" or "Malay ethnicity," and suggests that "Malay" might be better understood as a civilization rather than as a race or an ethnicity (Milner 2008]).

Other fascinating textual studies include Hendrik M.J. Maier's analysis of the reading of *Hikayat Merong Mahawangsa* (Maier 1988), Ariffin Omar's exploration of the concept of *bangsa Melayu* (Ariffin 1993) and Virginia Matheson Hooker's inquiry into social change through the novel in Malay (Hooker 2000). More recently, Syed Muhd. Khairudin Aljunied closely investigates Malay radicalism by focusing on a set of "mobilizing concepts" (Aljunied 2015). These studies all reinforce the argument that we should consider existing concepts and frames of reference as historical products.

These two approaches each have advantages and they are not incompatible. The present study therefore incorporates a socio-historical approach into a textual, discourse analysis. While it investigates social and historical context in which political discourse developed, it also provides a close reading of the texts with care for language and style as well as for intertextuality, that is, the interdependence of each text with the others. Furthermore, this research pays close attention to the consequences of political debate. Yet, as suggested earlier, it does not purport to be a comprehensive study of the history of identity politics in Malaya. This is basically a case study of the interplay of Malay vernacular education and *bangsa*-minded Malay political thought without denying the significance of other types of education and other ideological orientations.

There is a substantial collection of literature on the interplay of education for Malays and the emergence of modern Malay society and politics. As mentioned above, some previous studies on Malay politics in colonial Malaya, in particular Roff's *The Origins of Malay Nationalism*, are centrally concerned with the role of education in the making of Malay nationalism (Soenarno 1960; Roff 1994 [1967]; Nabir 1976; Firdaus 1985; Khoo Kay Kim 1991; Soh 1993; 2005; Rustam 2008; Ishak Saat 2011). Like the Malay College, Kuala Kangsar (MCKK), the SITC is a well-researched educational institution in colonial Malaya. Some works on the history of education for the Malays, such as Awang Had (1974; 1979), Loh (1975) and UPSI (2000), provide useful accounts of British education policy and the college's early development. These studies provide a detailed analysis of the development of education for the Malays in British Malaya and its transformative impact on Malay society. Yet they do not conduct an intensive investigation into the production and transmission of knowledge. There are also several significant studies that touch on the above-mentioned school textbooks in the context of the development of Malay literature and historiography (Zainal Abidin 1940; 1941a; Khoo Kay Kim 1979; Maier 1988; Cheah 1997; Gullick 1998; Milner 2005). But a close discourse analysis of the school textbooks is yet to be conducted. Such an analysis is necessary for a deeper examination of the transmission and appropriation of knowledge on the Malay world in education, and is therefore a theme on which this study seeks to shed light.

Several studies refer to Ibrahim and his nationalist thought. Some researchers have explored Ibrahim's leadership in the Malay leftist movement (Soenarno 1960; Roff 1994 [1967]; Abd. Malek 1975; Rustam 1986 [1976]; 2008; Firdaus 1985; Ramlah 1999; 2004a; Liow 2005; Mohamed Salleh 2006; Aljunied 2015). There have also been studies of his political thinking, as expressed in his newspaper articles and books (Cheah 1979; 2012 [1983]; Abdul Latiff 1981; Milner 2002 [1995]; Farish 2002; Roslan 2009; Ahmat 2013). Besides Cheah Boon Kheng's excellent intensive studies on Ibrahim's thought and behavior during the Japanese occupation (Cheah 1979; 2012 [1983]), several other standard works on Malaya under Japanese rule also touch on Ibrahim during the war (Itagaki 1962; Nagai 1978; Akashi 1980; Kratoska 2018 [1998]; Abu Talib 2003). Biographical essays about him are also available (Khoo Kay Kim 1979b; Bachtiar 1985; Ramlah 1999).

Many of these studies point out that nationalist thought and action in the Netherlands East Indies or Indonesia had a substantial impact on Ibrahim and his fellow leftist nationalists in British Malaya (Roff 1994 [1967]; Cheah 1979; 2012 [1983]; Abdul Latiff 1981; Liow 2005; Roslan 2009; Ahmat 2013; Aljunied 2015). Ibrahim personally stressed that publications in the Netherlands East Indies, such as newspapers, magazines, novels and almanacs, helped to foster his pan-Malay/Indonesian consciousness during his youth (Mss. 176 (2); (3)a). There is no room to doubt that Indonesian nationalists like Tan Malaka, Sukarno and Mohammad Hatta had a tremendous influence on Ibrahim and other SITC students and KMM members (Mss. 176 (2); (3)a; Roslan 2009; Ahmat 2013). After unsuccessful uprisings in Java in 1926 and 1927, some Indonesian communists including Tan Malaka, Alimin, Musso and Sutan Djenain took refuge in Malaya and contacted SITC students (Mss. 176 (3); Roff 1994 [1967]: 222–225; Cheah 2012 [1983]: 10). Roff argues that the KMM was modelled on Jong Java and Jong Sumatra, youth organizations in the Netherlands East Indies (Roff 1994 [1967]: 222).

Besides Indonesian anti-colonial movements, nationalist movements in other parts of the world also appealed to Ibrahim and other young Malay students and activists. For instance, the Turkish Revolution, or the Young Turk Revolution, had a significant impact on the Malay community in Malaya. Malay leftist leaders seem to have been impressed by the leadership of Mustafa Kemal Ataturk (Mss. 176 (3); Mustapha 1996: 195; Milner 1986; Aljunied 2015: 50–52). They also paid close attention to independence movements in other parts of the Islamic world such as Egypt and Morocco (Mss. 176 (3); Agastja 1948: 57). The influence of Indian anti-colonial movements led by prominent leaders including Gandhi and Nehru is also obvious (Mss. 176 (3); Aljunied 2015: 52).

While fully acknowledging that the rise of nationalism in the Netherlands East Indies and other parts of the world profoundly affected the political thinking of Ibrahim and his fellow nationalist leaders, we must not ignore the effect that colonialism in British Malaya may have had in their ethno-national identity formation. Hence, this study will provide an in-depth intellectual biography of Ibrahim in order to trace the development and transformation of his world-view, focusing on the interrelations between his acquisition of knowledge through education and his identity formation.

Organization of the study

This study consists of seven chapters (including this Introduction). Chapter 2 provides an overview of British Malaya as well as an outline of Malay vernacular education in colonial Malaya. It also looks at the British image of the Malays and the evolution of education policy towards the

Malays. Chapter 3 is an intensive inquiry into teacher training at the SITC. We investigate the formal curriculum, extra-curricular activities and dormitory life at the college to understand how college students accumulated knowledge and experience. Teacher training at the SITC is characterized by the reproduction of ethnic, class and gender relations. Chapter 4 analyses how knowledge of the Malay world was transmitted through Malay-school textbooks. It examines textbooks on the history and geography of the Malay world with special reference to conceptions of the Malay community, territoriality and history. In Chapter 5, the focus is on Ibrahim's political thought and behavior, paying special attention to the appropriation of knowledge in his advocacy of pan-Malay/Indonesian unity, named *Melayu Raya* or *Indonesia Raya*. Chapter 6 examines contending notions of Malayness in postwar Malaya. It deals with the rise and fall of pan-Malay/Indonesian nationalism as well as the formation and confrontation of Malaysia in the 1960s. Chapter 7 summarizes what has been discussed in the previous chapters and suggests some implications for contemporary Malay and Malaysian society and politics.

In general, English and Malay words are presented as they appear in source texts. However, transliteration from Jawi to Roman script is in accordance with current Malay spelling conventions.

2 Malay Vernacular Education in British Malaya

British education policy towards the Malays was formulated in a changing social, political and economic climate on the Malay Peninsula. Education of the Malays in turn contributed considerably to transformation of the social, political and economic landscapes of British Malaya. From this perspective, this chapter explores the development of Malay vernacular education in British Malaya.

This chapter is composed of four sections. The first section provides an overview of British Malaya. The second section outlines the British education policy towards the Malays, particularly on Malay vernacular education. The third section examines the image of the Malays cultivated by the British administrators who laid the basis of colonial education policy. The fourth section focuses on the Winstedt report of 1917, which became a guideline for British colonial policy on Malay vernacular education in Malaya.

British Malaya: Background

From the end of the eighteenth century, numerous Malay kingdoms in the Straits of Melaka were troubled by succession disputes in which the British and the Dutch became involved.[1] British colonization of the Malay Peninsula began with the cession of the island of Penang, originally a part of the sultanate of Kedah, to the English East India Company in 1786. In 1826, the British formed the Straits Settlements that included Penang, Singapore, which came under British control in 1819, and Melaka, which fell to the British as a trade-off under the Anglo-Dutch Treaty of 1824.[2] Following the Pangkor Treaty of 1874, signed between the British and Raja Abdullah of Perak, the British became involved in three other states: Selangor, Negeri Sembilan and Pahang. The four states, which were at first collectively known as the Protected Malay States, officially formed the Federated Malay States in 1896. Perlis, Kedah, Kelantan, Terengganu and Johor, which came under British control between 1909 and 1914, were called Unfederated Malay States. British Malaya means a set of the Straits Settlements, the Federated Malay States and the Unfederated Malay States, though these colonies and protectorates were not under a single unified administration before World War II.

The Malay Peninsula has a long history of migration from pre-colonial times. In the sultanate of Melaka and its successors, there were many migrants not only from other parts of the Archipelago but also from outside the region such as Arabia, India and China. Larger immigrant influxes, however, stemmed from European, particularly British, colonization. The expansion of the colonial economy, especially of tin mining and rubber plantation, and the development of colonial administration, induced new flows of people from China, India, Sri Lanka, Sumatra, Java, and so on.

The British colonizers officially formulated ethnic classifications in British Malaya. As Charles Hirschman shows, the population of British Malaya had gradually been classified according to "nationality" or "race" by the early twentieth century. Major ethnic categories, namely, "Europeans," "Eurasians," "Malays (Malaysians)," "Chinese," "Indians," and "Others," which were first introduced in the 1891 Straits Settlements census,[3] became conventional in the censuses of British Malaya (Hirschman 1987). It should be noted, however, that each "race" was far from culturally homogeneous. According to the 1931 census, the population of British Malaya consisted of "Europeans" (0.4 percent), "Eurasians" (0.4 percent), "Malaysians" (Malays and other indigenous peoples of the Malay Peninsula and Archipelago) (44.7 percent), "Chinese" (39.0 percent), "Indians" (14.2 percent), and "Others" (1.3 percent), as shown in Table 2.1. The population of the Federated Malay States was made up of 0.4 percent "Europeans," 0.2 percent "Eurasians," 34.7 percent "Malaysians," 41.5 percent "Chinese," 22.2 percent "Indians," and 1.0 percent "Others." While "Malaysians" formed a majority in Pahang (61.0 percent), they did not constitute the largest group in Perak (35.6 percent), Selangor (23.0 percent) and Negeri Sembilan (37.3 percent). Again, we should bear in mind that the population of what the British classified as "Malaysians" was culturally diverse, comprising of "Malays," which was itself a contested category, and various other indigenous peoples of the Malay Peninsula and Archipelago.

Table 2.1: Population of British Malaya, 1931

	Europeans	Eurasians	Malaysians[a]	Chinese	Indians	Others	Total
Singapore	8,147	6,937	71,177	421,821	51,019	8,352	567,453
	(1.4)	(1.2)	(12.5)	(74.3)	(9.0)	(1.5)	(100.0)
Penang	1,526	2,348	118,832	176,518	58,020	2,607	359,851
	(0.4)	(0.7)	(33.0)	(49.1)	(16.1)	(0.7)	(100.0)
Melaka	330	2,007	95,307	65,179	23,238	650	186,711
	(0.2)	(1.1)	(51.0)	(34.9)	(12.4)	(0.3)	(100.0)
Straits Settlements	10,003	11,292	285,316	663,518	132,277	11,609	1,114,015
	(0.9)	(1.0)	(25.6)	(59.6)	(11.9)	(1.0)	(100.0)
Perak	2,359	1,270	272,546	325,527	159,152	5,135	765,989
	(0.3)	(0.2)	(35.6)	(42.5)	(20.8)	(0.7)	(100.0)
Selangor	2,723	2,137	122,868	241,351	155,924	8,194	533,197
	(0.5)	(0.4)	(23.0)	(45.3)	(29.2)	(1.5)	(100.0)
Negeri Sembilan	878	699	87,195	92,371	50,100	2,556	233,799
	(0.4)	(0.3)	(37.3)	(39.5)	(21.4)	(1.1)	(100.0)
Pahang	390	145	111,122	52,291	14,820	1,343	180,111
	(0.2)	(0.1)	(61.7)	(29.0)	(8.2)	(0.7)	(100.0)
Federated Malay States	6,350	4,251	593,731	711,540	379,996	17,228	1,713,096
	(0.4)	(0.2)	(34.7)	(41.5)	(22.2)	(1.0)	(100.0)
Johor	722	302	234,422	215,076	51,038	3,751	505,311
	(0.1)	(0.1)	(46.4)	(42.6)	(10.1)	(0.7)	(100.0)
Kedah	411	108	286,262	78,415	50,824	13,671	429,691
	(0.1)	(0.0)	(66.6)	(18.2)	(11.8)	(3.2)	(100.0)
Perlis	3	11	39,831	6,500	966	1,985	49,296
	(0.0)	(0.0)	(80.8)	(13.2)	(2.0)	(4.0)	(100.0)
Kelantan	124	32	330,774	17,612	6,752	7,223	362,517
	(0.0)	(0.0)	(91.2)	(4.9)	(1.9)	(2.0)	(100.0)
Terengganu	35	15	164,564	13,254	1,371	550	179,789
	(0.0)	(0.0)	(91.5)	(7.4)	(0.8)	(0.3)	(100.0)
Brunei[b]	60	10	26,972	2,683	377	33	30,135
	(0.2)	(0.0)	(89.5)	(8.9)	(1.3)	(0.1)	(100.0)
Unlocated	60	22	149	794	408	63	1,496
	(4.0)	(1.5)	(10.0)	(53.1)	(27.3)	(4.2)	(100.0)
British Malaya (Total)	17,768	16,043	1,962,021	1,709,392	624,009	56,113	4,385,346
	(0.4)	(0.4)	(44.7)	(39.0)	(14.2)	(1.3)	(100.0)

Notes: Bracketed numbers represent percentages
[a]"Malaysians" means "all indigenous peoples of the Malay Peninsula and Archipelago."
[b]Though Brunei constitutes part of Borneo Island, the population of Brunei was included in that of British Malaya in the 1921 and 1931 censuses.
Source: Vlieland (1932: 126)

The education of Malays in the early twentieth century

The introduction of colonial education

The earliest form of schooling for Muslims in the Malay Peninsula was religious education which began with the introduction of Islam sometime around the fourteenth century. Muslim children learned the Arabic script and the Qur'an in Arabic at Qur'anic schools, located in the homes of religious teachers, in mosques, or in the *surau*.[4] While *pondok*-type boarding schools had developed from the early nineteenth century, modernized religious schools called *madrasah* began to grow in the early twentieth century (Rosnani 2004 [1996]: 21–31).[5] Even after secular education was introduced by the British in the early nineteenth century, Islamic religious education continuously played an important role in the Muslim community.

Secular education in British Malaya was divided according to the medium of instruction such as English, Malay, Chinese and Tamil (see Appendix 1). Malay children in the early twentieth century were expected to enter Malay schools, i.e. schools using Malay as the medium of instruction, by the age of seven and to pass through five standards for five years or more (*Education Code V 1927* 1927: 1). After completing Standard III or IV in Malay schools, a small number of excellent or privileged Malay children would have an opportunity to attend the Special Malay Class in order to enter English schools, i.e. schools using English as the medium of instruction.[6] English schools provided both primary and secondary education. Many of the English schools were in urban locations and thus inaccessible to the majority of Malays who resided in rural areas. The British also established English-medium higher educational institutions such as the King Edward VII College of Medicine[7] and Raffles College[8] as well as special schools for technical education like Technical School[9] and the School of Agriculture.[10] In contrast, there was no Malay-medium secondary school in prewar Malaya. Malay-medium post-primary education was only available at training colleges for Malay-school teachers[11] such as Sultan Idris Training College and Malay Women's Training College as well as at the School of Agriculture and some trade schools, which offered some special practical programmes in Malay.

Malay vernacular education was first introduced in the Straits Settlements around 1820, almost at the same time as English education started. The initiative was first taken by missionaries, and then followed by the British colonial government. As far as the Federated Malay States are concerned, Malay schools, which had been established since the 1870s, increased in significant number in the early twentieth century from 185 in 1901 to 322 in 1911 to 407 in 1921 to 535 in 1931 (see Table 2.2). The enrolment in Malay schools, the pupils of which were mostly Malays (or more precisely those who could be categorized as Malay), was almost fifteen times larger than the enrolment of Malay pupils in English schools (see Table 2.3). The number of Malay girls was much smaller than that of Malay boys, both in Malay and English schools. In 1931 the ratio of boys to girls in Malay schools was about seven to one while that of Malay boys to Malay girls in English schools was about eleven to one, as can be seen in Table 2.3. Since the number of girls' schools was very limited, many Malay girls studied at boys' schools. In British Malaya as a whole, there were approximately 46,000 pupils attending 757 Malay schools around 1920. The number is roughly 12 percent of the total "Malaysian" population (Malays and other indigenous groups of the Malay Peninsula and Archipelago) between the ages of 5 and 15 (Roff 1994 [1967]: 128). According to a report by Ormsby Gore in 1928, about 75 percent of Malay boys and about 9 percent of Malay girls of school age in the Federated Malay States received a Malay vernacular education (Cmd. 3235 of 1928–1929: 44).

One of the greatest problems with Malay vernacular education in British Malaya was the lack of trained teachers. In the late nineteenth century, the British authorities started to establish teacher training colleges as a remedy for the problem. The first training college for Malay-school teachers was founded in Singapore in 1878. After the college was closed in 1895, another training college was opened in Taiping, Perak, in 1898, but it only functioned for two years. These training colleges offered a one-year course for male teachers. The average enrolment of the college in Singapore was about 25 (Awang Had 1979: 27–32).

At the turn of the twentieth century, the training of male Malay-school teachers was made more systematic on the initiative of R.J. Wilkinson, who had served as Acting Inspector General of Schools in the Straits Settlements between 1898 and 1900. At his suggestion, a new Malay training college, the Malay Training College, Melaka, was established in 1900.[12] Another

Table 2.2: Number of Malay schools in the Federated Malay States,
1901–1931

	1901		1911		1921		1931	
Perak	110	(12)	181	(41)	217	(43)	274	(62)
Selangor	35	(2)	49	(2)	68	(7)	87	(10)
Negeri Sembilan	27	(0)	62	(3)	71	(4)	89	(8)
Pahang	13	(0)	30	(0)	51	(2)	85	(5)
Federated Malay States	185	(14)	322	(46)	407	(56)	535	(85)

Note. ( ): Number of Malay girls' schools
Source: AREFMS (1901: 2–6; 1911: 1–2; 1921: 19; 1931: 88)

Table 2.3: Enrolment in vernacular and English schools in the Federated
Malay States, 1931

	Enrolment	
	Boys	**Girls**
Malay schools	35,290	5,118
Chinese schools	14,394	4,488
Tamil schools	10,656	
English schools	13,169	4,875
Ethnic distribution of pupils in English schools		
Malays	2,525	222
Chinese	6,252	2,710
Indians	3,707	1,284
Europeans and Eurasians	576	492
Others	109	167

Source: AREFMS (1931: 76, 88–90)

training college was opened at Matang, Perak, in 1913. These two colleges, which provided a two-year course for male teachers, were dissolved in 1922 when the Sultan Idris Training College (SITC) was established at Tanjung Malim, Perak. The SITC was established along the lines laid down by R.O. Winstedt, who had served as Assistant Director of Education in charge of Malay schools since 1916.

The training of female teachers for Malay girls' schools was left far behind. It was not until 1935 that the colonial government established a

Table 2.4: The literacy rate for Malaysians[a], 1931

	Males (%)		Females (%)	
	All ages	**Over 15**	**All ages**	**Over 15**
Singapore	35.1	39.8	5.2	7.5
Penang	42.0	50.2	9.9	8.0
Melaka	47.8	53.8	4.0	3.3
Straits Settlements	41.9	48.2	7.1	6.3
Perak	42.2	51.6	9.9	8.8
Selangor	39.1	46.2	9.5	8.6
Negeri Sembilan	50.6	57.4	6.9	4.0
Pahang	29.8	34.9	4.9	4.6
Federated Malay States	40.7	48.3	8.4	7.2
Johor	23.6	28.6	3.1	2.9
Kedah	18.5	21.6	1.8	1.9
Perlis	23.0	25.5	2.5	1.7
Kelantan	6.0	8.0	0.4	0.5
Terengganu	6.2	7.9	0.6	0.7
Brunei[b]	14.0	19.0	2.6	3.5

Notes. [a]"Malaysians" means "all indigenous peoples of the Malay Peninsula and Archipelago."
[b]Though Brunei constitutes part of Borneo Island, the population of Brunei was included in that of British Malaya in the 1921 and 1931 censuses.
Source: Vlieland (1932: 93, 331, 337, 345–346)

college for training female Malay-school teachers, that is, Malay Women's Training College (MWTC), Melaka. Before World War II, the college's average intake per year was only 24. The situation was far from ideal considering that there had already been about 150 Malay girls' schools in British Malaya in 1935 (Awang Had 1979: 54–58).

Malay vernacular education and the development of Malay journalism

The spread of Malay vernacular education was closely related to the development of Malay journalism in colonial Malaya. Malay-medium education played a major role in providing literate Malays, who constituted potential Malay writers and readers. Yet the literacy rate for the "Malaysians" ("Malays" and other indigenous peoples of the Malay Peninsula and Archipelago) in 1931 differed markedly between states as well as between genders as presented in Table 2.4. While nearly half of the adult male "Malaysian" population of the Straits Settlements and the Federated Malay States was literate in Malay, the literacy rate for the same group of Kelantan and Terengganu was less than ten percent. The adult female "Malaysian" population of Malaya was far behind in literacy in Malay. The literacy rate for the adult female "Malaysian" population of every state was below ten percent. Though the majority of Malays were still illiterate in prewar Malaya, it does not necessarily mean that Malay journalism was completely out of reach of the illiterate. Literate readers could and often did orally pass on what was written in Malay newspapers and magazines to illiterate or less literate persons (Zainal Abidin 1941b: 249).

While Malay journalism may have begun in 1876 with *Jawi Peranakan*, a Singapore-based weekly newspaper in Malay, the publication of Malay newspapers and periodicals developed rapidly in the early twentieth century. The first group of Malay writers was called *penulis agama* (religious writers) who had received Islamic religious education either in the Malay Archipelago or in other parts of the world such as the Middle East. Under the influence of Middle Eastern Islamic reformism, they challenged the authority of the local traditional religious elite in the well-known dispute between the *Kaum Tua* (Old Faction) and the *Kaum Muda* (Young Faction). Religious reformists like Syed Sheikh Al-Hadi published Islamic-minded Malay periodicals such as *Al-Imam* (Singapore, 1906–1908 or 1909), *Al-Ikhwan* (Penang, 1926–1931) and *Saudara* (Penang, 1928–1941) (Ungku Maimunah 1987: 21).

The second group of Malay writers were known as *penulis guru* (teacher-writers) and *penulis wartawan* (journalist-writers). Malay-school teachers as well as teachers and students at teacher training colleges performed a significant role in the development of Malay journalism in the 1920s and 1930s. A number of these teacher-writers like Harun Mohd. Amin (Harun Amimurrashid), Abdullah Sidek and Ibrahim Haji Yaacob contributed articles, short stories (*cerita pendek* or *cerpen*), Malay classical verses (*syair*), etc. to Malay newspapers and magazines which had a comparatively secular outlook including *Warta Malaya* (Singapore, 1930–1941), *Majlis* (Kuala Lumpur, 1931–1941), *Utusan Melayu* (Singapore, 1939–1941) and *Majallah Guru* (Seremban, Kuala Lumpur, Penang, 1924–1940) as well as above-mentioned more Islamic-minded *Al-Ikhwan* and *Saudara* (Roff 1994 [1967]: 157–177; Ungku Maimunah 1987: 21–24). Malay-educated teachers and journalists highlighted various problems such as the socio-economic backwardness of the Malays and the erosion of Malay rights. It should be noted, however, that English-educated writers like Onn Jaafar, Zainal Abidin Ahmad (Za'ba) and Ishak Haji Muhammad and Arabic-educated journalists like Syed Sheikh Al-Hadi and Abdul Rahim Kajai also made great contributions to the development of Malay journals in which they tried to raise awareness of Malay problems.

British perceptions of Malays

In formulating a policy on the education of Malays, as William R. Roff argues, the British authorities had to find a compromise between preservation and innovation (Roff 1994 [1967]: 138). While the British authorities saw the need to provide modern secular education for the Malay populace in a spirit of rationalism, they carefully avoided "over-educating" the Malays.

The British applied a two-pronged education policy towards the Malays, apart from Islamic religious education, which was under control of the state religious authorities. Ordinary Malay children, mostly from the peasant class, were required to complete Malay-medium primary education. They were not, however, encouraged to enter English schools except for a small number of top-scoring students. Otherwise, the British intended to provide post-primary English-medium education only for a limited number of Malay children, particularly sons of Malay royal and aristocratic families. Many of the privileged English-educated Malay boys were to fill relatively minor posts in government departments.

This education policy closely reflected the British perceptions of Malays. To put it simply, the British intended to reproduce the Malay agricultural class within the context of an ethnic division of labour in British Malaya. Accordingly, the main purpose of British education policy towards the Malays was to educate the Malay populace to be "intelligent peasants." The Resident of Perak, Frank Swettenham, who laid down education policy in the Protected (later Federated) Malay States, wrote in 1891 in his report on Perak for 1890 that:

> The one danger to be guarded against is an attempt to teach English indiscriminately. It could not be well taught, except in a few schools, and I do not think it is at all desirable to give the children of an agricultural

population an indifferent knowledge of a language that to all but the very few would only unfit them for the duties of life, and make them discontented with anything like manual labour. At present the large majority of Malay boys and girls have little opportunity of learning their own language, and if the Government undertakes to teach them this, the Koran and something about figures and geography (especially of the Malay Peninsula and Archipelago), this knowledge and the habits of industry, punctuality and obedience that they will gain by regular attendance at school will be of material advance to them, and assist them to earn a livelihood in any vocation, while they will be likely to prove better citizens and more useful members of the community than if imbued with a smattering of English ideas which they would find could not be realized. (cited in Barlow (1995: 374))

From this account it is clear that Swettenham considered English education for the Malay populace as being harmful to the reproduction of the agrarian class. For him, English education would give ordinary Malays impractical knowledge that might generate unrealistic dreams. It would be more beneficial, he thought, if Malay vernacular education equipped rural Malay pupils with useful basic knowledge, skills and discipline.

About thirty years later, William George Maxwell, Chief Secretary to Government, Federated Malay States, presented similar views on education for the Malays. In his report on the Federated Malay States for 1920, he clearly stated that the main objective of education policy towards the Malays was to produce "intelligent peasants (or fishermen)":

> ...the aim of the government is not to turn out a few well-educated youths, nor numbers of less well-educated boys, rather it is to improve the bulk of the people, and to make the son of the fisherman or the peasant a more intelligent fisherman or peasant than his father had been, and a man whose education will enable him to understand how his own lot in life fits in with the scheme of life around him. (ARFMS 1920: 13)

Several factors contributed to the British education policy for the Malays. First, the British intended to maintain the existing order in Malay communities. The appearance of large numbers of English-educated Malays would have disturbed the hierarchical social structure in Malay states. The British authorities thus carefully controlled educational content and access in order to protect the established order from "over-educating" the Malay peasant population. British experience in India was behind this cautious attitude (Loh 1975: 2–4, 24, 82). After the well-known Orientalist-Anglicist debate over Indian education in the 1820s and 1830s, British education policy in India encouraged the English language and Western knowledge particularly at secondary and tertiary levels. This approach promoted the growth of the English-educated population and the dissemination of Western ideas in British India. Yet it also caused increasing unemployment or underemployment among English-educated Indians, which fuelled their frustration at British rule. The bitter lesson in India had sunk deep into the hearts of British administrators, as can be seen in Swettenham's statement in 1896:

> Nothing but good can, I think, come of teaching *in the native languages* what we call the three R's; and of greater value still are the habits of orderliness and punctuality, and the duties inculcated by teachers in the hope of making good citizens of their pupils. We have schools for girls as well as boys; and that, I think, is cause for congratulation in a Muhammadan country, where it will be understood that the only religious instruction is that of the Koran, at special hours, and usually by a special Koran teacher. I do not think we should aim at giving Malays the sort of higher education that is offered by the Government of India to its native subjects, but I would prefer to see the establishment of classes where useful trades would be taught. It is unfortunate that, when an Eastern has been taught to read and write English very indifferently, he seems to think that from that moment the Government is responsible for his future employment, and in consequence the market for this kind of labour is overstocked, while many honourable and profitable trades find difficulty in obtaining workmen, because of the prejudice against anything like manual labour. [Italics in original] (Swettenham 1983 [1896]: 186)

Ordinary Malays, therefore, were only expected to complete primary education in their vernacular, which stressed the 3R's (reading, writing and arithmetic) and good discipline, with the exception of a limited number of excellent students who were allowed some access to English education. In contrast, sons of the Malay ruling class had opportunities to study in English schools and thus prepare for future employment in the public services.

It should be noted that there were some differences among British officers' views about the education of Malays. Not all British administrators opposed more progressive education policy. For instance, R.J. Wilkinson, a notable educational administrator in British Malaya, appears to have been dedicated to the spread of education for the Malays as well as the expansion of popular education in English. Yet his view did not prevail and his successor, R.O. Winstedt, adopted more conservative education policy as discussed below. Furthermore, limiting access to English education seems to have been supported by royal and aristocratic Malay families who enjoyed their class privileges in the existing social order.[13]

Second, such a "rural-biased" education policy towards the Malays stemmed partly from the ethnic division of labour in British Malaya. Particularly after the late nineteenth century, a great immigrant influx from China, India and other parts of the world caused food shortages in British Malaya, which had been considerably dependent on imported rice from neighbouring countries like Siam and Burma. To improve the situation, the British encouraged the Malay populace to concentrate on producing food for the rapidly growing immigrant population, such as Chinese labourers in tin mines and Indian rubber plantation workers. In 1913, the Federal Council passed Malay Reservation Enactment, which enabled the residents to reserve certain areas of land, mainly for rice cultivation, exclusively for Malay owners (Roff 1994 [1967]: 122–123).[14] It was within this context that Malay vernacular education aimed at producing a large number of "intelligent peasants."

Third, British administrators, to a greater or lesser extent, shared colonial romanticist and paternalistic views about the Malay populace (Awang Had 1979: 132–134). Quite a few British administrators such as Swettenham, William Edward Maxwell, Hugh Clifford, Wilkinson and Winstedt were simultaneously well-known scholars in the field of Malayan and Malay studies. As Hendrik M.J. Maier rightly points out, British scholar-administrators like Swettenham, Maxwell and Clifford left a message to their successors such as Wilkinson and Winstedt that "the Malays were to remain Malay, Malayness should be strengthened, and the seeds for their improvement had to be found primarily in their own communities" (Maier 1988: 56–57). For British administrators, Malay vernacular education was a useful tool for the conservation of "Malay character," such as courteousness, obedience, ingenuousness and rusticity, among the indigenous populace.

The Winstedt Report of 1917

The standardization of Malay vernacular education was achieved following the appointment of R.O. Winstedt[15] in 1916 to the newly created post of Assistant Director of Education in charge of Malay schools. Winstedt was a scholar-administrator who published an enormous number of books and articles on the language, literature, religion and history of the Malays. Immediately after the appointment, he was sent to Java and the Philippines in order to survey vernacular and industrial education there and to make recommendations on Malay vernacular education. Upon his return in 1917, Winstedt produced a report[16] which would form the foundation for the British policy on Malay vernacular education in the 1920s and 30s.

In his report of 1917, Winstedt concluded that compared with vernacular education in Java and the Philippines, Malay vernacular education in British Malaya was considerably behind. "At present," he wrote, "the education afforded to the Malay of the Malay Peninsula is inferior to that provided for men of his race in Java and the Philippines" (No. 22 of 1917: C 120). This conclusion indicates that Winstedt regarded the indigenous peoples in Java and the Philippines to be of the "Malay" race. It is not surprising, therefore, if he thought that British educational administrators in Malaya could learn a lot from educational policies towards the indigenous populace in Java and the Philippines.

Winstedt recommended the standardization of Malay vernacular education. He proposed dissolving the small teachers' training colleges into one central college in the interests of uniformity, efficiency and cost-effectiveness. The proposed new college was expected to offer a course of three years instead of the two-year course provided by existing training colleges at Melaka and Matang (No. 22 of 1917: C 118). His plan was realized in 1922 when the two training colleges were integrated into one central college, namely, the Sultan Idris Training College (SITC) at Tanjung Malim, Perak. Winstedt also suggested standardizing school textbooks. The government was encouraged to prepare new standard textbooks and readers in various subjects (No. 22 of 1917: C 118). By introducing these reforms, Malay pupils would be taught using standard textbooks under a common method of teaching. These recommendations were subsequently realized. The Department of Education soon began to publish a series of textbooks, titled the "Malay School Series." Furthermore, a series of popular stories, mainly consisting of the Malay translation of European stories and novels, was also published under the name of the "Malay Home Library Series."

Two of the proposals in the Winstedt Report might be closely related to the official construction of Malayness. The first is the rationalization of the teaching of history and geography in Malay vernacular schools,

> We should follow the Dutch method. Only the geography of the district in which the school is situated should be taught in the lower standards; in the higher standards, the geography of the Malay Peninsula with just an outline of the Malay Archipelago and of the world beyond it. (No. 22 of 1917: C 97)

Along these lines, Winstedt recommended the authorities to use a simple textbook together with the following three maps: (i) a full map of the Peninsula, (ii) an outline map of the Malay Archipelago, and (iii) a very simple outline map of the world showing the continents, the important countries, the British colonies, and some chief towns. He was also sceptical about the existing method of teaching history in Malay vernacular schools. Following the Dutch method, he proposed omitting the subject, but this was not realized.

> Remembering that modern education is designed to develop the mind and not to deaden it with half-understood detail, I consider that the Dutch omission to teach the *kampong* boy history is sound and should be followed by us. It is useless to try to teach him European history: to teach him the fairy-tales that stand for history in Malay chronicles is futile, and, for teaching him scientifically the history of his own land, our books are founded on evidence too debatable and arrive at conclusions calculated too often to wound his susceptibilities. [Italics in original] (No. 22 of 1917: C 97)

Winstedt also suggested the method of teaching history and geography in teachers' training colleges.

> I think I am right in saying that the teaching of history and geography in our training colleges is far less intelligent. We require new text-books of geography and history of our colleges. Meanwhile history should be taught by lectures from Mr. WILKINSON'S pamphlet in the *Series of Papers on Malay Subjects* and no other should be studied. [Capitals and italics in original] (No. 22 of 1917: C 99)

In this way, Winstedt strongly proposed limiting the teaching of history and geography to "his own land," namely, the Malay Peninsula (Malaya) and the Malay Archipelago (Malay world) by a modern scientific method. Following his recommendations, several standard Malay textbooks were written in the form of modern historiography and geography, such as *Ilmu Alam Melayu* (Geography of the Malay World) and *Kitab Tawarikh Melayu*[17] (Book of Malay History), both of which were written by Winstedt himself, five volumes of *Sejarah Alam Melayu* (History of the Malay World), written by Abdul Hadi Haji Hasan and Buyong Adil, as well as other textbooks translated from English.[18]

The second important factor is his emphasis on practical education, popularly known as "rural bias." In this regard, Winstedt paid close attention to industrial works in schools in the Philippines. In primary and intermediate courses there, boys were taught manual works such as gardening and other industrial works including poultry-rearing, carpentry, pottery, carving, and basketry, while girls learned domestic works such as cooking, house-keeping, sewing, embroidery and lace-making (No. 22 of 1917: C 110–118).

> Horticulture and at least one other industry should be taught and a pass in one industrial subject required for a certificate. The Philippine system of school and home gardens should be adopted. Sewing will take the place of horticulture for girls, and if possible, cooking should be taught. (No. 22 of 1917: C 118)

What is obvious here is Winstedt's great persistence in industrial education. Also noticeable is his adherence to gender role differentiation between Malay males and females while he acknowledged that "Malay girls are more intelligent and industrious than the boys" (No.22 of 1917: C 116). Following his recommendations, practical subjects were gradually introduced into the curriculum of Malay vernacular schools in British Malaya. Training colleges for Malay-school teachers also introduced these subjects in order to produce teachers qualified to teach them. This strong emphasis on practical works in Malay vernacular education was along the lines of the above-mentioned British economic policy towards the ordinary Malay populace.

There is little doubt that the Winstedt report of 1917 embodied a characteristic feature of the British education policy towards the Malays, namely, a compromise between two contradictory orientations: preservation and innovation. The Malay populace were to maintain and strengthen their "Malayness" or "Malay character," which was closely associated with rurality and gender role differentiation, while they were encouraged to adopt the more "rational" and "practical" way of thinking.

3 Knowledge and Experience: The Case of the Sultan Idris Training College

The transmission of knowledge through Malay vernacular education should be understood with due consideration for the whole educational practice. Therefore, this chapter is a detailed investigation of teacher training at the SITC. It consists of five sections. The first section provides the college's historical background. To show how SITC students accumulated knowledge and experience, the second section explores the formal curriculum of the SITC, the third section looks at extra-curricular activities, and the fourth section examines dormitory life at the college. The final section interrogates the reproduction of ethnic, class and gender relations in the SITC teacher training.

Overview

As mentioned above, merging two training colleges at Melaka and Matang, the Sultan Idris Training College (SITC)[1] was established in 1922 at Tanjung Malim, a small town on the southern end of Perak. The SITC offered a three-year course for training male Malay-school teachers. The college was named after the late Sultan Idris of Perak, who was supportive of educating the Malays, including the establishment of the Malay College, Kuala Kangsar (MCKK) in 1905 and the Malay Training College at Matang in 1913. Though the SITC was not categorized as a higher educational institute, O.T. Dussek, the first Principal of the SITC (1922–1936), called the college "a Vernacular University in embryo" (Dussek 1939: 1).

Residential schools in British Malaya were modelled along the lines of British public schools. In prewar England and Wales, "public school" stood for a select group of old independent secondary schools for boys, like Eaton and Rugby, most of which had a boarding system.[2] British public schools were mainly concerned with producing gentlemen, who were expected to embody an aristocratic ethos. For this purpose, these public schools emphasized an all-round education. Teaching and learning the classics constituted the most important part of the formal curriculum while extra-curricular sporting, cultural and artistic activities were also encouraged. The majority of students admitted to Cambridge or Oxford came from these public schools. In British Malaya, the MCKK, called the "Eaton of the East," received a rich legacy from British public schools (Khasnor 1995: chap. 8).[3] The MCKK, one of the most prestigious English schools in British Malaya, was established in 1905 as a fully residential school mainly for Malay boys of royal and aristocratic families.

The SITC also followed the example of British public schools (Dussek 1939: 1). Like the MCKK, the SITC inherited some public-school traditions including a boarding system and extra-curricular sporting and cultural activities. The SITC, however, differed from the MCKK in several senses. The MCKK, on the one hand, was an English-medium school primarily for the sons of privileged families to become administrators in British Malaya. The SITC, on the other, was a Malay-medium teacher training college mainly for rural boys of humble origin. When the SITC was officially opened on 29 September 1922, W.G. Maxwell, Chief Secretary to Government, Federated Malay States, said:

> We really wanted to give the best possible education to the Malays of the village, and that would be the principal aim of this College, namely, to give the best possible education to the Malays of the agricultural class and the fisherfolk. (cited in Awang Had (1979: 77))

The site of the SITC, Tanjung Malim in Perak, was selected "for (a) its good soil, (b) its vicinity to rail, river, and small township, (c) its centrality" (Awang Had 1979: 73). Good soil was required because the SITC stressed a practical agricultural education, following the Winstedt report's recommendations. Dussek regarded its location in a rural area as necessary for safeguarding the mental well-being of rural-bred boys as well as enabling the acquisition of a sufficient area of land at a moderate price.

> The college is situated in a rural area, and not near a large town. This is considered important as affecting the mental outlook of the students. We do not desire to do anything to increase the lure which the towns undoubtedly exercise on the youth of all countries and races. (Dussek 1948 [1930]: 19)

Photo 3.1:   Teachers and students from Negeri Sembilan at the Sultan Idris Training College in 1930. (Courtesy of Arkib Negara Malaysia)

At the end of 1928, the SITC teaching staff comprised the Principal O.T. Dussek, one European Agricultural Instructor, three European and 15 Malay Assistant Masters, two Malay Religious Instructors and one Filipino Basketry Instructor (AREFMS 1928: 14). Most of these teachers were transferred from teaching colleges at Melaka and Matang, which were dissolved into the SITC.

Let us look at general regulations on admission of students to the SITC. According to the regulations of 1927 and 1936, a candidate "must be 16 years of age at date of entry" (*Education Code V 1927* 1927: 20) or "must be not under 16 and not over 18 years of age at date of entry" (*Education Code V 1936* 1937: 31). Students admitted to the SITC were usually former "pupil-teachers" in Malay schools. "Pupil-teachers" were pupils who had completed their Malay primary education and were employed as "untrained teachers" in Malay schools. Not until these pupil-teachers

Table 3.1: Salary scale for Malay-school teachers, 1924

Men		
	Special Class	$110–160
	Class I	$75–100
	Class II A (trained)	$50–70
	Class II B (untrained)	$30–45
	Class III A (trained)	$30–45
	Class III B (untrained)	$18–25
	Class IV (probationer)	$12–15
Women		
	Class I	$25–35
	Class II	$18–25
	Class III	$12–15

Source: *F.M.S. Government Handbook for 1924* as cited in Awang Had (1979: 20)

had completed the required course at teacher training colleges, were they officially recognized as "trained teachers" (Loh 1975: 135). Table 3.1 shows a considerable difference in salary between trained and untrained male Malay-school teachers in 1924. At that time, female teachers basically remained untrained and their average salary was far lower than the average salary for male teachers. The first training college for female Malay-school teachers was not established until 1935, at Melaka.

In the prewar era, about 120 to 130 boys entered the SITC annually and the total enrolment each year was approximately 360 to 400. The college was designed to accommodate 300 boys, namely, 200 from the Federated Malay States and 100 from the Straits Settlements. Each state was given a quota of students to be sent to the college. Additional students were accepted from the Unfederated Malay States in Malaya and the Borneo territories (*Education Code V 1927* 1927: 20). For instance, in 1930, the SITC had 388 students which consisted of 209 from the Federated Malay States, 99 from the Straits Settlements, 75 from the Unfederated Malay States and 5 from other political units (Awang Had 1979: 77–79).

In the Straits Settlements and the Federated Malay States, the respective Inspector of Schools selected candidates from pupil-teachers. Selected candidates were permitted to compete in the entrance examination. As listed in Tables 3.2 and 3.3, the entrance examination was held in the following subjects: reading in both Jawi (Arabic) and Rumi (Romanised)

Table 3.2: The entrance examination of the SITC, 1927

	Note	**Marks**
(a) Reading	Jawi and Romanised	Pass or Fail
(b) Dictation	Jawi	25
(c) Dictation	Romanised	25
(d) Composition	The candidate will be required to reproduce a story read twice over.	100
(e) Arithmetic	From *Kitab Hisab II*; and *Kitab Hisab III* (Chapters I–VII).	100
(f) The Geography of the Malay Peninsula and the Malay Archipelago	Textbooks: *Ilmu Alam*, Chapters VI to XIII inclusive. Simple questions only will be set to test a candidate's intelligence.	50
(g) The History of Malaya	Textbooks: *Tawarikh Melayu*	50

Note. Marks for Reading will be awarded by the Inspector of Schools; marks in the other subjects, by the examination staff of the College.
Source: *Education Code V 1927* (1927: 22)

Table 3.3: The entrance examination of the SITC, 1936

	Note	**Marks**
Part I		
(a) Reading	Jawi and Rumi	Pass or Fail
(b) Dictation	Jawi and Rumi	Pass or Fail
(c) Mental Arithmetic		Pass or Fail
Part II		
(a) Composition	The Examination will include some or all of the following: (i) Simple Essay, (ii) Simple Letter Writing, (iii) Reproduction of a short story, (iv) Simple Questions on Grammar and Syntax, etc.	100
(b) Arithmetic	From *Kitab Hisab II* and *Kitab Hisab III* (Chapters I–IX), omitting Square root.	100
(c) Geography	The Geography of the Malay Peninsula, the Malay Archipelago and Asia.	50
(d) History	History of the Malay Peninsula as contained in the simpler portions of *Sejarah Alam Melayu*. The four parts of the book should be distributed over 4 years, one each for each year in rotation.	50

Note. Part I of the examination will be conducted by Inspector of Schools while Part II of the examination will be conducted by College Examiners.
Source: *Education Code V 1936* (1937: 39)

alphabets, dictation in Jawi and Rumi, composition, arithmetic, geography, and history. The geography paper mainly covered the Malay Peninsula and the Malay Archipelago while the history paper focused on the Malay Peninsula (*Education Code V 1927* 1927: 22; 1936: 39). For candidates from the Unfederated Malay States, however, the entrance examination was not compulsory.

Although there is no data available regarding their parents' occupations, it appears that most of the SITC students were sons of the peasantry and commoners in Malay villages (Roff 1994 [1967]: 143). As mentioned, this was in sharp contrast with the MCKK, which aimed to educate the sons of Malay rulers and aristocrats to be public administrators. The typical career path for male Malay-school teachers was as follows. They completed their primary education at Malay schools at the age of 12 or 13 and started to work as untrained pupil-teachers. Around the age of 16, they entered the SITC to pursue the three-year course of training. After graduating from the college, they usually returned to Malay schools to serve as trained teachers. Later, some of them became headmasters of Malay schools or educational administrators. Borrowing the terminology of Benedict Anderson (1991 [1983]), we can say that the SITC was the centre of educational or, more specifically, learning "pilgrimages" for male Malay pupil-teachers in British Malaya. It is important to note, however, that their teaching pilgrimages were usually made within their home states, whereas Anderson was referring to administrative pilgrimages to the capital city.

Curriculum

The SITC aimed to achieve an educational standard somewhat higher than Malay-medium primary schools in which reading, writing and arithmetic skills (3Rs) and the basic knowledge of agriculture were regarded as most important. E.H.S. Bretherton of Malayan Education Department presented his view of the curriculum of Malay-medium primary schools and the SITC in the following terms:

> The Malay Population of the Peninsula is essentially agricultural. The curriculum of the vernacular schools does not, therefore, aim high, and has a definite agricultural bias... In ordinary school subjects, the three most important are, of course, Reading, Writing and Arithmetic; in addition it is

considered important that boys should have some knowledge of hygiene, of their own language and history, and of the geography of the Malay peninsula in particular and of Asia in general. The curriculum at the Sultan Idris Training College aims somewhat higher in all these subjects than that in the village schools, and the theory and practice of teaching is added. (Bretherton 1931: 4–5)

The SITC curriculum contains general academic subjects and various early morning activities. Distribution of subjects and activities as well as periods of instruction allocated per week can be seen in Table 3.4. Subjects were classified into several sections, namely, (a) General Literature (Language, Literature and History), (b) General Science (Arithmetic, Geometry and Geography), (c) Writing and Drawing, (d) Pedagogy (Theory of Teaching, Practice of Teaching and Hygiene), (e) Physical Training and (f) Manual Training (Theory and Practice of Gardening, Basketry, etc.). In order to obtain the SITC certificate, students were required to pass an examination in the above subjects. There was no examination in General Knowledge. A special certificate was issued for Religious Instruction, which was separated from other subjects *(Education Code V 1936* 1937: 33–35).

The curriculum at the SITC largely followed the major recommendations of the Winstedt report of 1917. We should pay special attention to the teaching of history and geography as well as gardening and manual training because these subjects and activities appear to have played a significant role in shaping "Malayness."

The SITC rationalized and systematized teaching in history and geography, following Winstedt's suggestions. Although the college's curriculum in 1936 indicates that history (*Tawarikh* or *Sejarah*) was still paired with literature (*Hikayat*), as can be seen in Table 3.4, according to the SITC's syllabus, different textbooks were used for literature and history. Malay classics like *Sejarah Melayu* (The Malay Annals) or *Hikayat Hang Tuah* (The Story of Hang Tuah) were no longer used as textbooks for history but remained among readings in language and literature. From the British educationists' perspective, the value of classical Malay literature lay in literary technique rather than historical accounts. Authorized history textbooks were Winstedt's *Kitab Tawarikh Melayu* and Abdul Hadi Haji Hasan's and Buyong Adil's *Sejarah Alam Melayu*. As discussed in detail in the following chapter, these history

Table 3.4: Subjects and activities (periods allocated per week) at the SITC, 1936

	Periods		
	1ˢᵗ yr	**2ⁿᵈ yr**	**3ʳᵈ yr**
Arithmetic (*Ilmu Kira-kira*)	4	4	3
Geometry (*Ilmu Jometri/Geometri*)	–	1	2
Geography (*Ilmu Alam*)	4	4	4
Language (*Bahasa*)	3	3	3
History and Literature (*Tawarikh/Sejarah dan Hikayat*)	3	2	3
Agriculture (*Ilmu Tanaman*)	3	3	3
Theory of Teaching and Criticism Lessons (*Teori dan Amalan Pengajaran*)	2	2	2
Hygiene (*Ilmu Kesihatan*)	2	2	2
Drawing (*Lukisan*)	2	2	2
Writing (Blackboard) (Tulisan (*Papan Hitam*))	2	2	2
Basketry (*Anyaman Bakul*)	2	2	2
General Knowledge (*Pengetahuan Am/Berjenis-jenis Pengetahuan*)	1	1	1
Religious Instruction (*Pengajaran Ugama*)	2	2	2
Sub-total for Subjects	30	30	31
Physical Training (*Latihan Tubuh*)	2	2	2
Gardening (*Perkubunan*)	3	3	4
Basketry (*Anyaman Bakul*)	1	1	–
Sub-total for Early Morning Activities	6	6	6
Total	36	36	37

Source: *Education Code V 1936* (1937: 33); UPSI (2000: 45–51); Awang Had (1974: 100–116)

textbooks purportedly gave an objective, scientific account of Malay history unlike the classical literature. As previously stated, students were not taught world-history beyond the Malay Peninsula and Archipelago *(Educational Code V 1927* 1927: 28; *Education Code V 1936* 1937: 36–37).

Geography (*Ilmu Alam*) was divided into political geography, or what we now call human geography, and physical geography. Let us focus on the former, which seems more important in the context of our discussion of identity formation. According to the 1927 regulations, students were taught the geography of: the Malay Peninsula in first year; the Malay Archipelago, Asia, and Africa (in outline) in second year, and; Europe (with special attention to Great Britain), America, Australia and New

Zealand and the British Empire in third year (*Education Code V 1927* 1927: 28–31). The territorial scope of political geography was thus much wider than that of history. Still, the main focus of geography teaching was the Malay Peninsula and Archipelago. To this end, Winstedt's *Ilmu Alam Melayu* was the most important geography textbook. For world geography, Malay translations of English books were used.

Teaching history and geography with a clear "Malay-orientation" seems to have contributed towards the students developing a Malay ethno-national consciousness. The narrative in history and geography textbooks and their role in identity formation will be closely examined in the following chapter. The role of a few charismatic teachers should be recognized as well. Some SITC alumni remembered Abdul Hadi Haji Hasan, who taught history at the college from 1922 until 1929, as a nationalistic teacher. Buyong Adil, an SITC history teacher who was taught history by Abdul Hadi at the college recalled that "he [Abdul Hadi] implanted nationalist sentiments (*perasaan kebangsaan*) and was surely regarded by his students as a man who developed their attachment for their own nation (*bangsa*) and homeland (*tanah ayer*)" (Buyong 1956: 14). Buyong himself was also remembered as a history teacher who stoked the pride of the Malay nation (*bangsa*) in his classes (Shaharom 1996: 94).

Another important subject was General Knowledge, comprising a series of lectures wherein SITC teachers delivered talks in rotation. Among the influential lecturers were Harun Mohd. Amin (Harun Aminurrashid), Ahmad Abdullah (Ahmad Bakhtiar), Zainal Abidin Ahmad (Za'ba) and Dussek. Harun, who was also well-known as a prolific writer and novelist, appears to have been the most popular speaker.[4] In his talks, he tried to raise students' consciousness of Malay nationalism, referring to growing nationalist movements in Indonesia and other countries of the world (UPSI 2000: 154–156: Shaharom 1996: 98–104).

The SITC also attached great importance to practical education, particularly gardening and manual training, in accordance with Winstedt's recommendations. Practical subjects such as agriculture and basketry were therefore included in the curriculum. More importantly, students were required to participate in gardening, manual training (basketry, carpentry, bookbinding, net-making, etc.) and physical training in the early morning. Four mornings per week from 6:30 to 7:30 a.m. and one afternoon from 4:45 to 6 p.m. were devoted to school gardening.[5] Gardening was taught by a European instructor and a Malay gardening teacher. The SITC's garden occupied 2 to 3 acres of land, which were divided into communal and individual plots. The students grew various vegetables including maize, sweet potato, groundnut, tomato, lettuce, Lima bean, long bean, and French bean as well as fruits like pineapple and banana. Economic crops such as tea and coffee were introduced as well (Bretherton 1931: 10–13; Dussek 1948 [1930]: 19–21; Awang Had 1979: 84–87).

Manual training or handicraft was similarly emphasized. As mentioned, Winstedt adopted the idea of handicraft training from the Philippines. The most important manual training was basketry, which was compulsory for all students. W. Olaguera, a Filipino teacher who had introduced basketry at the Malay Training College at Melaka in 1918, transferred to the SITC in 1922 to teach the same subject (Awang Had 1979: 108). In the Basketry course, selected students were also taught other handicrafts such as carpentry, bookbinding, net making and pottery (*Education Code V 1936* 1937: 54).

This emphasis on practical, industrial education broadly effected Malay vernacular education. First, SITC-graduates played an important role in disseminating knowledge and skill in gardening and handicraft. The British principal, Dussek, positively evaluated the effect of practical education.

> I can say with confidence that the introduction of manual training, and particularly of school gardening, has had a profound effect on the attitude of the Malay schoolboy towards manual work of all kinds… The attitude of the new teacher is reflected in the new pupil. The new pupil has begun to realize that his education in the school is a real preparation for life. There can be no doubt of the success of school gardening in the Malay Vernacular schools… (Dussek 1948 [1930]: 23).

Yazid Ahmad, an SITC teacher, shared Dussek's appraisal.

> The large number of exhibits sent to the agricultural shows throughout the country and the many prizes obtained by school children give proof of the good work which is being done in many of the schools. The beneficial effect of the "rural bias" in the school curriculum on the Malay children and the Malay community in general is already being felt, and as yet the work is but in its infancy. (Yazid 1948 [1930]: 55)

There may have been a secondary effect on villagers living near the SITC, too. An SITC graduate recalled that villagers had visited the college occasionally to learn crossbreeding techniques (Shaharom 1996: 76–77). The SITC's baskets were exhibited at the British Empire Exhibition at Wembley Park in London in the 1920s, and sold very well (AREFMS 1924: 13; 1925: 13). E.H.S. Bretherton of Malayan Education Department argued that basket-making served a useful purpose in manual training in Malay schools though there was still a lack of coordination in the work of villagers (Bretherton 1931: 9).

Practical education also seems to have had broad effects on the hearts and minds of the students. Early morning activities inculcated values such as discipline and diligence. Each student had to rise early in the morning for physical education, gardening and basketry. They were required to check the condition of their crops and to record their daily work in their notebooks and card-indexes. The gardening teacher awarded marks twice a term for individual and communal plots (Dussek 1948 [1930]: 22; Shaharom 1996: 74). Furthermore, group work in gardening may have strengthened a sense of camaraderie among the college boys. Not only did they have to cooperate with each other in these projects, but they also provided frequent and ample opportunities to talk about other topics such as educational practices, literature, nationalism and politics while working in communal plots (Shaharom 1996: 76).

Finally, let us briefly look at religious, namely, Islamic education at the SITC. SITC students had two period of religious instruction per week, although Winstedt had denied the need for religious instruction at teacher training colleges. Following the regulations of 1936, students were expected to learn Islamic theology, rules regarding religious rituals, practice in reading the Qur'an and the simple history of the religion in first year. Qur'anic phonetics and Islamic laws on commerce, property, etc. were taught in second year, while Islamic laws on family and common crimes, the administration of Islamic law and holy days for Muslims in third year (*Education Code V 1936* 1937: 54–55). As mentioned earlier, however, religious instruction and other subjects were not treated equally. The result of the subject was not mentioned in the SITC's certificate but in a separate certificate. Obviously, religious education was considered to be of secondary importance in the SITC's overall curriculum.[6]

Acquisition of knowledge outside the curriculum

SITC students had chances to acquire knowledge not only in school subjects but also outside the classroom. The focus of our investigation is on the students' reading environment as reading is a powerful means of acquiring knowledge. There was no special building or room used as the SITC college library before World War II. Yet students could borrow books located on the second floor of the Assembly Hall. Some books were donated while others were purchased by the college. They included religious books, collections of classical Malay literature (*hikayat*) and poetry (*syair*), school textbooks and newspapers (Awang Had 1979: 119–120). Special attention should be paid to Malay publications from the Netherlands East Indies and the Middle East. Among Malay periodicals were those published in Indonesia such as *Bintang Timur, Bintang Hindia* and *Soeloeh Ra'jat Indonesia* as well as those published in Egypt like *Seruan Azhar* (Awang Had 1979: 143).

Equally important were bookstores outside the campus. Special mention should be made of AHMY & Company, a bookstore in Tanjung Malim owned by Abdul Hadi Haji Hasan, the earlier mentioned history teacher of the SITC, and Md. Yusuf. Md. Sharif, a government clerk. The bookstore sold Malay books, newspapers and magazines published in British Malaya, the Netherlands East Indies and the Middle East. Students were exposed to Indonesian nationalism from various magazines as well as books and collections of speeches by political leaders and intellectuals in the Netherlands East Indies like Sukarno, Mohammad Hatta, Djamaluddin G.D.M. Adi Negoro, Muhammad Yamin, Sutan Sjahrir, Tan Malaka, etc. (Shaharom 1996: 92–93).

A department called the Translation Bureau was established at the SITC in 1924 to take over the task of publishing textbooks and readers for Malay vernacular schools from the Department of Education, the Straits Settlements and the Federated Malay States. Around 1930, the SITC had a board of General Editors that included R.O. Winstedt (Director of Education), O.T. Dussek (Principal of the SITC) and Zainal Abidin Ahmad (Za'ba) (Chief Translator). Other staff included seven translators (three under training) and two Malay writers (Bretherton 1931: 21). Dussek and Za'ba wanted to develop the Bureau into a large publisher of vernacular books like the Balai Pustaka in the Netherlands East Indies. Winstedt, however, did not support this idea (Abdullah Sanusi 1966: 54).

Photo 3.2: The Translation Bureau, Sultan Idris Training College, in 1929. Zainal Abidin Ahmad (Za'ba) and Abdul Hadi Haji Hasan are seated second and fourth from the left. (Courtesy of Arkib Negara Malaysia)

The Translation Bureau published school textbooks and readers in the "Malay School Series." While many of them were Malay translations of English textbooks, some were newly written, for instance, the five volumes of *Sejarah Alam Melayu* by Abdul Hadi Haji Hasan and Buyong Adil. Publications in The Malay School Series between 1924 and 1936 included 32 textbooks, 10 readers, two books on handicraft, and others. The Bureau also published Malay translations of famous stories and novels in the "Malay Home Library Series." Thirty-six publications were produced in the series between 1924 and 1936. Among them were Malay translations of *Treasure Island, Robin Hood, Adventures of Sherlock Homes, Cinderella, Aladdin and the Wonderful Lamp* and *Ali Baba and the 40 Thieves* (Zainal Abidin 1939: 157–158; Abdullah Sanusi 1966; UPSI 2000: 69–80). Some of these were included among the books that could be borrowed from the second floor of the Assembly Hall. The print runs generally ranged from

Photo 3.3: View of the Main Hall, Sultan Idris Training College. (Courtesy of Arkib Negara Malaysia)

5,000 to 10,000 and sometimes up to 40,000 for the Malay School Series and from 5,000 to 10,000 for the Malay Home Library Series (Yazid 1948 [1931]: 32).

As will be discussed in more detail later, it is widely acknowledged that some of the school textbooks in the Malay School Series, particularly history textbooks, played an important role in creating a Malay identity. The extent to which story books in the Malay Home Library Series contributed Malay identity formation is not as obvious, though. According to Za'ba, the Malay Home Library Series had a wide readership not only among students but also among the general public (Zainal Abidin 1939: 158–159). Some have argued, however, that books in the Malay Home Library Series provided little instruction and inspiration due to their foreign themes and the lack of depth. To them, reading materials from the Netherlands East Indies were much more influential (Abdullah Sanusi 1966: 57–58).

In addition to regular classes and reading, occasional lectures and speeches provided SITC students with opportunities to think about their ethno-national identity. These lectures were usually held on Saturday night in the college hall (*Chenderamata,* October 1930: 6). Teachers like Harun, Abdul Hadi and Buyong occasionally lectured about topics such as the history of the Malays and nationalism in other countries. It is notable, too, that Principal Dussek often tried to increase the students' awareness of their own language and race. In his speech to graduating students of SITC in 1935, he said:

> Your language is, I believe, spoken by some 70 millions of people. It forms one of the largest language groups in the world. Do not forget that fact. Cultivate your language; strive to raise it to the position it deserves amongst world languages. If the prestige of your language rises, so in equal measure rises the prestige of your race. (*Straits Times* 23 November 1935, cited in Awang Had (1979: 136))

Dussek, a graduate of London University, became interested in the Malay language after his arrival in Malaya in 1912. Some SITC graduates pointed out that Dussek was loved and respected by many boys as a devoted teacher who attempted to raise their consciousness of Malay identity (Buyong 1956: 15; Shaharom 1996: 64, 96–98). Shaharom Husain characterized Dussek as "a white (English) man in terms of his skin colour and physique but a Malay in terms of his heart"[7] (Shaharom 1996: 64). Of course, there is an internal contradiction in, and thus limits to, Dussek's advocacy of the awakening of Malay students in view of the fact that he was a British colonial teacher-administrator. Although he worked to raise the students' ethnic consciousness, he may not have gone so far as to support the idea of the political independence of Malaya. His strong attachment to the Malay language and culture, as Awang Had Salleh puts it, was based on his paternalistic and romanticist attitude towards the Malays, which was not much different from other British administrators (Awang Had 1979: 138–139). Despite these contradictions and limits, however, it is worth noting that Dussek was widely accepted by SITC students as a prime mover of Malay identity formation at the college.

House and extra-curricular activities

Fully residential British public schools are examples of "total institutions". "A total institution," according to Erving Goffman, "may be defined as a place of residence and work where a large number of like-situated individuals, cut off from the wider society for an appreciable period of time, together lead an enclosed, formally administered round of life" (Goffman 1961: xiii). For Geoffrey Walford, the public boarding schools are "total in that they provide everything that is deemed necessary for the pupils and exert control over pupils' activities day and night for periods up to three months" (Walford 1986: 174). He writes of life in public schools:

> Schools generally attempt to ensure that each day is full and structured, and that as much time as possible is "usefully" spent. Thus the rigorously timetabled academic activities of the school are extended into formal extra-curricular activities and then extended further into the formal social life of the houses, so that eating, going to bed, waking up and even brushing one's teeth become activities which, at least in theory, are conducted at set times of the day. Non-academic time is filled as much as possible by various forms of "useful" activity. Sports, which often occupy large slices of afternoon time, are there not simply so that boys can learn to play games well, or even enjoy playing, but to ensure that time is "usefully" spent. The range of extra-curricular clubs and societies and cultural activities is also designed to ensure that boys don't become idle. (Walford 1986: 71–72])

In that sense, British public schools share significant characteristics with other examples of total institutions, namely, prisons, mental hospitals, army barracks, etc. As a fully residential school, modelled on the line of public schools, the SITC can be characterized as a "total institution."

SITC's dormitories were called *rumah*, a Malay term equivalent to "house," which referred to dormitories in British public schools. There were six houses, named House A (*Rumah A*) to House F (*Rumah F*). Students from different states were mixed together in a house. As Awang Had Salleh points out, this boarding system may have helped to break down state provincialism among SITC students (Awang Had 1979: 139). This was a departure from the practice at the Malay Training College at Melaka, one of the SITC's predecessors, where the boys from each state were housed together. It is not surprising if the students of the Melaka College kept a stronger sense of belonging to their home states than SITC students (Zainuddin 1956: 36; Ramlah 1991: 52).

As in the case of British public schools, daily life at the SITC was strictly controlled. Students were required to follow a timetable throughout the

Table 3.5: The SITC daily timetable, 1936

7.00–8.00 a.m.	Gardening, physical training, etc.
8.00–9.00 a.m.	Breakfast
9.00–11.15 a.m.	Three periods
11.15–11.30 a.m.	Interval – tea and biscuits
11.30 a.m.–1.00 p.m.	Two periods
1.00 p.m.	Lunch
3.45 p.m.	Tea
4.45 p.m.	Preparation, etc.
5.00–6.00 p.m.	Games, etc.
6.15 p.m.	Bath
7.15 p.m.	Supper
8.15–9.30 p.m.	Indoor games, etc.
9.45 p.m.	Lights out (except for Thursday and Saturday nights – 10.15 p.m.)

Source: *Education Code V 1936* (1937: 32)

day. Table 3.5 shows the daily timetable of the SITC in 1936. Students had to wake up at 6 a.m. to take part in early morning activities, like gardening, physical training and basketry, which started 7 a.m. Breakfast began at 8 a.m. Starting from 9 a.m., they were to attend classes for three periods. Subsequent to a fifteen-minute break for tea and biscuits, they had another two periods until 1 p.m. when lunch started. Following a tea break, students had to prepare for classes from 4 p.m. Between 5 and 6 p.m. they were encouraged to take part in outdoor games, etc. After bath, supper began at 7.15 p.m. Boys were expected to play indoor games from 8.15 p.m. before lights out at 9.45 p.m. (*Education Code V 1936* 1937: 32).

Though not mentioned in the timetable, SITC students were required to follow Islamic religious practices, too. As for the five daily prayers, students had group prayers for *Maghrib* (after sunset until *Isyak*) and *Isyak* (dusk until *Subuh*) at *Surau Maktab*, the college's prayer hall, while they prayed individually at *Subuh* (dawn to sunrise), *Zuhur* (after true noon until *Asar*) and *Asar* (after the shadow of an object becomes equal to its length until sunset). On Friday, when no class work was scheduled, they could go out to perform the Friday prayer at a mosque in Tanjung Malim and to enjoy shopping and other activities after prayers (Shaharom 1996: 48–49). It should perhaps be noted that most British public schools were connected to one of the Christian denominations and required their students to attend chapel services, particularly on Sunday (Walford 1996: 9, 46). That is, the idea of incorporating religious instruction into extra-curricular activities was not unknown to British educational officers.

Discipline, control and surveillance were emphasized in the college's dormitory life. E.H.S. Bretherton, an officer at the Department of Education, emphasized the effects of discipline in strictly controlled dormitory life on SITC students in the following passages:

> The value of this discipline out of school hours as compared with discipline during school hours only is inestimable. A Malay youth, if left to his own devices, almost always leads a very irregular life: the effects of village life are particularly noticeable here during the first few weeks of a term when a strict medical supervision must be maintained. After the first few weeks of a term the students become accustomed to the regular hours and regular meals. (Bretherton 1931: 25)

Each house was supervised by a housemaster (*pengetua*) who was also an SITC teacher. Boarding students in a house were headed and represented by a senior student who became a head of house (*ketua rumah*), assisted by other senior students in the same house. These senior students took care of other boarders of the house. There were some privileges of seniority in dormitory life, as was the case in British public schools (Walford 1986: 49–50). Junior students were required to do the cleaning and other odd jobs under the supervision of senior students. They also had to call the senior students *Encik*, an honorific title for a man in Malay (Shaharom 1996: 46–48).

"Boarding schools," Walford writes, "differ from day schools in the extent to which 'extra-curricular' activities are formalized" (Walford 1986: 44). This clearly applies to the SITC, which sought to bring extra-curricular activities under the college's control. SITC students were required to take part in some activities after regular classes. In that sense, extra-curricular activities at the college were not optional but obligatory.

Sports constituted a significant part of extra-curricular activities at the SITC, as in British public schools. Public schools accord sports a major role in educating boys as "gentlemen." Sporting activities were emphasized not only for their physical training and health benefits, but also for fostering discipline, teamwork and obedience to the rules. Physical training was part of the early morning activities at the SITC.

Students had to take part in physical drill two periods a week from 6.30 to 7.30 a.m. (*Education Code V 1936* 1937: 51). They were required to play games four times a week in the afternoons, too. The main outdoor games were football, hockey, volleyball, badminton, rounders and *sepak raga* (*sepak takraw*). In the evening, indoor games such as ping pong, word building, chess, draughts, and snakes and ladders were played in the Assembly Hall (Bretherton 1931: 25).

Inter-house and inter-school matches and competitions were organized for most of these indoor and outdoor games (*Chenderamata,* April 1928: 13–25). At the SITC's annual sports festival (*Sukan Agung*), various matches and competitions were held between six houses. Some students represented the college in competitions against other schools such as MCKK, King Edward VII School, Anderson School and Victoria Institution[8] (UPSI 2000: 55–56). All of these schools were prestigious English schools. Inter-school contests were usually held between schools of equal status. The SITC was the sole Malay vernacular educational institution that was qualified to compete against those elite English schools.

Military training and scouting were also among the extra-curricular activities at the SITC. This was also in accordance with the tradition of British public schools. About half of the SITC students joined the Malayan Volunteer Infantry (MVI) and the remaining half became Scouts.[9] The MVI was an auxiliary volunteer defence force in British Malaya. SITC's MVI was established in 1924, and by 1927 had two platoons: Perak VII and Perak VIII. The MVI was later renamed the Sultan Idris Training College Company of the Federated Malay States Volunteer Force (Awang Had 1979: 115). In addition to the ordinary training, an annual camp was held at Port Dickson (AREFMS 1930: 26). Those who joined scouting learned Scout lore. After leaving the college, they would become Scoutmasters in Scout troops of Malay schools (Bretherton 1931: 19–20).

Military training and scouting may have contributed to make students internalize values of discipline, patience and obedience. It is also likely that these activities could give the boys chances to improve considerable skills in leadership and cooperation as well as to strengthen their solidarity transcending state boundaries. Military training and scouting probably inculcated some values favourable for the college's control over the students. It seems, however, that the students may have appropriated such values and skills for different, more voluntary activities.

The SITC's formal extra-curriculum included various activities other than sports, military training and scouting. There were, for example, cultural and artistic activities offered through various societies for debate, drama, music, geography, etc (Shaharom 1996: 78–82). The college published a magazine titled *Chenderamata* (Souvenir) twice a year. While the magazine reported the details of various college events and activities, SITC alumni, as well as teachers and students, contributed essays, poems and short stories to it (*Chenderamata*, 1928–1930; Awang Had 1979: 118; UPSI 2000: 54–55). The college also had a Students' Association (Persatuan Pelajar), but it was not very active, probably because the college authorities had established it and chosen its head (UPSI 2000: 158).

Though the SITC tried to control its students' everyday life through both curricular and extra-curricular activities, there was nevertheless room to escape from control and break or disregard the rules. For instance, some boys stole crops from the school garden while others secretly ate and drank after lights out (Shaharom 1996: 49, 74–76).

More importantly, it appears that some SITC students secretly organized political activities which were officially prohibited. According to Ibrahim Haji Yaacob, an SITC graduate who later became President of Kesatuan Melayu Muda (KMM) (Young Malay Union), when he studied at the college (1928–1931), he not only formed a secret student group named Ikatan Semenanjung/Borneo (Peninsular/Bornean Association) but also joined Partai Nasional Indonesia (PNI) (Indonesian National Party) with his college mates in 1929 (Agastja 1951: 60). This claim, however, is disputed by those who question whether a group of students could organize a secret association and join an Indonesian political party in view of the fact that teachers and students were under close surveillance by the authorities (Mustapha 1999: 207; Ahmat 2013: 66). Shaharom admitted that when he was an SITC student (1938–1940), a group of students joined the KMM and formed a small secret society named Kemeja Biru Hitam (Blue-Black Shirt) (Shaharom 1996: 105).

Some SITC students had an opportunity to meet political leaders of the Netherlands East Indies. After unsuccessful uprisings in Java in 1926 and 1927, some members of Partai Komunis Indonesia (PKI) (Communist Party of Indonesia) who took refuge in Malaya occasionally visited the SITC. Among them are Tan Malaka, Alimin, Musso, Sutan Djenain, Subakat, Djamaluddin Tamin and Natar Zainuddin (Mss. 176 (3); Roff 1994 [1967]: 222–225; Cheah 2012 [1983]: 10; Shaharom 1996: 95).

We should not presume that the college authorities were omnipotent or had full control of the students. SITC's teaching staff included local teachers, such as Abdul Hadi and Harun, who clearly demonstrated their nationalist sentiments, although they may not have explicitly voiced an anti-British position. As we have seen, even the British Principal Dussek was sympathetic to increasing awareness of Malay identity. Although as a "total institution," the college appears to have exercised effective control over the students, the boys still found ways to get around the rules and to become involved in volunteer activities which were neither organized nor sanctioned by the college.

Education policy and practice: Reproduction and beyond

School education performs a considerable role in the reproduction of social relations, as Pierre Bourdieu points out (Bourdieu 1977; Bourdieu and Passeron 1990 [1977]). Officially, British authorities in Malaya seem to have expected school education to play a key role in social reproduction. Malay-medium education and teacher training in colonial Malaya probably contributed to the reproduction of at least three types of social relations: ethnic, class and gender.

Ethnic reproduction

As discussed in Chapter 2, although the colonial government attempted to classify the population of British Malaya into various "races," such as "Europeans," "Eurasians," "Malays," "Chinese," "Indians" and "Others," each group was neither culturally homogeneous nor united by a single identity. "Malay" as an identity was one of the concepts under contestation. First, state provincialism (*kenegerian*), or the sense of belonging to one's own state (*negeri*), remained strong among the people who were called Malay. There was no single colonial state in prewar Malaya. "British Malaya" was just a generic term for Straits Settlements (Penang, Singapore and Melaka), Federated Malay States (Perak, Selangor, Negeri Sembilan and Pahang) and Unfederated Malay States (Perlis, Kedah, Kelantan, Terengganu and Johor). Second, Malay identity co-existed and competed with other ethno-cultural identities. As mentioned earlier, the Malay Peninsula had accepted a number of Muslim immigrants from other parts of the Archipelago such as Acehnese, Minangkabau, Javanese and

Bugis. While these immigrants and their descendants were gradually incorporated into "Malay" in a broad sense, many of them remained conscious of their immigrant origins. This is also the case for Muslims of Indian and Arab descent.

In this complex situation, education policy in British Malaya seems to have helped to formulate the concept of Malay. First, ethnic segregation in school education in line with the medium of instruction is likely to have contributed towards the formation of Malay identity. All children who were categorized as Malay were expected to receive a Malay-medium primary education. After completing three or four years at Malay primary schools, only a small number of excellent or privileged pupils were accepted into Special Malay Classes to work towards an English stream where they mixed with "non-Malay" pupils. Second, as mentioned, the British government emphasized the conservation of "Malayness" in the curriculum for Malay schools and training colleges like the SITC. The teaching of history and geography strongly focused on the Malay Peninsula and Archipelago. The promotion of practical industrial education such as gardening and basketry was another attempt for the colonial authorities to safeguard what they considered as "Malayness," which was tied closely to peasantry. In this way, education policy towards the Malays was expected to, and did, promote ethnic reproduction.

Class reproduction

Equally important is the role played by school education in fostering class reproduction. It is widely acknowledged that public schools, mainly for the elite, did, and continue to, play a significant role in class reproduction in England and Wales. Hence, it is worth examining the role of residential schools in British Malaya, modelled on the line of British public schools, in reproducing class relations. A brief comparison of the SITC and the MCKK would be useful. As argued above, Malay vernacular education mainly aimed to produce and reproduce "intelligent peasants." Even for Dussek, who was well known as a progressive educator, the main purpose of Malay vernacular education was "to equip happy, healthy, and contented youths for a pastoral or agricultural life" (CO 717/53: O.T. Dussek to Ormsby Gore, 22 December 1926). SITC graduates were required to educate Malay pupils to be rational and productive agricultural workers. As a fully residential school for Malay boys modelled on the lines of British public school, the

MCKK shared many characteristics with the SITC. Like the SITC, the MCKK emphasized extra-curricular activities like sports, art and culture as well as military training and scouting. There were also some similarities between the two schools in that students' dormitory life was under strict control and surveillance (Khasnor 1996: 137–158; Malay College 1965: 17–43).

Despite these similarities, there were notable differences in the medium of instruction and the contents of education between the SITC, which was established to train Malay-school teachers of plebeian origin, and the MCKK, whose main aim was to educate sons of the Malay ruling elite to be public officers.[10] First, the difference in the medium of instruction between the Malay-medium SITC and the English-medium MCKK was deeply connected with a class cleavage within the Malay population. Generally speaking, the social status of fully Malay-educated men, even SITC graduates, was lower than that of English-educated men like prestigious MCKK alumni. It should be added, however, that while the principle medium of instruction was English, Malay was taught as a compulsory subject at the MCKK to preserve "Malayness" among MCKK students as well as to meet the public services' requirement that all candidates must be bilingual. This is clearly different from other English-medium schools, where Malay was optional (Khasnor 1996: 154–155).

Second, the difference in the contents of education between the two institutions also corresponded to class disparity among the people who were called Malay. While the SITC emphasized the history and geography of the Malay world, history and geography classes at the MCKK focused on England, the British Empire and Europe (Khasnor 1996: 151–152). The MCKK followed the curriculum, including the history curriculum, for English schools of the Federated Malay States (Loh 1975: 80).[11] Unlike SITC students, students at the MCKK and other English schools had to cram knowledge about Euro/Anglo-centric history and geography to pass examinations such as Standard Seven Examination, Junior Cambridge Examination and Senior Cambridge Examination. MCKK students learned modern Malayan history only as a subset of the history of the British Empire (Loh 1975: 80–81). In contrast, it was not until 1938 that the history of the British Empire was introduced to the curriculum at the SITC (Awang Had 1979: 141). Though the MCKK introduced woodwork and carpentry in 1920 as extra-curricular activities (Khasnor 1996: 77), it put less emphasis on practical industrial education than the SITC, where students were taught gardening and manual training as school subjects. This also reflected class differences in education of the Malays. These differences between the two colleges illustrate that education policy helped to maintain class distinctions within the Malay population.

Gender reproduction

Colonial education and teacher training for the Malays seems to have promoted the reproduction of gender relations as well. Malay schools in British Malaya were officially divided into boys' schools and girls' schools although boys and girls studied together in several cases. This separation can also be seen in training for Malay-school teachers. Until World War II, the SITC only accepted male students. It was 1935 before the first training college for Malay-school female teachers, the Malay Women's Training College (MWTC), was established at Melaka.

As mentioned, Malay women in prewar British Malaya were left far behind in school education. Many Malay parents wanted their daughters to remain at home and were sceptical of formal school education for girls. To address this situation, the British authorities stressed domestic science and housekeeping in education of Malay women. M. Lomas, Principal of the MWTC, described the school's curriculum and the aim of Malay girls' schools as follows:

> The curriculum [of the MWTC] has a very definite bias towards domestic science and life in the home. As many, perhaps, as 95 per cent of Malay girls leave school to stay at home and later to marry and make a home of their own. Those who intend to enter a profession must of necessity go to the English schools, only the Malay teachers and midwives being drawn from the Malay schools themselves. The aim of the girls' vernacular schools is therefore to fit the pupils for home life, but at the same time to broaden their outlook and provide them with interests for their leisure time. (Lomas 1948 [1940]: 126)

It must be remembered that this emphasis on domestic science and home life not only reflected Malay parents' preference but reproduced the gender distinction of British schools in the prewar era. For instance, many girls' boarding schools in Britain were primarily concerned with "the making

Table 3.6: The MWTC daily timetable, 1936

6.00 a.m.	Rising bell
6.30–7.00 a.m.	Dressing and airing of beds
7.00–7.45 a.m.	Gardening; housework; cooking; laundry (4 divisions)
7.45–8.15 a.m.	Bath and dressing
8.15 a.m.	Coffee and bread
9.00–11.15 a.m.	Three periods (Friday: free)
11.15–11.30 a.m.	Interval (12.00–12.30: religious instruction)
11.30–1.00 a.m.	Two periods
1.15–1.45 p.m.	Lunch
1.45–3.45 p.m.	Ironing clothes: laundry section Crafts – other sections
3.45 p.m.	Tea
4.00–5.15 p.m.	Preparation
5.15–6.15 p.m.	Games and drill: badminton, tennikoit or basket-ball – 3 evenings Drill and rhythm – 3 evenings Brownies – 1 evening (Friday: Interschool matches)
6.15–6.30 p.m.	Bath
6.30 p.m.	Prayers
7.00–8.00 p.m.	Supper and washing of dishes
8.00–9.00 p.m.	Crafts and indoor games
9.30 p.m.	Lights out

Source: *Education Code V 1936* (1937: 61–62)

of a lady" to become future wives of the elite men who were educated in public schools (Walford 1986: 139–140).

A brief comparison of the SITC and MWTC might help us understand the role of teacher training in gender reproduction. Table 3.6 outlines MWTC's daily timetable. In order to secure the MWTC certificate, a student had to pass an examination in the following subjects: (a) general literature (history, literature, composition, grammar and reading (Rumi and Jawi)), (b) general science (arithmetic, geography and domestic science), (c) writing and drawing (on paper and blackboard), (d) pedagogy (theory and practice of teaching), (e) physical training (drill, hygiene, home-nursing, child welfare, instruction in Brownie and Girl Guide

Organization, net-ball, badminton and tennikoit[12]), (f) music (singing, rhythmic training and country dancing), and (g) manual training (laundry, cookery, housewifery, lacemaking, cloth weaving, mengkuang weaving, needlework, embroidery and gardening) (*Education Code V 1936* 1937: 62). Obviously, the MWTC and the SITC shared some features in terms of course of training and dormitory life. Like the SITC, the MWTC timetabled academic activities, formal extra-curricular activities and social life of the houses. In the formal curriculum, both colleges offered similar courses related to language, literature, history, arithmetic, geography, writing and drawing, pedagogy, etc.

Yet there were some notable distinctions between the two, as well. As discussed above, Winstedt suggested that practical industrial education should be promoted in Malay schools and training colleges. While the SITC stressed gardening and other manual training, the MWTC's manual training included gardening, but also various homemaking activities such as laundry, cookery, housewifery, lacemaking, cloth weaving, mengkuang weaving, needlework, and embroidery. Furthermore, unlike the SITC, the MWTC introduced music as a subject, consisting of singing, rhythmic training and country dancing. MWTC students were also required to engage in some sporting activities, such as badminton, basketball and netball, which were considered to be suitable for women. They were also expected to take part in Brownie and Girl Guide activities, which might be considered roughly equivalent to military training in the MVI and scouting for SITC students (*Education Code V 1936* 1937: 61–81; Lomas 1948 [1940]; Purdom 1948 [1931]; Taylor 1948 [1939]). Female gender roles can thus be seen in both formal subjects and extra-curricular activities, especially the strong emphasis on domestic science and housekeeping activities. The SITC and the MWTC seem to have represented male and female role-models, respectively, in Malay-medium education. It might be argued that these two training colleges were involved with gender differentiation in school education.

Beyond reproduction

The preceding analysis has shown that the SITC played a considerable role in the reproduction of ethnic, class and gender relations in British Malaya. More specifically, the SITC was tasked with reproducing

Malayness, peasantry and masculinity. It is necessary to recognize the hegemonic influence of the colonial educational policy on SITC teachers and students in the process of social reproduction. Undoubtedly, there was an asymmetry of power between the colonizer and the colonized in British Malaya. Colonial power structures played a significant role in identity formation among the colonized people. Nevertheless, there was ample room for active and creative construction of identities on the part of the individuals involved. It is indeed hardly conceivable that SITC teachers and students passively accepted whatever the colonial authorities suggested.

First, SITC teachers were not fully controlled by the British colonial power. They were able to redefine and reconstitute concepts of Malayness. As mentioned above, teachers like Harun and Abdul Hadi attempted to develop a strong Malay identity among students, hinting that the Malays could be regarded as a potential nation. Even Principal Dussek tried to inspire his students with a sense of ethnic pride. This seems to have been a considerable deviation from the official education policy which was stated in the Winstedt report of 1917.

Second, SITC students reinterpreted and reorganized knowledge learned at the college in order to construct their own identities. They accumulated knowledge from various sources such as lectures, books, newspapers and magazines, and daily discussions with their teachers and fellow students. Some future Malay nationalists reorganized and appropriated such knowledge as the foundations of their political thoughts. As will be argued in the following chapters, Ibrahim Haji Yaacob is a strong example of this appropriation of colonial knowledge.

Third, it is likely that communal life at the SITC provided enduring comradeship among its students and improved their organizational skills. Friendships could be formed through all kinds of experiences such as group life in dormitories and teamwork in gardening, sports, art and cultural activities, military training and scouting. In this environment, students could increase their ability to organize group activities and to exercise leadership. Some of them, like Ibrahim and his college mates, may have learnt how to establish and run political organizations from their experiences at the college.

In this way, though the SITC performed a considerable role in ethnic, class and gender reproduction by the colonial authorities, there remained substantial space for SITC teachers and students to reconstitute their knowledge and utilize their experiences for their own sake. To understand the paradoxical relationship between colonial education and Malay nationalism, we will conduct a close examination of the transmission and appropriation of colonial knowledge in Malay vernacular education in the following chapters.

4 The Malay World in Textbooks: The Transmission of Colonial Knowledge

As we have seen, British education policy for the Malays seems to have played a considerable role in disseminating perceptions of "Malayness." To understand the foundations of popular Malay nationalism, we need to grasp the dissemination of standardized knowledge about the "Malay world," particularly about Malay history and geography.[1] We must pay particular attention to the teaching of history and geography in Malay vernacular schools and teaching colleges if we are to understand the transmission of knowledge about the Malay world from British colonizers to the local populace.

The main question of this chapter is how and to what extent British conceptions of Malay history and geography were transmitted to Malay-educated people. A close examination of history and geography textbooks used in Malay-medium educational institutions will help us address this question. The importance of school textbooks lies in their potential influence on ordinary Malay-educated people. School textbooks provide frames of reference for their readers, mostly teachers and students. More specifically, Malay-educated students acquired new understandings of Malayness through studying Malay history and geography with authorized textbooks. A discourse analysis of these writings requires not only reading the texts closely – examining intertextuality, or the interdependence of each text with the others – but also examining the historical context in which they were produced and studied.

This chapter consists of five sections. The first briefly surveys the background of the publication of history and geography textbooks for Malay-medium schools and training colleges in British Malaya as well as basic characteristics of the authors and the textbooks themselves. The second section discusses the conceptions of community expressed in the textbooks, especially the authors' adoption of the idea of Malay as a race.

The third section is an inquiry into conceptions of space, highlighting how the authors defined Malay territoriality. The fourth section investigates conceptions of time, focusing on the periodization of Malay history. The final section reviews the discussion in this chapter.

The main sources are four textbooks on Malay history and geography: one written by a Briton in English, two by a Briton in Malay, and one by a Malay in Malay. The textbooks are R.J. Wilkinson's *A History of the Peninsular Malays, with Chapters on Perak and Selangor*, R.O. Winstedt's *Kitab Tawarikh Melayu* (Book of Malay History), which is also known simply as *Tawarikh Melayu* (Malay History), and *Ilmu Alam Melayu* (Geography of the Malay World), and Abdul Hadi Haji Hasan's three-volume *Sejarah Alam Melayu* (History of the Malay World). These textbooks were once standard in Malay schools and teacher training colleges in British Malaya.

History and geography textbooks in perspective

Background

Before the 1910s, the history taught in Malay schools was not clearly distinguished from the classical Malay literature like *Sejarah Melayu* and *Hikayat Hang Tuah*. As we have seen, the 1917 Winstedt report proposed that history based on Malay chronicles be replaced by a more scientific method. Winstedt suggested that the history taught in training colleges should be based on R.J. Wilkinson's English-language series, *Papers on Malay Subjects*, until new textbooks in Malay became available (No. 22 of 1917: C 97).

In 1918 *tawarikh* (history) was introduced as a subject at the Malay Training College at Melaka (Ramlah 1991: 11, 36). Also in 1918, Winstedt (with the assistance of Daing Abdul Hamid Tengku Muhammad Salleh) wrote the Malay-language textbook *Kitab Tawarikh Melayu* (Book of Malay History). In the late 1920s, this textbook was gradually replaced by the three-volume *Sejarah Alam Melayu* (History of the Malay World) written by Abdul Hadi Haji Hasan. A graduate of the Malay Training College at Melaka, Abdul Hadi taught history at the College and the SITC. His series was subsequently extended to five volumes by Buyong Adil, another prominent SITC teacher of history and former student of Abdul Hadi. Until the early 1950s, *Sejarah Alam Melayu* was used as a standard history textbook in Malay schools and teacher training colleges (Khoo Kay Kim 1979a: 305;

1991: 224). As previously discussed, the history taught in Malay schools and teacher training colleges was strongly Malay-oriented, focused almost exclusively on the Malay Peninsula and the Malay world. This was clearly different from the Euro-centric or Anglo-centric history taught in English schools in Malaya.

It appears that instruction in geography began earlier than history in Malay schools. As early as 1855, a geography textbook in Malay, *Hikayat Dunia* (A Story of the World), was published by a Singapore printing and teaching establishment run by Benjamin Keasberry, a Protestant missionary.[2] This book refers only to certain regions of what we now call Malaysia, Indonesia and Australia, although its subtitle describes it as a geography of the Asian and African continents as well as the Malay Archipelago (Milner 2002 [1995]: 59–60).

As mentioned, the Winstedt report suggested that the geography taught in Malay vernacular schools should cover the district surrounding the school and the Malay Peninsula together with an outline of the Malay Archipelago and the world. Not satisfied with the level of geography instruction in Malay training colleges, Winstedt called for new geography textbooks and soon published one himself, *Ilmu Alam Melayu* (Geography of the Malay World), which was later used at the SITC. According to the SITC syllabus, the instruction of geography covered the Malay Peninsula, the Malay Archipelago and all areas of the world.

Authors and textbooks

R.J. Wilkinson, *A History of the Peninsular Malays*

R.J. Wilkinson[3] was a prominent British scholar of Malay studies and a colonial administrator who played an important role in Malay education and publication as Acting Inspector of Schools, Straits Settlements, and Inspector of Schools, Federated Malay States. Highly dissatisfied with the quality of teaching staff in Malay schools, Wilkinson took the initiative in establishing the Malay Training College at Melaka in 1900 (Ramlah 1991: 19–23). Largely through his efforts, the Malay Residential School, too, was founded in 1905. The Malay Residential School later became known as the Malay College, Kuala Kangsar (MCKK) (Khasnor 1996: 41–49). William R. Roff describes Wilkinson as a man who "possessed one of the most able intellects among British Malayan officials of the time, allied to a real love for and sympathy with the Malay people" (Roff 1994 [1967]: 130).

Photo 4.1: R.J. Wilkinson. (Courtesy of Arkib Negara Malaysia)

Wilkinson was reportedly "the first to put forward the idea of publishing a collection of studies on the Malays" (Burns 1971: 1). In 1907 he published the first pamphlet in the series of *Papers on Malay Subjects*, which he edited. The series continued until 1927, covering fields such as Malay literature, law, history, life and customs and industry, as well as some aspects of the "aboriginal tribes," the people who are now called the Orang Asli[4] (lit. original people). Other famous works of Wilkinson include *A Malay-English Dictionary* (1903).

Wilkinson's "A History of the Peninsular Malays" first appeared in *Papers on Malay Subjects* in 1908 as the first two parts of the history section, that is, Part I "Events Prior to British Ascendancy" and Part II "Notes on Perak History.". In the revised 1920 edition, titled *A History of the Peninsular Malays, with chapters on Perak & Selangor*, he bound these two parts together in one volume and added chapters on the history of Malay kingship and British intervention in Perak and Selangor. A third, corrected edition was published under the same title in 1923 (Burns 1971: 7, 9).[5]

Wilkinson intended to edit *Papers on Malay Subjects* to produce a textbook for British cadets in Malaya and to meet the needs of outstation officers (Burns 1971: 2, 6). In other words, it appears that *A History of the Peninsular Malays* was originally intended for British readers. As mentioned, however, the Winstedt report suggested that Wilkinson's papers on history be used as a textbook or instruction manual for Malay training colleges until a "scientific" history textbook in Malay became available. As there is no available information about the circulation of the book, it is unclear how widely it was read.

R.O. Winstedt, *Kitab Tawarikh Melayu* and *Ilmu Alam Melayu*

R.O. Winstedt,[6] another influential British scholar-administrator, was closely associated with Wilkinson in the early years of his career in Malaya. There is little doubt that Winstedt's interest in Malay education and Malay studies was significantly influenced by Wilkinson.

Winstedt's impact on educational policy for the Malays was two-fold. On the one hand, his proposal to standardize and unify the system of Malay vernacular education led to the establishment of the SITC in 1922. On the other hand, he recommended that Malay vernacular education be elementary (limited to four years of primary education) and rural-oriented.[7] As previously discussed, one of his innovations in this regard was to introduce into the Malay school curriculum subjects for industrial education, such as gardening, basketry and needlework.

Winstedt's contribution to Malay studies has been widely acknowledged. He wrote more than fifteen books and brochures and more than two hundred articles and notes in various fields, such as Malay language (dictionaries, grammars and readers), history, literature, Islam, beliefs and customs, laws and arts.[8] Nevertheless, there have also been criticisms of his service and research. "A man of very different caliber from Wilkinson," William Roff argues, "Winstedt showed a fundamental lack of concern for Malay intellectual development" (Roff 1994 [1967]: 139). Moreover, "charges have been levied by present-day historians against his unanalytical style and predominant interest in court history" (Choy et al. 1995: 122). In the postwar era, Winstedt, like Wilkinson, has been criticized by both Malay(si)an and non-Malay(si)an scholars for his "Euro-centric" or "imperialist" standpoint,

Photo 4.2: R.O. Winstedt. (Courtesy of Arkib Negara Malaysia)

though he claimed to write from the Malay point of view (Cheah 1997: 42, 46–47; Choy et al. 1995: 121–122; Maier 1988: 69).[9]

As mentioned, Winstedt's contribution to textbook development centred on the introduction of "scientific" history textbooks in the Malay language. His 1918 *Kitab Tawarikh Melayu* (Book of Malay History)[10] was highly praised by Za'ba as "the first scientific work on general Malay history ever produced in the Malay language" (Zainal Abidin 1940: 151). Za'ba wrote of *Kitab Tawarikh Melayu*:

In spite of an artificial style, it was undoubtedly *the* book which, by popularising the Arabic word *tawarikh*, first opened the eyes of the average Malay to the meaning of history as distinct from legend. Before it, all Malay history and biography had been styled *hikayat* or "stories," and there had

been no clear distinction in the Malay mind between fact and fiction. [italics
in original] (Zainal Abidin 1940: 151)

Although there is some disagreement on this,[11] it is generally accepted that
Kitab Tawarikh Melayu was the first influential history textbook in the
Malay language that claimed to adopt a scientific approach.

Kitab Tawarikh Melayu was in essence a textbook of Malay history
written by a British scholar-administrator for teachers and students in
Malay schools and training colleges.[12] In the same year as the first edition
of *Kitab Tawarikh Melayu*, Winstedt also produced a geography textbook,
*Ilmu Alam Melayu, iaitu Sa-buah Kitab Pemimpin bagi Segala Guru-Guru
Melayu* (Geography of the Malay World: A Guidebook for All Malay
Teachers).[13] As per its subtitle, the book was for teachers in Malay schools
as well as teachers and students in teacher training colleges. Tables 4.1 and
4.2 give some indication of the circulation of these two texts.

Table 4.1: Print runs: R.J. Winstedt, Kitab Tawarikh Melayu

	No. of copies printed
First edition (1918)	2,000
Reprint (1919)	(No print run given)
Second edition, revised (1920)	(No print run given)
Third edition, revised and corrected (1921)	(No print run given)
Fourth edition, revised and corrected (1925)	10,000
Reprint (1927)	10,000

Source: Winstedt (1927 [1918]: ii)

Table 4.2: Print runs: R.J. Winstedt, Ilmu Alam Melayu

	No. of copies printed
First edition (1918)	10,000 (estimated)
Second edition (1922)	3,000 (estimated)
Reprint (1924)	(No print run given)
Third and revised edition (1925)	5,000
Reprint (1926)	5,000

Source: Winstedt (1926 [1918]: 2)

Photo 4.3: Abdul Hadi Haji Hasan. (Ramlah 1991: 83)

Regardless of the number of copies printed, we should not overestimate the textbook's readership. Za'ba pointed out that textbooks printed in Rumi or Romanized script were not popular among the Malay public at large who preferred Jawi. To his knowledge, "being text-books they are seldom read outside the schools even by the teachers" (Zainal Abidin 1940: 157). The readership of this textbook is therefore likely to have been limited to teachers and students in Malay schools and training colleges.

Abdul Hadi Haji Hasan, *Sejarah Alam Melayu*
Though not as prominent as Wilkinson and Winstedt, Abdul Hadi Haji Hasan[14] was a historian of the Malay world. While teaching history at the SITC, Abdul Hadi published the first, second and third volumes of *Sejarah Alam Melayu* (History of the Malay World) in 1925, 1926 and 1929 respectively. Buyong Adil, who also taught history at the SITC, produced the fourth and fifth volumes of the book in 1934 and 1940.

Abdul Hadi's *Sejarah Alam Melayu* is reportedly to be the first book of Malay history written by a Malay writer in the style of modern historiography. "The honour of producing the first 'national' history," writes Khoo Kay Kim, "belongs to Abdul Hadi bin Haji Hasan, a graduate of the Malay College, Melaka" (Khoo Kay Kim 1979a: 304–305; 1991: 216). Hendrik M. J. Maier not only describes Abdul Hadi as "the first Malay to attempt to write a historiography of the Malay Peninsula as a whole" (Maier 1988: 148), but also as "the first Malay intellectual who was given the task of imposing British concepts of history on Malay teachers through his text-books for vernacular schools" (Maier 1988: 127). As a textbook for teachers and students in Malay schools and teacher training colleges, the original three volumes of the book were reprinted several times.[15] Tables 4.3, 4.4. and 4.5 provide an indication of the circulation of the first three volumes of the textbook.

From "their" history to "our" history

From this brief survey of the authors and textbooks, we can see changing author-reader relations although the social categories "British" and "Malay" were not given, but socially constituted. R.J. Wilkinson wrote *A History of the Peninsular Malays* as a manual for British cadets in Malaya, though it was temporarily recommended as a textbook in Malay teaching colleges. Hence, it was basically a history of the Malays by a British author for

Table 4.3: Print runs: Abdul Hadi Haji Hasan, Sejarah Alam Melayu, vol. 1

	No. of copies printed
First edition (1925)	2,000
Reprint (1927)	2,000
Reprint (1928)	3,000

Source: Abdul Hadi (1928a [1925]: ii)

Table 4.4: Print runs: Abdul Hadi Haji Hasan, Sejarah Alam Melayu, vol. 2

	No. of copies printed
First edition (1926)	3,000
Reprint (1928)	3,000

Source: Abdul Hadi (1928b [1926]: ii)

Table 4.5: Print runs: Abdul Hadi Haji Hasan, Sejarah Alam Melayu, vol. 3

	No. of copies printed
First edition (1929)	5,000
Reprint (1930)	(No print run given)

Source: Abdul Hadi (1930 [1929]: ii)

British readers. R.O. Winstedt, who succeeded Wilkinson, produced *Kitab Tawarikh Melayu* and *Ilmu Alam Melayu* as textbooks for students in Malay teaching colleges and Malay schools. In this case, each text was a history or a geography of the Malays by a British author for Malay readers. Finally, Abdul Hadi Haji Hasan's *Sejarah Alam Melayu,* a history textbook for students in Malay teaching colleges and schools, was a history of the Malays, by a Malay, for the Malays.

Thus, it was not until Abdul Hadi that an author of a Malay history textbook could unhesitatingly claim to describe "our" history. Though Wilkinson may have attempted to constitute Malay history by drawing on Malay vernacular writings as much as possible, there is no doubt that he wrote Malay history as "their" history. For him, the Malays were clearly "others" even if he "loved" them very much. As Wilkinson belonged to the same community as the target audience of his book, it was probably unproblematic for him to write Malay history as a history of "others."

In this light, Winstedt's history and geography textbooks merit special attention because they were written for the Malays, a community to which the author did not belong. Despite his status as a British administrator, his readers expected to read "our" history and geography. In other words, he had to imagine himself to be a Malay. Such role-playing can be seen in his use of *kita* (we) in the following passage of *Ilmu Alam Melayu*:

> It has been said that in ancient times, our Malaya/Malay Land (*Tanah Melayu kita ini*) was inhabited only by wild races, namely, the Semang and the Sakai: when we Malays (*orang kita Melayu*) came, these races retreated to inlands and mountains.[16] (Winstedt 1926 [1918]: 26)

As we can see, Winstedt referred to *Tanah Melayu* and *orang Melayu* as "our" land and people. He even used Islamic terminology such as "*insha Allah* (God willing)" (Winsted 1926 [1918]: 11) and "*Amin! Amin! ya rabba'l-'alamin!* (Amin! Amin! Lord of the Universe!)" (Winstedt 1927 [1918]: 116). In short, Winstedt attempted to narrate Malay history and geography as if he belonged to the Malay Muslim community. He pretended to be an insider among the Malays, the object and audience of his study. Nevertheless, Winstedt did not try to present himself as an insider every time he wrote Malay history. Such a pretence was not necessary when he wrote Malay history in English, mainly for British readers. For instance, in *A History of Malaya,* he portrayed Malays as "others," as Wilkinson did in *A History of the Peninsular Malays* (Winstedt 1935).

"Scientific" textbooks

As mentioned, the Winstedt report stressed the need to publish new "scientific" textbooks for Malay schools and training colleges. For Winstedt, scientific textbooks were based on reliable "evidence" and "facts," in contrast to Malay classical literature, which was considered to be full of "myths" and "fairy tales." To understand what "scientific" textbooks are really about, it is useful to analyze the authors' approaches.

Looking briefly at the evidence used, there are three notable points. First, each textbook depended on its predecessors. Winstedt cited Wilkinson and both were quoted by Abdul Hadi. Second, while Malay historical literature (*hikayat*) and English historiography were the main references, the authors also drew on historical records written in Javanese, Chinese, Arabic, Portuguese and Dutch. Third, all the authors depended on the census for statistical data. This variety of evidence provided many opportunities to cite "facts" endorsing the arguments presented, thus constructing a "scientific" Malay history.

In *A History of the Peninsular Malays*, Wilkinson critically examined classical Malay literature or legends in terms of historical accuracy. He eagerly sought "historical truth," as distinguished from "myth," as in the following passages on the origin and development of the kingdom of Melaka:

> In its outline of events the legend [of Sang Sapurba] approaches very closely to historical truth. (Wilkinson 1971 [1923]: 30; 1975 [1923]: 20)

> The corroborative detail that the "Malay Annals" give to an unconvincing genealogy must also be rejected as untrue. It is made up of myths. (Wilkinson 1971 [1923]: 33; 1975 [1923]: 25)

In a passage on the early history of Perak, his attempt to find "reliable evidence" was frustrated:

> It is unfortunate that repeated Achehnese invasions and some internal dissensions have left no reliable evidence of the XVI century history of Perak but only a few tangled genealogies and stories attaching to regalia and legendary graves. (Wilkinson 1971 [1923]: 80; 1975 [1923]: 88)

Like Wilkinson, Winstedt's "scientific" approach to history was clearly expressed in his textbooks. For instance, Winstedt took a skeptical view of the historical accuracy of Malay historical literature (*hikayat*) in his *Kitab Tawarikh Melayu*:

> Although some hikayats narrate events of ancient times, they are not so useful because all the stories about gods and persons of supernatural power narrated in these hikayats seem to be nothing but tales which are merely agreeable to the ear. They are neither acceptable nor valuable in respect of historical value (*nilayan tawarikh*).[17] (Winstedt 1927 [1918]: 16)

Later, Winstedt questioned the historical authenticity of *Sejarah Melayu*, an authoritative Malay text, on the origin of the Malay rulers:

> And, what is the related evidence (*saksi*)? It is obvious that the story narrated in the *Sejarah Melayu* is false (*salah-nya*)![18] (Winstedt 1927 [1918]: 29)

As an educational officer, Winstedt praised the introduction of "scientific" method of teaching in Malay vernacular education. "The revised curriculum 'awakened students' intelligence'," wrote Winstedt in 1923, "and the text-books caused the Malay vernacular press to talk of the New Learning. For the first time the Malay was introduced into modern scientific method" (Winstedt 1923a: 26–27).

Finally, Abdul Hadi sought to write as "scientifically" as his British predecessors. As Maier points out, Abdul Hadi often posed questions about the historical accuracy of Malay hikayats, especially *Hikayat Merong Mahawangsa* (Maier 1988: 148). For instance, he was skeptical about *Hikayat Merong Mahawangsa*'s narrative on what he called *Orang Liar*, an Orang Asli group:

> Also in this case, we cannot depend on it [*Hikayat Merong Mahawangsa*], because most [of the story] is not logical in the light of our reason (*tiada munasabah pada 'akal kita*).[19] (Abdul Hadi 1928a [1925]: 15)

He also wondered about the historical truth of the description in the *Hikayat Merong Mahawangsa* of Kedah's presentation of a *bunga emas* (gold flower) to Siam:

> However, also in the case of this story in the *Hikayat Merong Mahawangsa*, any evidence or witness to ensure its truth is still not found (*belumlah diperoleh apa-apa keterangan atau saksi hendak meyakinkan benar-nya*).[20] (Abdul Hadi 1928b [1926]: 175)

As in the above passage, Abdul Hadi often used words related to a "scientific" approach, such as *saksi* (witness, evidence), *dalil* (evidence, proof), *keterangan* (explanation, evidence) and *akal* (reason, intelligence).

In search of historical evidence, Wilkinson, Winstedt and Abdul Hadi crosschecked the descriptions of historical events in Malay sources with those in Chinese, Javanese, Arabic, Portuguese, Dutch and English sources. For instance, Winstedt discussed his references in the author's note of *Kitab Tawarikh Melayu*:

> This *Tawarikh Melayu* was written by comparing some Malay hikayats with Arabic books [*kitab-kitab Arab*], Javanese chronicles [*babad Jawa*], Chinese historical records [*tawarikh China*], Portuguese historical literature [*hikayat Portuguese*], and Dutch historical literature [*hikayat Belanda*]. Most quotations are made from an English book [*kitab Inggeris*] on the history of the Peninsular Malays, written by Mr. R.J. Wilkinson, C.M.G., in the English language.[21] (Winstedt 1927 [1918]: v)

In this way, a "scientific" approach to history, or an emphasis on historical evidence, seems to have been transplanted from British scholar-administrators to a Malay teacher. It should be emphasized that in the late 1920s even a Malay teacher no longer placed full confidence in the narratives of Malay historical literature from the viewpoint of historical accuracy, critically reading Malay historical literature in comparison with other materials. To find "historical truth," he sought the "facts" to endorse, or disprove, their narratives. As Maier calls Winstedt's perspective "evolutionary positivism" (Maier 1988: 59), so can we call Abdul Hadi's "scientific" approach "positivism," meaning "the view that all true knowledge is scientific, in the sense of describing the coexistence and succession of observable phenomena" (Quinton 1988: 669). Such positivism paved the way for a new conceptualization of the Malay world.

Conceptions of community: Identifying the Malay as a race

Anthony Milner identifies three contesting ideological orientations that "promote allegiance, respectively, to three distinct forms of community in Malay society—the sultanate or *kerajaan*, the Islamic congregation or *umat* and the Malay race or *bangsa*" (Milner 2002 [1995]: 6). By the early 1930s, *bangsa*-based identity had become more important in Malay society, while the other two forms of Malay identity sought to accommodate the growing *bangsa* consciousness. The purpose of this study requires a detailed examination of the conceptions of community represented in textbooks on Malay history and geography, focusing on two factors. First, we will consider how the authors adapted racial distinctions and "systematic quantification" (Anderson 1991 [1983]: 168) from the British colonial authorities' censuses. Second, we will examine the authors' narratives on the Malay race or *bangsa Melayu*.

Adopting racial classification from the census

Under British administration, the census classification of "Malay" changed under the influence of late nineteenth-century racial theory and social evolutionism. Hirschman notes that the term "nationality" was used in the Straits Settlements censuses between 1871 and 1891; the term "race" first appeared in the 1891 census; and the transition from "nationality" to "race" was completed by 1911. The category of "race" was used in the censuses of 1921 and 1931 (Hirschman 1987: 561–562, 567–568).

Similarly, the Malay category was a gradual construct. The Straits Settlements censuses of 1871 and 1881 separately listed the Aborigines of the Peninsula (1881 census only), Achinese, Boyanese, Bugis, Dyaks, Javanese, Jawi Pekan (Jaweepekans), Malays and Manilamen. It was not until 1891 that these were rearranged as subcategories under the more comprehensive "Malays & other Natives of the Archipelago." This comprehensive Malay category was then used continuously in the censuses of the Straits Settlements, the Federated Malay States and British Malaya before World War II.[22] Between the 1891 census of the Straits Settlements and the 1931 census of British Malaya, this category was successively titled "Malays & other Natives of the Archipelago," "Malays & Allied Races," "Malay Population by Race" and "Malaysians by Race" (Hirschman 1987: 571–576). Thus, there were two definitions of "Malay" represented in census classifications: the narrower and more specific concept referring to the Muslim inhabitants of the Peninsula or of Sumatran origin, on the one hand, and the broader, comprehensive one embracing all the indigenous groups of the Archipelago, on the other (Vlieland 1932: 75). We should then proceed to investigate how and to what extent a racial ideology was transmitted to the Malay populace. Let us outline the conceptions of community presented in the textbooks.

In the first chapter of *A History of the Peninsular Malays,* titled "The Peninsular Aborigines," Wilkinson introduced the Negrito, one of the subgroups of Orang Asli, as follows:

> The Negrito aborigines, collectively known as Semang, are believed to have been the first race to occupy the Peninsula. As they are closely akin to the Aetas of the Philippines and to the Mincopies of the Andamans they must at one time have covered large tracts of country from which they have since disappeared; at the present day they are mere survivals and play no part in civilised life. Slowly and surely they are dying out. Even within the last century they occupied the swampy coast districts from Trang in the north to the borders of Larut in the south; and yet at the census of 1891 only one Negrito – who, as the enumerator said, "twittered like a bird," – was recorded from Province Wellesly, and in 1901 not one was found. Of the purest and most primitive Semang tribe only 113 were enumerated at the census of 1911, most of them in territory ceded to Perak in 1909. (Wilkinson 1971 [1923]: 15; 1975 [1923]: 1)

Here it is evident that Wilkinson regarded the "Semang" or Negrito as a race. Also clear is the fact that his conclusion – that "[s]lowly and surely they are dying out" – was drawn from the data and classifications of the censuses taken in 1891, 1901 and 1911.

The best example of the adoption of racial classifications can be found in Winstedt's 1926 edition of *Ilmu Alam Melayu*. It gave information about the population of each state or colony by "race" (*bangsa*), mostly extracted from the 1921 census. Such information was presented in the section titled "*bumi-putera-nya*" of each state or colony. The population of Selangor is explained in the following passage:

> The population (*isi*) of the state of Selangor, according to the census of A.D. 1921, amounts to more than four hundred thousand: one hundred and seventy thousand Chinese, one hundred and thirty thousand Indians and ninety thousand Malays... Then, Biduanda or Mantera, who are a Proto-Malay race (*bangsa Melayu asli*), are one thousand in number. Also [one thousand in number] are Besisi, that is, a mixed race (*bangsa kachokan*) of Proto-Malays and Sakai.[23] (Winstedt 1926 [1918]: 92)

It should be noted that in the section titled "*bumi-putera-nya*" Winstedt applied the term *bumi-putera,* which literally means "sons of the soil," to all the inhabitants of each state regardless of "race." This is quite distinct from the current usage in Malaysia, where the term *bumiputera* only refers to Malays and other indigenous groups. Elsewhere in the book, however, Winstedt uses the same term *bumi-putera* to refer to only the "natives" and not including Chinese, Indians and other "immigrant" groups (Winstedt 1926 [1918]: 26–319). Whether Winstedt's usage of the term was exceptional or not is beyond the scope of our enquiries. Suffice to say that the term *bumiputera* had not yet been strictly defined in the 1920s.

It is no surprise that Abdul Hadi also embraced racial distinctions, considering the extent to which he relied upon the Wilkinson and Winstedt textbooks, the censuses of British Malaya and other English sources. On the population of the "Jakun," or Proto-Malays, Abdul Hadi wrote:

> The Jakun race (*bangsa Jakun*) mentioned above are decreasing in number. Thus, one could say that the race is almost disappeared. In the state of Pahang the data from the census (A.D. 1921) has shown that only fifty persons of the race still live there[24]... (Abdul Hadi 1928a [1925]: 35)

Unlike Winstedt, Abdul Hadi restricted the term *bumi-putera* to only the "natives." For instance, he argued that the "Jakun" was the *bumi-putera* of the population of Pahang, Johor, Riau Lingga, Bengkalis, and the east coast of Sumatra (Abdul Hadi 1928a [1925]: 27). His usage of *bumi-putera* was thus not dissimilar to the current usage of the term.

In this way, the interpretation of the population as "race" is the most characteristic feature of the conception of community shared by Wilkinson, Winstedt and Abdul Hadi. It is also noticeable that all three writers depended very much on the census and its classifications to explain each "race." Thus, through their textbooks on Malay history and geography, these authors seem to have played a considerable role in popularizing the racial distinctions that had already appeared in census classifications devised by the British colonial government.

Malay as a mixed race

If all three authors accepted the racial classification of the population, how did they understand the boundaries and origins of the Malay race? Wilkinson's title, *A History of the Peninsular Malays*, bounds its subject geographically. In that sense, the definition of Malay in the book is close to the narrower definition of Malay in the census. His discussion of the Malay race, however, not only includes Malay Muslims but also non-Muslim indigenous groups, basing the concept of Malayness on race rather than religion. With his strong interest in racial genealogies in the Malay Peninsula, Wilkinson explained the origins of "modern Malays":

> We need not infer that every modern Malay is a descendant of Proto-Malayan tribesmen. He comes of a mixed race. The Malays differ among themselves in physical type as much as a carthorse differs from a polo-pony. In the towns they have absorbed whole communities of foreign settlers and in the country-districts they have intermarried with the older aboriginal tribes. There is no such thing as a true Malay racial type and the expression "real Malay" must be used guardedly. (Wilkinson 1971 [1923]: 22; 1975 [1923]: 10)

Here we not only understand that Wilkinson was concerned about racial distinctions, but also that he perceived the Malays as a "mixed race." His observation was that especially since the fourteenth century, the Malays of Sumatran origin "have been in constant contact with the aboriginal races of the Peninsula and with the peoples and civilisations of Arabia, India and Europe. There has been much intermarrying and much borrowing" (Wilkinson 1971 [1923]: 22–23; 1975 [1923]:11).

While the discussion about the Malays in Winstedt's history textbook (*Kitab Tawarikh Melayu*) was limited to the Malay Peninsula or Malaya, his geography textbook (*Ilmu Alam Melayu*) mentioned the Malays both inside and outside the Peninsula. In *Ilmu Alam Melayu*, he describes all the indigenous groups in the Malay Archipelago as belonging to one and the same stock:

> In fact all of them [Proto-Malays] mentioned above were originally pure Malays (*Melayu belaka*), but they have their own language and customs, which are different from the language and customs of the Malays, because they have greatly mixed with other races (*berchampor dengan bangsa-bangsa asing*), that is, Hindus and others. Then, until now their race has spread through the whole Malay world and the Malay Archipelago (*sa-luroh 'Alam Melayu dan Pulau-Pulau Melayu*), that is, in the Malay Peninsula, the Percha [Sumatra] Island, the Land of Java, the Lesser Sunda Islands, the coast of the Land of Bugis, the coast of the Borneo Island, and the Philippine Islands.[25] (Winstedt 1926 [1918]: 14–15)

Winstedt's description of the Malays as a "mixed race" can be found in *Kitab Tawarikh Melayu* as well:

> It is only after settling in the Percha [Sumatra] Island that they became the Malay race (*bangsa Melayu*) of today. They lived very close to other races such as the Hindu race (*bangsa Hindu*) and the races who had settled earlier in the Sumatra Island, the Borneo Island, and other islands. Therefore, since ancient times the Malay race has been a mixed race (*bangsa champoran*) just like the British (*orang Inggeris*).[26] (Winstedt 1927 [1918]: 7)

While the Peninsular Malays were his focus in *Sejarah Alam Melayu*, Abdul Hadi followed Winstedt's broader definition. For Abdul Hadi, the Malay race was made up of indigenous groups not only in the Malay Peninsula but also in other parts of the Malay Archipelago. For instance, in the chapter titled "Proto-Malays" (*Orang Melayu Asli*), he observed not only the "Jakun" (*orang Jakun*) in the Malay Peninsula but also the Dayak in Borneo, the Batak in Sumatra, the Toraja in Sulawesi and the Alifuru in

Maluku. In the same chapter, he referred to the main ethnic groups in the Philippines (Bontok, Igorot, Tagalog, Pampango and Bisaya) as Malays (Abdul Hadi 1928a [1925]: 25–52). Regarding their origins, Abdul Hadi regarded the Malays as a mixed race, as did Wilkinson and Winstedt:

> In fact, a mixture (*perchamporan*) of other races (*lain-lain bangsa*) (especially Hindus) and the original ancestors of the Malays (*beneh pancharan nenek moyang orang Melayu*) developed into the current Malay race (*bangsa Melayu*), which turned into inhabitants in all parts of the Malay World (*Alam Melayu*).[27] (Abdul Hadi: 1928a [1925]: 27)

In this way, the interpretation of the Malays as a "race" is the most characteristic feature of the conception of community shared by Wilkinson, Winstedt and Abdul Hadi. Furthermore, in their dependence on census classifications for explaining "race" in their textbooks, each author seems to have played a successive role in popularizing those classifications devised by the colonial government. Second, these authors, especially Winstedt and Abdul Hadi, by employing both the narrower and broader definitions of the Malay race, extended the concept of Malay to indigenous groups in other parts of the Malay Archipelago. Third, it is important to note that all three writers considered the Malays to be a "mixed race." They did not seek to posit "pure" Malays.

Conceptions of space: The constitution of the Malay territories

One of the important elements of nationhood is territoriality, or what Thongchai Winichakul calls the "geo-body" (Thongchai 1994: 16). If "[t]he nation is imagined as *limited*" (Anderson 1991 [1983]: 7), territorial identity limits nationhood spatially. In order to understand the popularization of the territorial identity of Malay, we must explore the conceptualization of Malay territoriality in these textbooks.

Regarding the territorial identification of "Malay" or *Melayu* (*Malayu*), it is hard to find a clear definition of a specific territory regarded as Malay from pre-colonial court writings in the Malay language (Matheson 1979: 369). It appears that in the seventh century, the term *Malayu* referred to a place on the Jambi River just north of Palembang in Sumatra (Andaya & Andaya 2017 [1982]: 26). During the years of the Melaka sultanate, from around 1400 to 1511, *Melayu* probably became applied to a line of royal descent from Bukit Seguntang in Sumatra as well as a small group of loyal subjects of rulers (Andaya & Andaya 2017 [1982]: 50; Reid 2004: 4–5). It was during the colonial period that the notion of the territorial stretch of the Malay community became standardized.

Malay territoriality in three tiers

According to Milner, in the late nineteenth century, an important innovation was introduced into the political vocabulary of the Malay language. The word *kerajaan*, which had in older times usually meant "king", "royalty" and "kingdom," began to be defined as "government" (Milner 2002 [1995]: 103–104). In the same period, the term *negeri* was increasingly being used as a word equivalent to "state," in contrast to its earlier use in court texts "more in the sense of a 'settlement' than of a political entity" (Milner 2002 [1995]: 104). As Milner puts it, "[w]ith growing frequency, publications of the 1870s and 1880s employed the term to refer either to individual Malay sultanates or any political state in the world beyond the Malay territories" (Milner 2002 [1995]: 105).

The word *Tanah Melayu* literally means "Malay Land(s)" or "the land(s) of the Malays." It is not clear when the term *Tanah Melayu* began to imply the Malay Peninsula. As Virginia Matheson's study shows, the term *Tanah Melayu* in a Malay classic *Hikayat Hang Tuah* was used to refer to a wide area including the Malay Peninsula and Sumatra in a certain context, but it also referred to Melaka in a different context (Matheson 1979: 361). The application of *Tanah Melayu* to the Peninsula had already been mentioned in history books by William Marsden and John Crawfurd published in 1811 and 1820 respectively (Reid 2004: 11–12). Crawfurd explained that "[t]he country which Europeans denominate the Malay Peninsula, and which, by the natives themselves, is called '*the land of the Malays*' ('Tanah Melayu'), has, from its appearing to be wholly occupied by that people, been generally considered as their original country" (Crawfurd 1967 [1820]: vol. II, 371). Anthony Reid claims that "Malaya," an English term for the Peninsula, was already used in English writings in the early eighteenth century (Reid 2004: 11).

It is difficult to trace how the concept of the Malay world (*alam Melayu* or *dunia Melayu*) developed as a term which refers to the Archipelago. Let us begin with the different meanings of the terms *alam* and *dunia*. While both *alam Melayu* and *dunia Melayu* refer to "the Malay world," *alam Melayu* is used much more frequently than *dunia Melayu* in the Malay textbooks that we investigate. Although both terms *alam* and *dunia* can be translated as "the world" in English, the two terms have considerably different meanings. While *alam* implies "the natural world" or "geographical world," *dunia*, which originally means "the present world" (as an antonym of *akhirat*, or "the next world"), connotes "the human world." [28]

It seems that European colonizers played an essential role in popularizing the concept of the Malay world, the broadest territorial stretch of the Malay community. Although advocating pan-Malay solidarity in the Malay world, Ismail Hussein, a Malaysian expert on Malay literature, acknowledges that the broader concept of "Malay" was in essence a colonial product. Ismail highlights the role of the Spanish since the seventeenth century and the British since the eighteenth century in identifying the Archipelago as the Malay world (Ismail 1993).[29] Reid points out that Thomas Stamford Raffles "should probably be regarded as the most important voice in projecting the idea of a 'Malay' race or nation, not limited to the traditional Malay sultans or even their supporters, but embracing a large if unspecified part of the Archipelago" (Reid 2004: 10). William Marsden, another British "merchant-scientist," classified the inhabitants of the Archipelago as Malays, based on religion (Islam), language (Malay) and origin (the kingdom of Minangkabau) (Marsden 1986 [1811]: 41).

To put it simply, in British Malaya, there were at least three available frames of reference to conceptualize Malay territoriality, namely, the Malay states (*negeri-negeri Melayu*), Malaya (*Tanah Melayu*) and the Malay world (*alam Melayu*). How, then, did these authors illustrate the territorial stretch of the Malay community?

Wilkinson preferred the term "state" to refer to an administrative or territorial unit in the Malay Peninsula in his time, while using the word "kingdom" or "sultanate" for a Malay polity of older times. For example, in *A History of the Peninsular Malays*, he used the term "state" in the following passage on the Proto-Malays:

> In the Southern States of the Malay Peninsula, in the Riau-Lingga Archipelago, in the isle of Bangka, and in certain districts of Eastern Sumatra there are a number of primitive pagan communities who speak Malayan dialects. (Wilkinson 1971 [1923]: 21; 1975 [1923]: 9)

While Wilkinson often used "the Peninsula" or "the Malay Peninsula," he also called the Peninsula "Malaya." His use of the word "Malaya" occasionally included not merely the Peninsula under British rule but also the parts under Siamese rule. For instance, we find the phrase "Siamese Malaya" (Wilkinson 1971 [1923]: 15; 1975 [1923]: 1–2). To refer to the Archipelago, Wilkinson not only used "the Archipelago" or "the Indian Archipelago" but also "the Malay world," which may have carried more socio-cultural connotations. "States of the Malay world" in the following passage applied to kingdoms in the Archipelago:

> The greatest local power of its day, the Javanese kingdom of Majapahit decided suddenly to play a part in history and to take a memorable place among the conquering States of the Malay world. (Wilkinson 1971 [1923]: 35; 1975 [1923]: 28)

Among the textbooks under investigation, Winstedt's *Ilmu Alam Melayu* presents the clearest picture of the territoriality of the Malay community. As expressed in the title, "Geography of the Malay World," Winstedt attempted to cover most of the Archipelago. He described not only the British colonies and protectorates in the Malay Peninsula and Borneo, but also the Netherlands East Indies and the Philippines. Southern provinces of Siam, however, were not discussed (Winstedt 1926 [1918]).

His notion of space was clearly reflected in the structure of the book. Titled "The Overview of the Malay World" (*Keadaan Alam Melayu*), the second chapter of the book discussed primordial ties within the Malay world (*alam Melayu*), or the Malay Archipelago (*Pulau-Pulau Melayu* or *Gugusan Pulau-Pulau Melayu*). According to Winstedt, *Tanah Melayu* (Malaya) and other territories of the Malay world were of the same stock (*sa-rumpun*), a conclusion he based on shared features such as topography (*keadaan tanah-tanah*), people (*manusia*), animals (*binatang-binatang*) and plants (*tumboh-tumbohan*) (Winstedt 1926[1918]: 9). In the third through eighth chapters, Winstedt discussed some aspects of the Peninsula (*Semenanjong*) or Malaya (*Tanah Melayu*) such as overview (*keadaan*), indigenous peoples (*bumi-putera*), climate (*iklim atau hawa*), mineral products (*isi bumi*), plants (*tumboh-tumbohan*) and handicrafts (*pertukangan*). The ninth through eleventh chapters focused on the political units of the Straits Settlements, the Federated Malay States and the Unfederated Malay States. Every state (*negeri*) in the Peninsula was discussed here. In these chapters the word *negeri* implied "territorial state," while the word "*kerajaan*" was used for "kingdom" or "monarchy." The twelfth chapter was for the Netherlands East Indies.[30] The final chapter provided a brief examination of the Philippines.

The structure of *Ilmu Alam Melayu* reflects the three-tiered constitution of the Malay world which this geography textbook sought to convey. The Malay world (*alam Melayu*) was divided into sub-regions, namely, Malaya (*Tanah Melayu*), the British Borneo territories, the Netherlands East Indies and the Philippines. Malaya, in turn, was made up of the Malay states (*negeri-negeri Melayu*). It is also important to note the standardization of geographical knowledge in this book. All states in the Peninsula, the main islands and areas of the Netherlands East Indies and all of the Philippines were systematically discussed through the common topics of overview (*keadaan*), towns (*bandar-bandar*), products (*hasil-mahsul*), inhabitants (*bumi-putera*) and history (*tawarikh*) (Winstedt 1926 [1918]). Such a systematic and comprehensive catalogue of geographical knowledge could convey an image of the Malay world as a territorial entity.

Abdul Hadi presented a very similar view of the Malay world. For Abdul Hadi, too, the Malay territories are made up of the Malay states (*negeri-negeri Melayu*), Malaya (*Tanah Melayu*) and the Malay world (*alam Melayu*). Of the twelve chapters in the three volumes of Abdul Hadi's textbook, chapters I, III, VII and VIII focused on the history of the Malays in Malaya, while other chapters dealt with the history of the Malays in both Malaya and other parts of the Malay world. It is also worth noting that the history of each colony or state (*negeri*) in the Straits Settlements and the Federated Malay States was fully explained in the fourth and the fifth volumes of the book published by Buyong Adil in 1934 and 1940 (Buyong 1951 [1934]; 1952 [1940]). Thus, both British and Malay authors conceptualized Malay territoriality in three tiers, that is, the Malay states (*negeri-negeri Melayu*), Malaya (*Tanah Melayu*) and the Malay world (*alam Melayu*).

A Malaya-centric view of the Malay territories

Though all three authors shared the view of the Malay territories in three tiers, it is also important to note that their discussion of the Malay territories centered around Malaya or *Tanah Melayu*.[31] As mentioned earlier, Wilkinson's *A History of the Peninsular Malays* limited its examination to the history of the Malays in Malaya. This is also the case with Winstedt's history textbook, *Kitab Tawarikh Melayu*. Though his geography textbook, *Ilmu Alam Melayu,* covered the entire Malay Archipelago, nine of its thirteen chapters describe the geography of *Tanah Melayu* or Malaya. Only two chapters deal with the Netherlands East Indies and the Philippines, respectively. Abdul Hadi's *Sejarah Alam Melayu* was more expansive on the history of the Malay Archipelago outside Malaya than Wilkinson and Winstedt. While four of twelve chapters deal exclusively with the history of the Malays in *Tanah Melayu* or Malaya, the other eight chapters cover both Malaya and the other territories of *alam Melayu* or the Malay world, mainly Sumatra and Java. Thus, although his primary interest was still *Tanah Melayu* or Malaya, Abdul Hadi broadened the sphere of the history of the Malays (Abdul Hadi 1928a [1925]; 1928b [1926]; 1930 [1929]).

Thus, on the one hand, Malaya was the most important among the three tiers of the Malay territories, a focal point for the three authors although it was not a single political unit. On the other hand, Abdul Hadi gave more emphasiis to the history of the Malay world outside Malaya than the two British authors, who tended to limit their scope to Malaya.

Conceptions of time: The periodization of Malay history

Along with the sense of a common territory, the sense of a shared history is a crucial component of nationhood (Chatterjee 1993: chaps. 4 & 5). Reid contends that "[m]odern nationalisms have been no exception in their synchronic reassessments of history and national destiny" (Reid 1979: 281). Hence, examining the periodization of Malay history in these textbooks will be worthwhile.

Most pre-colonial Malay historical literature took the form of genealogies of Malay kings. They were basically collections of stories about rulers, chiefs, and events in courts (Khoo Kay Kim 1979a: 299–300; 1991: 211–212). By contrast, history textbooks in colonial Malaya claimed to deal with the history of the Malay people and their territories. In order to write the history of the Malay people and their territories, the authors had to reorganize Malay history according to their own historical views. Before discussing the structure of Malay history in these textbooks, we must first look at their conceptions of time: their adherence to calendrical time and chronology, their progressivist view of history and their periodization of Malay history.

Calendrical time and chronology

Unlike modern historiography, most classical Malay historical writings, especially those written before the eighteenth century, do not specify the dates of historical episodes (Khoo Kay Kim 1979a: 299: 1991: 211–212). In contrast, Wilkinson, Winstedt and Abdul Hadi sought to fix the dates of principal historical events. Then, with few exceptions, they described Malay history in chronological order.

For a full account of the construction of this chronology, two appendices of Winstedt's *Kitab Tawarikh Melayu* merit attention. Appendix I is a note on "*Menukar-nukarkan Tahun Hijrat dan Tahun Masehi*" or "Conversion between the Muslim Year (*Anno Hegirae* or A.H.) and the Gregorian Year (*Anno Domini* or A.D.)," which presents a conversion formula from the Muslim to Gregorian year and vice versa. For instance, it shows that A.H. 1021 is approximately equal to A.D. 1612 and that A.D. 1409 is more-or-less equivalent to A.H. 811 (Winstedt 1927 [1918]: 117–121). This conversion formula was an important mediator between the traditions of Malay historical literature and European historiography, making it possible for the reader to connect Malay history with Euro-centric "world" history.

A remarkable product of such a conversion is Winstedt's Appendix II, a sixteen-page "Chronological Table" (*Daftar Tawarikh*). It outlines historical events related to the Malay world in chronological order from B.C. 5004 (the establishment of a kingdom in Egypt) to A.D. 1925 (the visit of some Malays, including rulers, to London during the "British Empire" exhibition). Of the 143 events listed in the chronological table, twenty-nine are presented in bold type as particularly important.[32] Most of the historical events in the table occurred in the "Malay world" and are listed chronologically alongside historical events outside the area that had significance for the Malay world. For instance, the chronological table includes important dates in Islam (e.g. the birth of prophets), Indian civilization (e.g. the compilation of *Ramayana* and *Mahabharata*, the birth of Buddha) and the industrial revolution (e.g. the introduction of railway transport and steamships) (Winstedt 1927[1918]: 122–137).

The chronological table presents a bird's eye view of Malay history through calendrical time, according to the Gregorian calendar. It is not unlike what Anderson calls "'homogenous, empty time', in which simultaneity is, as it were, transverse, cross-time, marked not by prefiguring and fulfilment, but by temporal coincidence, and measured by clock and calendar" (Anderson 1991 [1983]: 24).[33]

Although neither Wilkinson nor Abdul Hadi present a chronological table such as Winstedt's, they conform to the same chronological order. For instance, at the end of each chapter in the third volume of *Sejarah Alam Melayu*, Abdul Hadi listed main historical figures together with the (Gregorian) year of their significance, e.g. Confucius, B.C. 552; Affonso d'Albuquerque, A.D. 1508; Captain Light, A.D. 1786; and so on (Abdul Hadi 1930 [1929]). These lists of historical figures likewise generate a sense of homogenous time.

A progressivist view of history

All three authors also present a progressivist view of history, based on these concepts of calendrical time and chronology. By progressivism I mean the idea of gradual progression to higher forms of life.

In *A History of the Peninsular Malays*, Wilkinson assumed that surviving "primitive" peoples represented earlier stages in the development of modern Malay society. From this perspective, he says, "the Peninsula presents us with a historical museum illustrating every grade of primitive culture" (Wilkinson 1971: 19; 1975: 8). His criteria for judging whether a people are "primitive" or "civilized" can be seen in the following accounts:

> The boundary between primitive culture and civilisation cannot be said to be reached, until habitations become permanent and a comparatively small area can support a large population. That boundary is crossed when a people learn to renew the fertility of land by irrigation, by manuring, or by a proper system of rotation of crops. The Malays with their system of rice-planting – the irrigated rice, not hill rice – have crossed that boundary. But no Sakai unaided has ever done so. (Wilkinson 1971 [1923]: 20; 1975 [1923]: 8)

Wilkinson thus differentiated "primitive" peoples from "civilized" ones based on criteria of development or progress such as mode of habitation – nomadic or permanent – and mode of production – hunting, shifting cultivation or repeated cultivation. He also referred to criteria such as the ability to process metal, the rationality of beliefs and customs, cleanliness and the complexity of the numeral system (Wilkinson 1971 [1923]: 15–23; 1975 [1923]: 1–11). Wilkinson's notion of civilization or progress was strongly related to rationalization of the way of life leading to increases in productivity supporting larger populations.

This progressivist view of history is also evident in Winstedt's *Kitab Tawarikh Melayu*. For instance, he argued that the Malays were at a higher stage of progress than the "Semang" (Negrito):

> The reason why they [*Semang*] are said to have originally lived in Malaya (and the Malay Archipelago) is [as follows]: if the Malays had already lived here before them, how could these weak and stupid races (*bangsa-bangsa yang lemah lagi bebal itu*) have come later? [That was impossible.] [This is] because the Malays were surely much more intelligent and progressive (*terlebih cherdek dan maju*) and were also much more able to make efforts to resist enemies' attack than the Semang people (*orang bangsa Semang*) who were wild (*liar*) and always afraid of [other] human beings.[34] (Winstedt 1927 [1918]: 1–2)

Winstedt's criteria of progress or development are very similar to Wilkinson's, focusing on mode of habitation – nomadic (*berpindah randah, merayau*) or permanent (*berumah yang tetap*), mode of production – hunting (*mencari makanan-nya pada segenap hutan rimba*) or cultivation (*bercucok tanam*), the ability to process metal, the rationality of beliefs and customs, diligence, and so on. To quote his passage on the Negrito:

> None of these wild people (*orang-orang liar*) has inhabited a permanent village or resides perpetually. And nobody knows how to sink a well and to crop a paddy field unlike the people who have already crossed over from the boundary of wildness (*manusia yang telah keluar dari-pada sempadan keliaran*).[35] (Winstedt 1927 [1918]: 4)

Abdul Hadi, also accepted the classification of human beings according to stages of progress, providing criteria of progress quite similar to Wilkinson and Winstedt. In *Sejarah Alam Melayu*, he described the difference between the *Orang Liar* ("Wild People," i.e. the Negrito and the Senoi) and the Proto-Malays:

> Even so, if we look into some aspects of condition and figure of their [Proto-Malays'] stock, there are differences from the *Orang Liar* mentioned earlier. [This is] because actually the ancestors of the Malays (*nenek moyang orang*

Melayu) made efforts to form villages, to crop paddy fields, and to know how to process metal.[36] (Abdul Hadi 1928a [1925]: 25)

On the racial affinity between the "Jakun" and other peoples in the Archipelago:

> The Jakun race (*bangsa Jakun*) mentioned here belongs to one and the same race (*sa-bangsa*) with the Kubu in the Percha [Sumatra] Island, the Kalang in Java, the Bajau who reside in the whole area of gulfs in the Borneo Island, and the people who live in the Philippine Islands, that is, the Bontok and the Igorot – *Melayu Liar* [Wild Malays] – and the Tagalog, the Pampango and the Bisaya – *Melayu Jinak* [Tame Malays].[37] (Abdul Hadi 1928a [1925]: 27)

It is important to note Abdul Hadi's dichotomy between *Melayu Liar* and *Melayu Jinak*, literally "wild" and "tame." In Abdul Hadi's usage, *liar* referred to isolation from the influence of "higher" cultures or civilizations, while *jinak* meant familiarity with external cultures or civilizations.

It is useful to briefly outline the ideology underlying this progressivist view of history. Maier points to the influence of the theory of social evolution in Wilkinson's and Winstedt's studies (Maier 1988: 57–58). In the second half of the nineteenth century, evolutionary theory was increasingly applied to social sciences. "In one form, evolutionary theory keeps close to biology in speaking of increasing complexity and differentiation; in another, a series of phases or stages of development is posited, although not all societies are expected to go through all of them" (Freedman 1988: 293).

In the preface to *Shaman, Saiva, and Sufi: A Study of the Evolution of Malay Magic* (1925), Winstedt explained the structure of the book as follows:

> Chapters i.-iv. deal with the Malay's evolution from animist to Muslim; chapters v. and vi. with his animism; chapters vii. and viii. with his shamanism; chapter ix. with rites largely infected with Hindu magic; and chapters x. and xi. with Muslim accretions. (Winstedt 1925: v)

Here, the "evolutionary" is explicit in the subtitle of the book and elucidated in the preface. Winstedt's *A History of Malay Literature*, published in 1940, is based on similar ground. Of its fourteen chapters, the second through sixth are titled: Folk Literature, The Hindu Period, A Javanese

Element, From Hinduism to Islam and The Coming of Islam and Islamic Literature (Winstedt 1940). It is apparent that Winstedt assumed that Malay culture had progressed through various cultural stages, that is, folk, Hindu, Javanese and Islamic (Maier 1988: 57). The structure of *A History of Malay Literature* is quite similar to the same author's *Kitab Tawarikh Melayu,* except that the former includes a chapter on the Javanese influence and the latter discusses European elements.

In his preface to *Shaman, Saiva and Sufi,* Winstedt acknowledges his debt to the works of E. B. Tylor, father of evolutionary anthropology (Winstedt 1925: v).[38] Maier rightly stresses the similarities between Tylor, Wilkinson and Winstedt in their interest in human "mental development" (Maier 1988: 58). Abdul Hadi may have been indirectly influenced by this evolutionary approach through the writings of his British predecessors.

From this brief discussion, it is clear that all three writers shared a progressivist view of history. They divided Malay history into stages of development or progress and assumed that Malay history should be understood as an evolution from a "primitive" to "civilized" life-style. Furthermore, they used similar criteria for judging the state of progress or civilization, criteria that had much to do with the productivity and rationality pursued by the British colonial government. Finally, their progressivist view of history was strongly influenced by the theory of social evolution influential in Western scholarship at the time.

Periodization of Malay history

As we have seen, these authors applied ideas of calendrical time, chronology and a progressivist view of history in their textbooks. Let us turn now to examine how they organized and periodized Malay history in their narratives. Wilkinson's notion of Malay history in the Peninsula was expressed in the following passage:

> ...the first great conquering Sumatran kingdom was Palembang or Sri Vijaya, of Hindu and particularly Buddhist civilization.[39] In the seventh century it annexed the *Malayu* country, probably Jambi. In the thirteenth century Langkasuka, Trengganu, Pahang, and Kelantan were subject to its sway. Singapore was one of its colonies. In the middle of the fourteenth century A.D. the Javanese empire of Majapahit wrested its sovereignty. The superficial character of those early Sumatran settlements is shown by the fact that the

wilder aborigines of the archipelago have never been completely absorbed. From Singapore Sumatran civilisation spread to Malacca, where there was already a village of Proto-Malayan "Celletes". This was after the sack of Singapore about 1360. Between that day and this the Malays have been converted to Islam and have been in constant contact with the aboriginal races of the Peninsula and with the peoples and civilisations of Arabia, India and Europe. There has been much intermarrying and much borrowing. [italics original] (Wilkinson 1971 [1923]: 22–23; 1975 [1923]: 11)

In Wilkinson's historical view, "primitive" and "animistic" aborigines and Proto-Malays formed the basis of Malay culture. After that, large Malay kingdoms were built in Sumatra by accepting Hindu-Buddhist civilization. The migration of large numbers of Malays from Sumatra to the Peninsula was followed by the Malays' conversion to Islam and the establishment of the Malay sultanate of Melaka. Melaka and other Malay sultanates were in contact with foreign merchants or settlers. Finally, European powers politically intervened in these sultanates.

Moreover, Wilkinson argued that the Malays did not abandon elements of former historical stages. Rather, all the historical stages accumulated to constitute layers of Malay history. Writing about Malay life and customs, he explained this stratification of Malay history as follows:

> [The Malay] keeps the old while adopting the new. He has gone on preserving custom after custom and ceremony after ceremony till his whole life is a sort of museum of ancient customs – an ill-kept and ill-designed museum in which no exhibit is dated, labelled or explained. (Wilkinson 1925 [1908]: 42)

Therefore, to understand Malay customs,

> We can best begin by eliminating the modern Moslem elements... Of the Hindu elements we cannot speak so positively... But when we have eliminated these Hindu and Moslem details, we are still far from the bedrock of Indonesian custom; we have to distinguish between essentials and accessories. (Wilkinson 1925 [1908]: 42)

Wilkinson thus presented Malay history as the accumulation of Islamic and Hindu influences layered upon the indigenous "bedrock of Indonesian custom."

This historical view is clearly discernible in the structure of *A History of the Peninsular Malays*. Its original eight chapters can be classified into the following categories: the substratum of Malay culture (chapters 1–2), the arrival of Indian civilization and the migration of the Malays (chapters 3–4), the arrival of Islam and the establishment of the Malay sultanate of Melaka (chapter 5) and the ascendancy of the European powers (chapters 6–8) (Wilkinson 1971 [1923]; 1975 [1923]).[40] The additional five chapters (9–13) on Perak and Selangor, which he added in the 1920 and 1923 revised editions, give special reference to the history of Malay kingship and British intervention in Perak and Selangor.

The structure of Winstedt's *Kitab Tawarikh Melayu* is not much different. Its eight chapters can be divided into: the substratum of Malay culture (chapters 1–2), the arrival of Indian civilization and the migration of the Malays (chapters 2–3), the arrival of Islam and the establishment of the Malay sultanate of Melaka (chapters 4–5) and the ascendancy of the European powers (chapters 6–8) (Winstedt 1927 [1918]).[41]

Abdul Hadi's *Sejarah Alam Melayu* is presented in twelve chapters over three volumes.[42] These chapters might be classified into the following categories: the substratum of Malay culture (chapters 1–2), the arrival of Indian civilization and the migration of the Malays (chapters 3–5), the arrival of Islam and the establishment of the Malay sultanate of Melaka (chapters 6 & 8), the ascendancy of the Siamese (chapter 7), the arrival of the Chinese (chapter 9) and the ascendancy of the European powers (chapters 10–12) (Abdul Hadi 1928a; 1928b; 1930).

The similarity in structure of these three textbooks is striking, largely agreeing on at least four phases of Malay history. First was the making of the substratum of Malay culture, that is, the cultures of the Orang Asli. A discussion of the "Semang" (Negrito) and the "Sakai" (Senoi) is followed by an explanation of the "Melayu Asli" (Proto-Malays). Second, the authors looked at the arrivals of Indian civilization, Hinduism and Buddhism, as well as the migration of the Malays from Sumatra to the Peninsula. The large kingdoms of the Malay world, such as Srivijaya established in the seventh century and Majapahit in the thirteenth century, arose during this stage. The third is marked by the coming of Islam and the establishment of the Malay sultanate of Melaka between about 1400 and 1511. The fourth stage is characterized by the ascendancy of the European powers, the Portuguese, the Dutch and the British.

The characterization of historical periods

Having established the strong similarities between the three authors' periodization of Malay history, we turn now to how they characterized each period. As we have seen, all the authors regarded the first stage of Malay history, the formation of the substratum of Malay culture, as its "primitive" age. Notably, all three authors addressed this stage of Malay history by examining the ways of life of the Orang Asli groups extant at the time of writing. That is, they assumed that the existing "primitive" culture of the Orang Asli was more-or-less the remnant of the ancient culture of the Malays. As mentioned, all three authors divide this "primitive" age of Malay history into two stages of civilization, namely, the period of the "Wild People" (Orang Liar) and that of the more "civilized" Proto-Malays (Wilkinson 1971 [1923]; 1975 [1923]: chaps. 1 & 2; Winstedt 1927 [1918]: chaps. 1 & 2; Abdul Hadi 1928a [1925]: chaps 1 & 2).

The second stage of Malay history in these texts was characterized by the inflow of Hindu-Buddhist civilization of Indian origin. For Wilkinson, the earliest civilization in the Archipelago began with the spread of Hindu and Buddhist influences, which were then introduced to the Peninsula with the emigration of the Malays from Sumatra. His focus was on the kingdom of Srivijaya or Palembang, which "was a civilized and important state, owing its culture to Indian sources" (Wilkinson 1971 [1923]: 31; 1975 [1923]: 23). Like Wilkinson, Winstedt acknowledged the initial influence of Hindu civilization on the Peninsular Malays:

> The teachers (*guru*) who first came and presented examples or models (*tiruan dan tuladan*) to the Malays regarding progress, civilization and new ideas (*kemajuan dan tamaddun dan fikir-fikiran baharu*) which the Malays had never possessed at that time were Hindus (*Orang Hindu*). It has been said that they [Hindus] began to come [to the Peninsula] in the second century (A.D. 200) when Hindus had already inhabited Java.[43] (Winstedt 1927 [1918]: 7)

At the same time, Winstedt described the teachings of Hinduism as irrational. He castigated the belief in magical power in Hinduism as "stupid" (*bodoh*) and pointed out that such "stupid" ideas survived in Malay classical literature (Winstedt 1927 [1918]: 13).

In *Sejarah Alam Melayu*, Abdul Hadi wrote more on the Hindu-Buddhist influence in Malay history than Wilkinson and Winstedt, paying special attention to the Javanese empire of Majapahit and its large sphere of influence in the Malay world under the leadership of Gajah Mada in the mid-fourteenth century. Abdul Hadi contended that "it is the contact with Hindus that brought the Javanese the wisdom which advanced the race (*kepandaian yang memajukan bangsa-nya*)" (Abdul Hadi 1928a [1925]: 133). As traces of Hindu-Buddhist civilization in the Malay Peninsula, Abdul Hadi pointed to the existence of old statutes and gravestones of Hindu-Buddhist origin, Malay words of Sanskrit origin and Malay rituals and customs of Hindu origin (Abdul Hadi 1928b [1926]: 45–49). Abdul Hadi, however, also identified "stupid elements" (*perkara bodoh-bodoh*) and "absurd beliefs" (*keperchayaan bukan-bukan*) in Hinduism (Abdul Hadi 1928b [1926]: 4).

The influx of Hindu-Buddhist civilization gave way to the third stage of Malay history, the coming of Islam. The authors' chief focus was on the establishment of the Malay sultanate of Melaka together with the conversion of the Malays to Islam. Wilkinson claimed that "the Permaisura," or the king of Melaka, "made his power secure by paying one or more visits to China to secure recognition from the Emperor, and by conversion to Islam, the accepted religion of Pasai" (Wilkinson 1971 [1923]: 36; 1975 [1923]: 29–30). While Wilkinson acknowledged that the Malay people have always praised the glory of the Malay sultanate of Melaka, he also commented on what seemed "strange" about Melaka:

> It was a strange sentiment, this loyalty of the old Malays. A man might murder a hero or a saint, or betray a relative or friend, or abduct an innocent girl: if he did it in the interest of a royal intrigue, it was a noble act of self-sacrifice according to his ethical code. (Wilkinson 1971 [1923]: 39; 1975 [1923]: 34)

On the narrative in *Hikayat Hang Tuah*,

> The fight between the champions is the subject of two famous passages in Malay literature, but it makes little appeal to European taste. (Wilkinson 1971: 40; 1975: 35)

In sum, for Wilkinson, although the Malay sultanate of Melaka was politically ascendant and enjoyed economic prosperity, various elements of it were strange or irrational.

In *Kitab Tawarikh Melayu* Winstedt did not present the coming of Islam to the Malay community in a consistently good light. His focus was on the early stage of the dissemination of Islam in the Peninsula. Arguing that it was Indians, not Arabs, who brought Islam and its civilization, Winstedt insisted that the Islam brought to the Malays was unorthodox and contained many misinterpretations. He also argued that religious teachers were not well respected by the Malay populace during the initial stages of conversion to Islam (Winstedt 1927 [1918]: 41–63). On the Malay sultanate of Melaka, while acknowledging its economic prosperity, he also noted its harsh and despotic rule (Winstedt 1927 [1918]: 73).

Abdul Hadi followed Winstedt's argument that it was not Arabs but Hindustanis and Persians who first brought Islam to the Malays (Abdul Hadi 1928b [1926]: 124–137). Abdul Hadi's view of the role of the Melaka sultanate in the Islamization of the Malays also concurred with Winstedt's. On the one hand, he described the sultanate of Melaka as the main force promoting the development of Islam in the Peninsula (Abdul Hadi 1928b [1926]: 91) and briefly outlined material aspects of ancient Islamic civilization, such as the distinctive architecture, especially of mosques (Abdul Hadi 1928b [1926]: 139–152). On the other hand, he agreed with Winstedt that the majority of the Malays in the Melaka sultanate did not sincerely observe the teachings of Islam and that religious teachers were not necessarily respected by ordinary Malay people (Abdul Hadi 1928b [1926]: 86–91).

The final stage of Malay history was the ascendancy of European powers in the Malay world from the early sixteenth century. All the authors accepted that the aim of the European powers in Asia was basically commercial. For instance, as Wilkinson put it, "[t]he aim of all European powers in the Far East – whether Portuguese or Dutch or English – was to capture the rich trade" (Wilkinson 1971 [1923]: 49; 1975 [1923]: 48), although the imperialisms of the Portuguese, the Dutch and the British differed in character.

They stressed the harshness of Portuguese colonial policy. For instance, Winstedt referred to the unsuccessful Portuguese policy of conversion to Christianity in Melaka:

> The Portuguese, in their character, too much liked to promote their religion (Christianity), and advised persons of other religions and of other groups to convert to their religion. Therefore, Muslims intensely hated them.[44] (Winstedt 1927 [1918]: 84)

He also attributed the fall of the Portuguese in Asia to their rudeness:

> The fall of the Portuguese power was increasingly rapid due to cruel and rude behaviours of all the Portuguese crews and captains. They were almost like pirates and robbers...[45] (Winstedt 1927 [1918]: 88)

Like Winstedt, while Abdul Hadi acknowledged Portuguese economic power in the Malay world in the sixteenth century, he also stressed the harshness of Portuguese rule and the antipathy engendered amongst the Malays by Portuguese policies. Abdul Hadi pointed out that the Malays strongly opposed the Portuguese because of their promotion of Christianity, which contrasted with the Dutch and the British, who were seen to be more liberal about religion (Abdul Hadi 1930 [1929]: 104). He wrote:

> But if Islam had not come to most Malay states earlier [than Christianity], probably all the inhabitants in our Malay world would have been attracted by Christianity like the Filipinos who were converted to Christianity by the Spanish... In fact it is Islam that blocked the Portuguese attempt to spread and develop Christianity among the Malays.[46] (Abdul Hadi 1930 [1929]: 111)

Generally, the writers were more sympathetic to the Dutch than the Portuguese. According to Winstedt, Dutch rule in the Archipelago was more commercial-minded and less religion-oriented than Portuguese rule:

> At first the aim of the Dutch [East India] Company was not like the intention and ambition of the Portuguese and the Spanish. For the Dutch Company, from the beginning, neither intended to conquer any state nor to promote Christianity but merely wanted to trade. However, the Dutch Company often had to intervene in the affairs of Malay states because some kings of these states obstructed them while others granted the desire of the Company.[47] (Winstedt 1927 [1918]: 94)

Winstedt argued that although the Dutch introduced some harsh policies in Java, exemplified by the cultivation system, without such policies the large population in Java could not have been supported (Winstedt 1927 [1918]: 106–107). As a result of this,

> Now that the Javanese enjoy comforts, the Dutch government begins to refrain from using harsh methods. And their rule and British rule are more or less the same.[48] (Winstedt 1927 [1918]: 107)

Abdul Hadi dealt with the coming of the Dutch mainly in the context of their commercial activities led by the Dutch East India Company. Yet Abdul Hadi also touched on the Dutch administration in Melaka. Citing *Hikayat Abdullah*, he explained that Dutch rule in Melaka had been rigorous in taxation and punishment (Abdul Hadi 1930 [1929]: 217–222).

Finally, British rule tended to be described most uncritically. For Wilkinson, the British, who had originally intended to pursue commercial interests, inevitably intervened in the Malay states as a benevolent protector for the Malays. On the Pangkor Treaty in 1874, he explained that social disturbances had forced the British to intervene in the Malay states:

> In the year 1873 Larut was being torn in two by rival secret societies; Perak proper was in a state of anarchy; Selangor was in the throes of civil war, even in the Negri Sembilan there were serious disturbances. The whole Peninsula, as Sir Harry Ord pointed out, was in the hands of the lawless and the turbulent. (Wilkinson 1971 [1923]: 102; 1975 [1923]: 118)

He argued further that British intervention was welcomed by local societies. "Local feeling," he wrote, "was all in favour of intervention" (Wilkinson 1971 [1923]: 102; 1975 [1923]: 118). British colonial paternalism is notable in the following passage:

> The policy laid down by that Governor [Sir Andrew Clarke] in his dispatch on the Pangkor Treaty can be summed up in his words: "The Malays, like every other rude Eastern nation, require to be treated much more like children, and to be taught." (Wilkinson 1971 [1923]: 111; 1975 [1923]: 131)

Winstedt, too, emphasized that the British originally had not intended to intervene in the Malay states. Only after their disturbances affected British colonies, he argued, did the British government feel the need to intervene in order to secure peace (Winstedt 1927 [1918]: 115–116). Finally, although Abdul Hadi was not uncritical of British activities in the Malay world,[49] he portrayed the British as relatively more benign than the Dutch (Abdul Hadi 1930 [1929]: 258–259). He argued that the original concern of the British was not military expansion but commerce and trade (Abdul Hadi 1930 [1929]: 254). The British intervention in the Malay world as well as in India was described as a passive response to pressure from the Dutch in the Malay world and from the French in India (Abdul Hadi 1930 [1929]: 276–301).

Unlike the Hindu-Buddhist, Islamic and European elements, relations between the Malays and their Siamese and Chinese neighbors were only occasionally discussed in the histories written by Wilkinson and Winstedt. In contrast, Abdul Hadi's *Sejarah Alam Melayu* contains two independent chapters on the Siamese and the Chinese. His interest centered on two aspects: the migration of Siamese and Chinese to the Malay Peninsula on the one hand and tributary relations between Siamese and Chinese overlords and their vassal states in the Peninsula on the other. But he did not conceptualize either a "Siamese period" or a "Chinese period" in his history textbook, probably due to the view that neither civilization built an enduring empire in the Malay world. There was neither a Siamese nor a Chinese equivalent of "Srivijaya", "Majapahit" or "Melaka" in the Malay world.

Our examination of the Malay history textbooks has revealed significant similarities in the authors' perceptions of time. First, Wilkinson, Winstedt and Abdul Hadi shared the conceptions of calendrical time and chronology. Second, their historical views were progressivist in that they believed in the gradual progression to higher forms of life. Finally, the authors divided Malay history into identical periods on the scale of progress and civilization. For all three, Malay history evolved through distinctive periods, from "primitive" to Hindu-Buddhist to Islamic. After the ascendancy of European powers, it kept moving onward through three colonial periods, from Portuguese to Dutch to British.

Transmission of colonial knowledge

We have traced the transmission of colonial forms of knowledge from British scholar-administrators (Wilkinson and Winstedt) to a Malay teacher (Abdul Hadi) through a discourse analysis of Malay school textbooks. These textbooks transitioned from "their" history to "our" history, that is, from a history of the Malays by a British writer for British readers, to a history (and a geography) of the Malays by a British writer for Malay readers, and finally to a history of the Malays by a Malay writer for Malay readers. In terms of methodology, a "scientific," positivist approach was transplanted from British to Malay writers. In this approach, any argument should be founded on "evidence" or "facts." From this perspective, the authors reconstructed the Malay world in terms of community, territory and time.

First, these writings are based on the concept of Malay as a *bangsa* or race. The textbooks played an important role in popularizing racial classifications which had been originally introduced in population censuses. In this sense, the textbooks can be regarded as mediating the gap between official census classifications and the popular consciousness. Furthermore, these textbooks share an image of the Malays as a "mixed race."

Together with the coexistence of narrow and broad definitions of Malay, the sense of the hybridity of the Malay race seems to have led to open-ended debates about the boundaries of Malay identity. One example of this is the dispute over the categorization of Indian and Arab Muslims in the late 1930s. Abdul Rahim Kajai, a prominent Malay journalist, claimed to purify Malayness by arguing that Muslims whose fathers were of Indian or Arab descent should be excluded from the social category "Malay" (Abdul Latiff 1984: 105–112). Kajai's frustration came from the fact that Indian and Arab Muslims played a dominant role not only in commerce but also in Malay journalism and public administration in British Malaya in the early twentieth century.

Secondly, the authors shared a notion of Malay territoriality. All three referred to geographical data which were systematically catalogued for each political unit in a similar way. The standardization of geographical knowledge and "systematic quantification" served to objectify the territoriality of the Malay community. By absorbing the concept of territorial boundary, the authors described the Malay territories at three levels, namely, the Malay states (*negeri-negeri Melayu*), Malaya (*Tanah Melayu*) and the Malay world (*alam Melayu*). Furthermore, these textbooks presented Malaya or *Tanah Melayu* as the focal point of the Malay territories. This Malaya-centric view reflected the substantialization of the colonial territorial boundary. Yet we should note that Abdul Hadi made a modest attempt to depart from this Malaya-centric view by providing a more extensive account of the history of the "Malay world" outside the Peninsula.

This new objectification of space seems to have played an important role in conceiving a potential national territory. These three territorial identities, namely, Malay states, Malaya and the Malay world probably shaped the different strands of Malay nationalism. On the one hand, in the late 1930s, Malay aristocrats and their supporters began to organize Malay state associations. For them, Malay states were the focus of territorial identity. In postwar Malaya, these state-based Malay associations were dissolved into a Malaya-based Malay political party, that is, the United Malays National Organisation (UMNO). Their territorial identity gradually shifted from Malay states to Malaya or *Tanah Melayu*. On the other hand, in the late 1930s, some Malay non-aristocrat intellectuals formed a pan-Malay-oriented association, that is, Kesatuan Melayu Muda (KMM) (Young Malay Union). As indicated by its President, Ibrahim Haji Yaacob, their imagined homeland seems to have stretched to cover the whole territory of the Malay Archipelago.

Finally, Wilkinson, Winstedt and Abdul Hadi had a shared conception of time. They wrote Malay history according to calendrical time and chronology, and their historical views were progressivist. They believed in a gradual progression to higher forms of human life and accordingly divided Malay history into distinctive periods on a scale of progress and civilization, from "primitive" to Hindu-Buddhist to Islamic, and then to Portuguese, Dutch and finally British. At the same time, the authors also understood Malay history to be clearly stratified, with older layers retained as new layers were added on.

Despite its colonial origin, such a progressivist view of history would pave the way for what Anthony D. Smith calls "the cultural evolutionism of nationalism," in which "the nation is multilayered, and the task of the nationalist historian and archeologist is to recover each layer of the past and thereby trace the origins of the nation from its 'rudimentary beginnings' through its early flowering in a golden age (or ages) to its periodic decline and its modern birth and renewal" (Smith 2000: 64). Some readers of these books, like Ibrahim Haji Yaacob, imagined that British rule in Malaya would be transient, as Portuguese and Dutch rule had been, and that these history textbooks would be revised in the future to add a new chapter on the post-British or independent era.

Thus, by the early 1930s not only British scholars but also a Malay teacher had begun to reformulate the Malay world in the form of modern historiography and geography. Race and territorial state became increasingly important as basic components of the Malay world. Malay history and geography were made comparable with the national history and geography of other parts of the world. These changes would pave the way for the identification of "Malay" as a potential nation. Of course, this was not what the British administrators had intended.

5 Ibrahim Haji Yaacob and Pan-Malayism: The Appropriation of Colonial Knowledge

We have closely investigated the transmission of colonial knowledge about the Malay world from British to Malay writers. Yet this knowledge transmission constituted only a part of the process of localizing the British concept of Malayness. To avoid over-simplification, we should explore the Malays' accommodation to the modern concept of Malayness.

For this purpose, this chapter enquires into the interrelations between the acquisition and usage of knowledge and the search for Malay ethno-national identity through the intellectual biography of a political leader, Ibrahim Haji Yaacob. Our focus is on the interplay between the transmission and construction of knowledge and the formation of ethno-national identity by tracing the origins and development of Malay identity in the writings of Ibrahim. As well as a close examination of his texts, we will explore the social, political and economic contexts in which he wrote.

This chapter is presented in five sections. The first deals with Ibrahim's life and times in the prewar period. The second carefully analyzes his pre-war writings. The third traces his wartime and postwar political behavior. The fourth conducts a textual analysis of his postwar publications. The final section summarizes our findings in this chapter.

The main sources for this study are Ibrahim's writings, particularly his books (Ibrahim 1941; 1951; 1957; Agastja 1951), newspaper articles, particularly the ones in *Majlis*, and private papers (Mss. 176). We must, however, treat his reminiscences, particularly his postwar writings, with care – they may include a number of omissions and/or fabrications. Other sources include official documents on education in British Malaya, textbooks used in Malay-medium primary schools and teacher training colleges, and memoirs and articles written by Malay-educated intellectuals.

The life and times of a young activist: Ibrahim in prewar Malaya

Home and school learning

Ibrahim Haji Yaacob was born on 27 November 1911 in Kampung Tanjung Kertau, a village in the Temerloh District, near the center of the State of Pahang. Ibrahim's mother, Hawa Husin (Hussein), raised him after divorcing his father, Haji Yaacob Tok Lebai Saat (Saad), when Ibrahim was two years old.[1] Apparently, Hawa married several times. While Ibrahim was the only child of Yaacob and Hawa, he had an elder brother who had a different father. After their divorce, Yaacob and Hawa both remarried and had more children. Hawa belonged to an ordinary peasant family holding a paddy field, coconut trees and an orchard. She nurtured Ibrahim with assistance from her female relatives and Ibrahim's elder brother. Despite the divorce, Ibrahim had a good relationship with his father, who was well known for his knowledge of Islam and the Arabic language (Mss. 176 (1); Bachtiar 1985: 31–32).

In his writing Ibrahim portrayed his home village as a microcosm of the Malay Archipelago. He observed that the villagers were of "Malay stock" (*rumpun Melayu*) with origins tracing to various ethnic groups in the Malay Archipelago, such as Bugis, Javanese, Riau-Lingga Malays, Minangkabau and Balinese. Ibrahim was of Bugis descent. His ancestors came from Wajo, South Sulawesi. His father and relatives liked to tell him how brave the Bugis were as anti-colonial fighters and defenders of Islam. Ibrahim loved these legends and enjoyed repeating them to his school friends (Mss. 176 (1); (3) a). Significantly, Ibrahim belonged not only to the humble peasant class but also to the immigrant "Malays" of Bugis origin.

Like other boys in his village, Ibrahim began his formal education by attending both a private Qur'anic class and a government primary school. When he was seven years old, he started to learn the Qur'an, the rudiments of Islam, and the Arabic alphabet under his father's younger brother, who served as a religious teacher. He later recalled that his mother had also strictly practiced Islam (Mss. 176 (2)). A year after beginning to attend the Qur'anic class, Ibrahim entered Sekolah Melayu Tanjung Kertau, a Malay-medium primary school. As a pupil, he showed a remarkable talent particularly in reading and writing (Mss. 176 (1)).

School education seems to have had a significant impact on Ibrahim's conceptualization of Malayness. In his reminiscences, Ibrahim recalled

Photo 5:1   Ibrahim Haji Yaacob. (Semangat Asia *August 1943: 3*)

that he had seen a map of the Malay Archipelago (*Gugusan Pulau-Pulau Melayu*) in a classroom of his primary school. The map showed the Malay Peninsula (*Semenanjung Tanah Melayu*) stretching from the southern part of mainland Asia to the Archipelago, comprising Sumatra, Borneo, Java, the Lesser Sundas, Sulawesi, Maluku, Papua and the Philippines. He wrote:

> My teacher taught us that the whole territory in the map of the Malay Archipelago was the homeland (*tanah air*) of the Malays, which had been divided under the ascendancy of European colonial powers...[2] (Mss. 176 (3) a)

> Taken in connection with the learning of geography (*ilmu alam/bumi*), my school friends and I were of the opinion that the map of the Malay Archipelago was the map of the homeland of the Malays, and the name of *Melayu* was regarded as the name of my race (*bangsa saya*). Moreover, a history book titled

Tawarikh Melayu analyzes the Malay kingdom of Srivijaya and subsequently
the territory of the Javanese-Malay kingdom of Majapahit.[3] (Mss. 176 (3) a)

Thus, he attributed his concept of Malayness, derived – at least in part –
from learning geography and history at school, as can be seen from his
reference to a map of the Malay Archipelago and a history textbook.

Political awakening of a young student

After completing the fifth standard at a Malay-medium primary school in
1925, Ibrahim started a teaching apprenticeship as a pupil teacher at the
same school before transferring to another primary school. In 1928 he was
admitted to the Sultan Idris Training College (SITC). A close examination
of his college days is worthwhile, as college life seems to have played a
crucial role in shaping his concept of Malayness.

As we have seen, SITC students had various opportunities to learn about
the Malay world through lectures, textbooks and other publications, and
daily conversations with teachers and friends. As for Ibrahim, some of
the lectures given by SITC teachers deeply influenced his ethno-national
identification. In his books as well as unpublished memoirs and letters,
he often named teachers who had delivered impressive lectures. In an
unpublished memoir written in 1976 or 1977, for example, he recounts the
impressive lectures that he had attended:

> I was a student who had just started to recognize and feel nationalist sentiment
> (*rasa kebangsaan*) after I heard lectures given by history teachers Cikgu[4]
> Abdul Hadi bin Haji Hassan and Cikgu Buyong bin Adil, a geography teacher
> Cikgu Abdul Rahman bin Haji Sahabuddin [*sic*],[5] and an agriculture teacher
> Cikgu Nordin bin Haji Harun as well as lectures by Cikgu Harun bin Mohd
> Amin and in particular lectures by Cikgu Zainal Abidin bin Ahmad (Za'aba
> [Za'ba])…[6] (Mss. 176 (2))

These teachers strongly influenced the thinking of Ibrahim and other
concerned SITC students. Some of the teachers were also widely known as
writers in the field of Malay history, literature and language, namely, Abdul
Hadi Haji Hasan, Buyong Adil, Harun Mohd. Amin (Harun Aminurrashid),
and Zainal Abidin Ahmad. In addition to these Malay teachers, Ibrahim
also mentioned the Principal of the SITC, O.T. Dussek, as a teacher who

promoted Malay national identity (Mss. 176 (2); (3) c). In 1935, four years after graduating from the SITC, Ibrahim wrote in *Majlis*, a Malay newspaper, on Dussek's contribution to the Malay community:

> In short, I felt as if Mr. Dussek's body had been divided into two sides, namely, English on the one side, and Malay on the other. Therefore, he did not forget to cultivate good sentiments among Malay students, urging that the Malays should love their race (*bangsa*), homeland (*tanah air*) and rulers (*raja*).[7] (*Majlis,* 29 August 1935)

Certain textbooks also contributed to framing Ibrahim's worldview. In one of his writings, Ibrahim specifically discusses the history textbooks that he read in Malay schools and the SITC.

> Likewise, in history lessons, we learned from books *Tawarikh Melayu* and *Sejarah Alam Melayu*. Then, at the SITC, Tanjung Malim, history lessons are mainly on the history of the Malay world (*Alam Melayu*), namely, histories of the ages of Srivijaya, Majapahit, and the spread of Islam to the whole Malay Archipelago (*Gugusan Pulau² Melayu*), that is, to Sumatra, to Java, to Borneo (Kalimantan), to Celebes (Sulawesi), to the Maluku Islands, to Papua, to the Lesser Sunda Islands, and to the Philippine Islands.[8] (Mss. 176 (2))

In his college days, Ibrahim had access to *Kitab Tawarikh Melayu* and the first three volumes of *Sejarah Alam Melayu*. His writings occasionally mention these books as important sources of his knowledge on the history of the Malay people and homeland.

Apart from authorized textbooks, SITC students also had reading materials like books, magazines and newspapers. Although the college did not have a dedicated library when Ibrahim studied there, as we mentioned, it did have a collection of books for borrowing. Bookstores at Tanjung Malim, particularly AHMY Bookstore, also provided books and periodicals for the SITC students. The bookstore was owned by a history teacher Abdul Hadi Haji Hasan and a clerical employee Md. Yusuf Md. Sharif (Shaharom 1996: 92–93). For Ibrahim and other students fond of reading, the bookstore seems to have been an important source of knowledge (Ramlah 1999: 42).

Importantly, there were also strong Indonesian influences on Ibrahim and his fellow SITC students. As well as Malay classics, religious books, light readings, newspapers and magazines published in Malaya, their reading materials also included those published in the Netherlands East Indies. Ibrahim recalled these Indonesian publications helping to foster his pan-Malay/Indonesian consciousness. Publications in the Netherlands East Indies that he claimed to have read included almanacs, periodicals such as *Pandji Poestaka, Bintang Hindia, Pandji Islam, Bintang Timor, Pertja, Pertja Selatan, Pewarta Deli* and *Persatuan,* and novels like *Siti Nurbaya, Salah Pilih, Salah Asuhan, Djumpa Atjeh,* and *Melati van Agam.* Ibrahim and his fellow students enthusiastically praised Indonesian nationalists like Sukarno, Hatta, Tan Malaka, Dr. Soetomo and Ki Hadjar Dewantara (Mss. 176 (2); (3)a).

His extra-curricular activities included military training as a member of the Malayan Volunteer Infantry (MVI). He recalled enjoying camping at Port Dickson, Negeri Sembilan, as part of his MVI obligations (Mss. 176 (1)).

During his college days, Ibrahim became involved in journalism and politics. He contributed several articles to Malay periodicals, particularly to *Warta Negeri,* a Kuala Lumpur-based Malay newspaper, under the pen name "IBHY." As mentioned, Ibrahim claimed that he and other SITC students had formed a socialist-oriented secret society in 1929, and the following year, developed it into a student organization called Ikatan Semenanjung/Borneo (Peninsular/Bornean Association).[9] He noted that the inner circle of the association aimed to incorporate Malaya into *Indonesia Raya,* a state covering all the territories from Sabang to Papua (Agastja 1951: 60). If we accept his account, Ibrahim and some of his friends also became members of the Sukarno-led Partai Nasional Indonesia (PNI) in 1929 (Ibrahim 1957: 24). As noted above, however, some former SITC teachers and students were skeptical about whether Ibrahim and his friends had really managed to organize an underground association and join an Indonesian political party because the authorities had kept them under constant surveillance (Mustapha 1999: 207).

Formation of the Kesatuan Melayu Muda

After graduating from the SITC in 1931, Ibrahim began teaching at a Malay school in Bentong, Pahang. According to Bachtiar Djamily, Ibrahim learned English while teaching there (Bacthiar 1985: 39). In 1934 he moved to Kuala Lumpur to teach the Malay language at the Police Depot. Ibrahim continued to write various articles on the interests of the Malays, frequently under pen names like "IBHY," "Silawatan," "Agastya (Agastja)" and "Indera," in several Malay newspapers and periodicals including *Majlis* (Kuala Lumpur), *Warta Ahad* (Singapore), *Warta Jenaka* (Singapore) and *Bulan Melayu* (Johor Bahru). Between 1936 and 1937, he also attended night classes of a private trade school in Kuala Lumpur to study the English language. In 1936 or 1937 he quit the job at the Police Depot to become a full-time journalist for *Majlis*. He was promoted to chief editor in 1939. After resigning from his post at *Majlis* in 1940, he went to work for *Utusan Melayu*, a Singapore-based Malay newspaper (Mss. 176 (3)b; Fortnightly Intelligence Report, Nos. 10 & 13 (CO273/669/50744/7); Agastja 1951: 71–72; Abdul Latiff 1981: 213; Cheah 1979: 87, Bakhtiar 1985: 15–16). Ibrahim claimed that after completing his study at the SITC, he had continued his underground political activities with other graduates scattered across Malaya (Agastja 1951: 71).

Ibrahim was once a member of two state Malay associations, the Kesatuan Melayu Selangor (Selangor Malay Association) and the Persatuan Melayu Pahang (Pahang Malay Association), both of which were established in the late 1930s, primarily on the initiative of Malay aristocrats and administrators to protect Malay rights. Yet Ibrahim soon left both associations. He argued that he had broken away from them not only because of their pro-British stance but also due to their "narrow-minded nationalism (*kebangsaan sempit*)," characterized by state (*negeri*)-based feudalism, and the narrow definition of Malay by which "Malays" of mixed descent and of non-Peninsular origin could be marginalized or excluded (Agastja 1951: 67–72). It should be noted that Ibrahim had been a member of these state Malay associations despite being a "foreign Malay" of Bugis descent. Nevertheless, he might have felt somewhat marginalized within the associations because traditional Malay elites usually controlled the leadership of them.

In 1937 Ibrahim and some former college mates joined Persatuan Belia Melayu (Malay Youth League), a Kuala Lumpur-based informal organization formed by students and graduates of the School of Agriculture, Serdang, and Technical School, Kuala Lumpur (Mss. 176 (3) b). When Ibrahim was elected as its President in 1938, the Persatuan Belia Melayu was renamed and officially registered as Kesatuan Melayu Muda (KMM) (Young Malay Union). KMM was modeled on youth movements in other parts of the world such as the "Jong Java" and "Jong Sumatra" leagues in the Netherlands East Indies (Ibrahim 1957: 24; Roff 1994 [1967]: 222) as well as the "Young Turks" of Turkey (Mustapha 1999: 195; A. Samad

Ahmad 1981: 110–111). The leadership of the KMM included Ibrahim Haji Yaacob (President), Mustapha Haji Hussain (Vice President), Hassan Haji Manan (Secretary-General), Othman Mohd. Noor (Secretary), Idris Hakim (Treasurer). Other committee members included: Ishak Haji Muhammad, Onan Haji Siraj, Abd. Karim Rashid, Bahar Abik, Sulong Chik, Abdullah Kamil, Abd. Samad Ahmad, Mohd. Salehudin and Abdullah Thani (Abdullah Sani) Raja Kecil or Ahmad Boestamam (Mustapha 1999: 206–227; Abd. Malek: 1975: 99–100, 358).

These people all came from similar backgrounds. First, as the organization's name Kesatuan Melayu Muda (Young Malay Union) indicates, its core leaders were young men in their twenties. For Ibrahim, however, "*Muda* does not mean Youth, but young in ideas, that is, progressive" (Agastja 1951: 72; Cheah 1979: 89). It should be added that the KMM was male-dominated with no females in its top leadership.

Second, the KMM's leadership belonged to the newly risen intelligentsia of ordinary origin. They were drawn from non-privileged, mostly peasant, classes. Unlike the leadership of state Malay associations, none of the KMM's core leaders were from the ruling class. Some, like Ibrahim, Hassan and Othaman were basically Malay-educated while others like Mustapha, Ishak and Boestamam had both Malay and English education. Many of them were Malay schoolteachers, teaching staff or students of the SITC, the School of Agriculture, Technical School and Trade School, and journalists for Malay periodicals. At the grass roots, however, Islamic-educated religious teachers and students also played a considerable part (Agastja 1951: 72–73; Abd. Malek 1975: 98–100, 144–146, 151, 156; Khoo Kay Kim 1979b: 36–37; Firdaus 1985: 18, 22; Roff 1994 (1967): 231).

Finally, most of the KMM's top leadership were descendants of immigrants from various parts of the Archipelago. For instance, like Ibrahim, Ishak was of Bugis descent, Mustapha, Abd. Karim and Boestamam of Minangkabau, Idris of Mandailing, Onan of Javanese, and Bahar of Bawean (Mustapha 1999: 206–227). They were frequently not regarded as indigenous Peninsular Malays but as "Foreign Malays" (*Melayu Dagang*). Though the KMM's pan-Malayism should not be understood merely in terms of the member's immigrant origins,[10] we should consider their broader definition of Malay and their advocacy of *Melayu Raya / Indonesia Raya* as their strategy of survival in order for "foreign Malays" to hold a legitimate position in the Malay community.

It is unlikely that KMM members shared a single, homogenous political ideology. For Roff, "it seems clear that there was among the members considerable confusion of opinion about what they were trying to do. KMM, in short, meant different things to different men" (Roff. 1994 [1967]: 232). Nevertheless, Abd. Malek Hj. Md. Hanafiah attempts to present a more consistent KMM ideology. He argues that the KMM's struggle policy could be divided into short-term and long-term policies.[11] The former comprised three factors: anti-colonialism, anti-feudalism, and anti-Malay bureaucratic elite, while the latter was made up of the following six principles in English: unity, humanity, liberty, democracy, fraternity, and honesty (Abd. Malek 1975: 106).[12] Abd. Samad Ahmad, a former KMM member, also noted these six principles in his memoir (A. Samad Ahmad 1981: 153). As Abd. Malek acknowledges, however, even core members were not in complete agreement about the KMM's principles (Abd. Malek 1975: 127). Without its own medium to promote their cause, local people's deep-rooted loyalty to their state rulers prevented the KMM from mobilizing mass support in Malay society. Roff estimates that the prewar KMM membership numbered no more than a few hundred (Roff 1994 [1967]: 234).

Whatever their differences, though, it seems likely that most KMM members intended to overcome state provincialism (*kenegerian*) as well as the narrow definition of Malays which excluded Malayo-Muslims of immigrant origins. For Ibrahim, besides its anti-colonialist and anti-feudalist approach, the KMM's distinctiveness lay in its advocacy of *Melayu Raya / Indonesia Raya*, a concept of the pan-Malay/Indonesian nation covering all the territories in the Malay Archipelago (Agastja 1951: 73; Ibrahim 1951: 59–60; 1957: 24–25). Though we should not uncritically accept Ibrahim's self-reflections, particularly in his postwar writings, there is little doubt that the KMM membership generally supported the broader definition of Malay which included immigrant Malayo-Muslims.

After quitting his post as editor of *Majlis* in June 1940, Ibrahim travelled around the Malay Peninsula for nearly one year. The aim of this tour was to survey the socio-economic realities of the Malays in British Malaya and to mobilize support for the KMM-led Malay nationalist movement through frequent discussions with the Malay populace, especially with students of various schools (Ibrahim 1941: 5–7; 1975 [1941]: 13–14). He recorded his observation in a book entitled *Melihat Tanah Air* (Surveying the Homeland).[13] *Melihat Tanah Air*, the only book that he published before the Pacific War, consists of two parts. Part one is basically an overview of the government and the socio-economic history of Malaya. Part two is a journalistic reportage on the condition of the Malay people, including the "Sakai" or Orang Asli, and their territories in the Straits Settlements and the Federated Malay States, based on his observations and interviews during his tour of Malaya.

There were considerable contradictions and inconsistencies in Ibrahim's political behavior. If we accept his account, he contacted some Malay members of the Malayan Communist Party (MCP) during that year-long tour (Agastja 1951: 79; Ibrahim 1957: 25–26; Nagai 1978: 59).[14] At the same time, he also acted as an agent for the Japanese in his own and the KMM's interests.[15] Ibrahim was in touch with Japanese intelligence agents, who were seeking to obtain British military secrets from local collaborators in Malaya. Nagai Shin'ichi argues that Ibrahim obtained financial assistance from Tsurumi Ken, the Japanese Consul-General in Singapore, in August 1941 to purchase a Singapore-based Malay newspaper, *Warta Malaya*, originally owned by Syed Hussein Al-Sagoff, for anti-British propaganda (Nagai 1978: 59–60).[16] In November 1941, the Fujiwara Kikan (Fujiwara Agency) or F Kikan (F Agency),[17] a Japanese intelligence agency headed by Major Fujiwara Iwaichi, began approaching Ibrahim and other KMM leaders (Fujiwara 1966: 71). Later Ibrahim justified his collaboration with the Japanese as an effort for the Malays to compete with other pro-Japanese groups in Malaya such as the Indian Independence League and the Chinese pro-Wang Ching-wei group (Agastja 1951: 83–85; Cheah 1979: 93). According to Cheah Boon Kheng, Ibrahim attempted to play the role of a "double agent", working for both the Japanese and the British (Cheah 1979: 91), hoping to enlist British support for his project to achieve independence for the Riau islands from the Dutch (Cheah 1979: 93–94; Agastja 1951: 81–83).

Awareness of Malay problems

In his prewar writings, Ibrahim repeatedly urged the Malays to be aware (*sedar, insaf*) of the problems that they faced.[18] As early as 1930, when he was an 18 year-old SITC student, he claimed that Malays should have awareness (*kesedaran*) in order to not be left behind as the world progresses (*kemajuan dunia*) (*Warta Negeri*, 5 May 1930). He insisted that the Malays should take a more positive attitude to progress. He regretted that Malays tended to say that it was still not the time (*belum masa-nya*) for them to make progress (*maju*) in many areas such as education, politics and business and prompted them to say instead that it was the time (*inilah masa-nya, inilah waktu-nya*) for them to advance (*Warta Negeri*, 17 February 1930). Ibrahim considered the three main problems faced by the Malay to be: (1) socio-economic backwardness, (2) the erosion of rights, and (3) the lack of unity among the Malays.

The Malays' socio-economic backwardness

In his prewar writings, Ibrahim frequently cautioned that the Malay people were far behind in socio-economic terms. Coincidentally, he started writing during the Great Depression, which hit the Malayan economy as well. As mentioned earlier, the vast majority of Malays in prewar Malaya belonged to farming classes in rural villages. Among 241,754 working Malays in the Federated Malay States in 1931, no fewer than 204,644 were categorized as engaged in "agricultural pursuits" (Roff 1994 [1967]: 121). Roff argued that among Malay peasant farmers, the majority of whom were indebted to Chinese or Indian moneylenders, "[t]hose Malays who took their livelihood mainly from padi cultivation, with small subsistence or cash crops of fruit, coconuts, tapioca, and the like grown in home gardens, were least affected by the depression; those whose dependence on rubber was greatest suffered most" (Roff 1994 [1967]: 205).

From his student days at the SITC, Ibrahim had persistently called attention to the fact that the Malays were economically left behind, particularly in commerce and industry. He argued that Europeans came to the Malay world (*alam Melayu*) mainly to promote their business and commerce. Chinese and Indian immigrants were also active in business. In contrast, it seemed that the Malays were totally marginalized in business despite their status as the natives (*anak negeri, bumiputera*) of Malaya.

> But, what are the Malay races (*bangsa-bangsa Melayu*), that is the natives (*anak bumi putera*)? Their field of commerce becomes increasingly so small that it is no longer visible in the world today.[19] (*Warta Negeri*, 24 February 1930)

One situation he found particularly deplorable was that the Malays themselves preferred shopping in Chinese and Indian shops to Malay stores.

He therefore suggested that the Malays should respect and promote business and commercial activities of their own race (*bangsa*).

> Hey, my race (*bangsa-ku*). Develop the commerce and business of your own race. Don't be ashamed to buy in the shops of your own race. A little help, even a quarter cent, would be very beneficial.[20] (*Warta Negeri*, 24 February 1930)

Ibrahim contended that the Malays' economic backwardness stemmed mainly from the fact that they had been oppressed by "foreign" economic forces. As Milner points out, Ibrahim attempted to analyze the Malays' economic backwardness from a socialist perspective, using analytical terms such as capital (*modal*) and labor (*buruh*) (Milner 2002 [1995]: 266–268). Many of his newspaper articles in the 1930s argued that the influx of foreign capital (*modal bangsa-bangsa asing*) was the main cause of the Malays' poverty and marginalization. He wrote in 1938, "we have to be aware (*sedar*) now of how we have been cheated by the capitalists of foreign races (*kaum modal bangsa asing*)" (*Majlis*, 7 January 1938). In his book *Melihat Tanah Air*, published in 1941, he claimed again that the Malays were economically marginalized owing to pressure from outside, adding that they should not become xenophobic but rather co-operate with all the foreign races (*bangsa asing*) in Malaya (Ibrahim 1941: 8–9).

> My people are in the situation where they feel as if their homeland (*tanah air*) does not exist because their life is oppressed. Sources of the oppression are: (1) capital from the outside (*modal luar*), (2) labor from the outside (*buruh daripada luar*) following the inflow of capital from the outside, and (3) products from the outside (*barang-barang luar*) following the inflow of capital and labor (working people) from the outside. [These factors are] to open this country as wide as possible without considering the life of my people (Malays).[21] (Ibrahim 1941: 9)

Ethnic and national consciousness can only arise and flourish by contrast with "others." It is therefore necessary to define what Ibrahim meant by "foreign." For him, "foreigners" consisted of those who could be categorized as Chinese, Indians, Europeans, Eurasians, Arabs,[22] Japanese, etc. Note, however, that he tried to avoid directly criticizing British economic dominance in Malaya in his prewar writings. During that period, Ibrahim's main targets tended to be "foreign eastern races" (*bangsa-bangsa timur asing*), which were also called the "Malayan races" (*bangsa Malayan*²³), namely Chinese and Indian immigrants in Malaya.

As a schoolteacher, Ibrahim vigorously wrote about the Malays' education. He expressed regret that the Malays were left behind in education in a series of articles in *Majlis*.

> The ordinary Malays are extremely low in educational standards. They leave Malay schools at the age of 14 at the most, usually at the age of 12. Their thinking is still incomplete. Due to this, after leaving schools, they go back home with the expectation that they would be protected by their parents, and they get used to being lazy...²⁴ (*Majlis,* 5 November 1934)

For Ibrahim, Malay participation in commerce and industry was limited because education for the Malays, either in Malay or in English, did not encourage them to enter modern sectors of the economy except for public services. He argued that the Malays were not given enough opportunities to study commerce, engineering or special skills (*Majlis,* 5 November 1934; 12 May 1937).

Despite his image as a secular nationalist, Ibrahim paid considerable attention to religious matters as well. He regretted that some Malays started to look down Islam (*merendahkan ugama Islam*) while they blindly accepted anything from the West as "modern." For him, Islam was not an obstacle but a guide to progress (*Majlis*, 9 September 1935).

> I am very sad to hear that some Malays say, "Malays cannot make progress (*maju*) if they believe in Islam" … Islam does not hinder progress (*kemajuan*) at all. Islam urges us to progress…²⁵ (*Majlis*, 9 September 1935)

Ibrahim urged Malay rulers, aristocrats and religious officers at the Majlis Ugama Islam (Islamic Religious Council) to play a more important part in the development of progressive Islam. He also suggested that the government put more emphasis on Islamic religious education in Malay schools and English schools. Religious teachers were expected to guide Muslim students to a correct understanding of Islam (*Majlis*, 12 September 1935; 13 December 1937).

Erosion of Malay rights

The British colonial government introduced a so-called "Pro-Malay" policy in the early twentieth century. In 1919, only 10.5 percent of the 1,001 clerks of all grades in the General Clerical Service of the Federated Malay States were Malay. The share of Malay officers in the specialist services was even smaller. In 1924, there were only 11 Malays among more than 5,500 subordinate officers in the railways, postal, and medical department. Under these circumstances, the Federated Malay States adopted "Pro-Malay" policy due to which Malays were to be recruited preferentially to the lower ranks of public services (Roff 1994 [1967]: 113-121). In the late 1920s and early 1930s, non-Malay residents, particularly long-domiciled Chinese, increasingly called for equal rights with the Malays. Some Chinese and Indians regarded themselves as "Malayans" who were qualified to have substantial political rights in Malaya while the majority of the Malays disliked the term "Malayan" as a threat to Malay sovereignty (Ariffin 1993: 17). The Chinese representatives in the Legislative Council of the Straits Settlements and in the Federal Council demanded a greater share in government and administration such as the intake of non-Malays in the Malayan Civil Service. The Malayan Civil Service, dominated by European administrative officers with a small number of Malay officials,[26] was at the apex of a bureaucratic hierarchy in British Malaya. In 1931, Lim Ching Yan, a member of the Legislative Council of the Straits Settlements, remarked to a Penang Chinese association that the Peninsula was not a Malay country but their own country. Malays reacted strongly to these and similar claims (*Majallah Guru*, March 1931: 57–58; Roff 1994 [1967]: 207–210).

It was under these circumstances that Ibrahim claimed that Malay rights (*hak-hak Melayu*) were under attack. Ibrahim had two primary concerns about the erosion of Malay rights. First and foremost, he claimed that "foreign races" (*bangsa-bangsa asing*) were trying to deprive the Malays of their rights as the natives (*anak negeri, bumiputera*) of Malaya. Continuing his critique of the dominance of foreign races in socio-economic fields, his concern was mainly about the growing demands by Chinese and Indian residents for a greater role in government and administration.

Malaya has already become an object of competition between the native race (Malays) (*bangsa anak negeri (orang Melayu)*) and foreign Eastern races (Chinese and Indians) (*bangsa timur asing (iaitu Cina dan India)*).

For these five or six years, these foreign races (*bangsa asing*) continuously raised their voices to demand rights (*hak*) as if they were not satisfied with the British government which is eternally loyal to Malay rulers. The shameless and greedy foreign races (*bangsa dagang*[27]) lack understanding at all times ... and demand what should not be given to them.[28] (*Majlis*, 16 November 1933)

Ibrahim contended that these "foreign races" demanded:

1. to make their rights (*hak mereka*) equal with [the rights of] the natives (*anak negeri*) in the government sector.
2. to create the Malayan race (*bangsa Malayan*) in Malaya as if they wanted the Malays to vanish.
3. to have paddy fields.
4. to abolish the Jawi script.
5. to run their vernacular primary schools with government expenditures.[29] (*Majlis*, 16 November 1933)

Ibrahim did not accept the demands of Chinese and Indians in Malaya for equal rights (*hak persamaan*) with the Malays, nor their effort to legitimize their status as "Malayans." For Ibrahim, only the Malays, the natives (*anak negeri, bumiputera*) of Malaya, were entitled to political rights in Malaya while "foreign races (*bangsa-bangsa asing*) should not demand rights (*hak*)" (*Majlis*, 22 December 1932).

While openly rejecting Chinese and Indian claims for equal rights with the Malays, though, Ibrahim tended to refrain from directly criticizing British colonial rule in his prewar writings.[30] Indeed, in his articles in the 1930s, he frequently praised the British government as the protector (*penaung*) of Malay rulers and subjects. As early as 1930, as a young student, Ibrahim described the British as "the most just government (*kerajaan yang maha adil*)" (*Warta Negeri*, 1 March 1930). He even attempted to stoke the Malays' affection for paternalistic British rule in an article in 1933.

...but don't forget that we must express our sentiment of love (*perasaan kasih sayang kita*) toward the supreme government, namely the British (*pemerintah agung iaitu British*), as our foster father (*bapa angkat kita*) who pampers us very much.[31] (*Majlis*, 25 September 1933)

Later in 1937, he wrote an article entitled, "The Malays must defend the British Empire"[32] (*Warta Jenaka*, 16 December 1937). In *Melihat Tanah Air*, too, he expressed thanks to the British colonial government (Ibrahim 1941: 38–39). Though he occasionally commented critically on particular government policies, such as the liberal policy towards the Chinese and Indians in Malaya, he did not question the legitimacy of British rule in Malaya in his prewar writings.

For those whose image of Ibrahim is of an ardent anti-colonialist, it might be surprising that Ibrahim took a "pro-British" stance in his prewar writings. As we have seen, he was much more animated by the conflict between Malays and non-Malays than that between the colonizer and the colonized. It was not until the Pacific War that he began to openly criticize British colonialism in Malaya. Some might suggest that he practiced self-censorship when writing about British colonial administration in the prewar period because of the colonial restrictions on freedom of expression. It is more likely, however, that he had not yet developed a staunch anti-colonial stance at this earlier stage, at least partly accepting the political legitimacy of British colonial rule in prewar Malaya.

The second major concern was that most Malay rulers and aristocrats, including representatives on the Federal Council, had largely disregarded the demands of the Malay populace (*Majlis,* 12 July 1937). Perak, Selangor, Negeri Sembilan and Pahang originally had separate State Councils.[33] Each State Council was an advisory body in which the ruler (Sultan) and selected chiefs sat as members. The creation of the State Councils was, in fact, a British effort to assuage rulers and chiefs who felt the loss of power. These four states formed the Federated Malay States in 1896. The establishment of the Federal Council in 1909, which was superordinate to the State Councils, was an attempt to unify and centralize administration in the Federated Malay States. The Federal Council, which was conducted in English, was comprised of the High Commissioner, who chaired the Council, the Resident-General, the four rulers, the four residents and four nominated "unofficials." The first council consisted of six British officials (the High Commissioner, the Resident-General and the four residents), four Malay rulers, three British "unofficials" and one Chinese "unofficial." In 1927 the four Malay rulers were replaced on the Council by four Malay "unofficials" (Puthucheary 1978: 7–8). Malay "unofficial" members were usually prominent aristocrats from component states.

Ibrahim was openly skeptical about the Malay "unofficial" members'
role in defending Malay rights. He was frustrated that they appeared to be
lacking both the will and the ability to promote and protect the interests of
ordinary Malay people (*rakyat, orang ramai, orang kebanyakan*). "Most of
the Malay representatives (*wakil-wakil Melayu*) in the Council," he claimed,
"always forget their responsibility to the public (*umum*) and just express
their ideas only for their own interests" (*Majlis*, 11 June 1937). Therefore,
he argued, most of the Malay "unofficials" in the Council did not deserve
the status of Malay representatives (*wakil Melayu*). He did, however,
acknowledge that some of the Malay ruling elite had dedicated themselves
to the defense of people's rights and welfare (*Majlis*, 28 June 1937).

Ibrahim demanded the introduction of a more democratic system which
would enable the common Malay people to more actively participate in
the government and administration of the Federated Malay States. He
questioned the procedures for nominating "unofficial" members to the
Council. pointing out that there was no mechanism by which ordinary
Malay people could influence the selection of representatives. He posited
the following questions in *Warta Ahad* in 1936:

1. Are these members of the Council selected on approval by popular vote
   (*undi rakyat umum*)?
2. Are these members of the Council truly the persons who are not
   connected with government posts?
3. Are these members of the Council from among the ordinary people
   (*orang kebanyakan*)?[34] (*Warta Ahad*, 29 March 1936)

He wrote a series of essays on democracy in *Majlis* in 1937. In one essay,
he observed a trend from autocracy (*otokrasi*) to democracy (*demokrasi*)
in the world and praised England or Britain as a democratic country where
the people have a significant voice in politics although she still maintained
a kingdom (*Majlis*, 28 July 1937; 13 August 1937). Interestingly, Britain
was portrayed here as an ideal democratic constitutional monarchy which
the Federated Malay States could emulate. He then indicated the Federated
Malay States was not a democratic country (*negeri demokrasi*) which
respected the rights of the Malay people (*hak rakyat Melayu*) (*Majlis*,
30 July 1937). Yet we must also note that despite his later image as anti-
feudalist, in his prewar writings, he neither denied the legitimacy of Malay
royalty and aristocracy nor demanded the abolition of Malay monarchy.

Disunity among the Malays

In prewar writings, Ibrahim had occasionally cautioned that the Malay people were divided, lacking a sense of unity. Three kinds of disunity caused considerable dissatisfaction on his part. First, there was a class distinction between the traditional ruling elite and the ordinary people. As we have seen, Ibrahim considered that most Malay aristocrats, including representatives in the Federal Council, had not paid heed to the demands of the local populace. Second, and closely related, state provincialism (*kenegerian*), or the sense of identifying with one's own Malay sultanate, was still strong in Malaya. Ibrahim believed that rivalry among Malay states had hindered the formation of *Melayu Raya* consciousness. Third, there were also divisions according to (sub-) ethnic origin. This is particularly the case between "indigenous" Malays, immigrants from the Archipelago (Javanese, Bugis, Minangkabau, Acehnese, etc.), and Malayo-Muslims of Indian and Arab descent.[35] Ibrahim criticized "narrow-minded nationalism" in the forms of state (*negeri*)-based provincialism and a narrow definition of Malay.

In the 1930s, and particularly the late 1930s, Ibrahim's writings warned of disunity among the Malays. An article in *Majlis* in 1938 clearly presented his deep anxiety about the disunity of the Malays, who still maintained a strong sense of belonging to either particular states or areas.

> The Malays have national spirit (*semangat kebangsaan*), but such sentiments have already become fragmented (*berpecah belah*) because of the lack of initiative and certain management.
>
> In fact, we wish the Malay national spirit (*semangat kebangsaan Melayu*) were still firm in the hearts of our people (*orang-orang kita*). But, our spirit is fragmented (*berpecah*) and is still narrow (*sempit*). Part of the spirit is still provincial (*bernegeri-negerian*), like Perak-minded (*berperakan*), Terengganu-minded (*berterengganuan*), Kelantan-minded (*berkelantanan*), Sumatra-minded (*bersumateraan*), Java-minded (*berjawaan*), and so forth.[36] (*Majlis*, 20 July 1938)

An editorial by Ibrahim in *Majlis* in 1939 also touched on the fragmentation of the Malay community.

> In fact, there are more than two million of our people (*orang-orang kita*) in Malaya (*Tanah Melayu*). Additionally, there are more than 60 million of our

Malay people (*orang-orang kita Melayu*) in the whole Malay Archipelago (*Gugusan Pulau-Pulau Melayu*) and more than two million of our people who have migrated to India, Ceylon, South Africa, China, Japan, Siam and so on. Thus, obviously our Malay race (*bangsa kita Melayu*) amounts to not less than 65 million, and accordingly we are a populous race (*bangsa yang ramai*). But, due to weaknesses in national spirit (*semangat kebangsaan*), experience and other various points, the Malay race (*bangsa Melayu*) has become a backward and fragmented one. This is because most of our people only love subgroups (*puak-puak*), not the race (*bangsa*)…[37] (*Majlis*, 16 November 1939)

In the passages above, Ibrahim, on the one hand, portrayed the Malays as a large race (*bangsa*) incorporating the entire Malay Archipelago. But on the other hand, he deeply deplored the realities of the Malays, who were backward and disintegrated mainly because they maintained a strong sense of belonging to their subgroups (*puak-puak*), lacking Malay identity in a broader sense. In the same article, however, Ibrahim also dreamed that the Malays would be united in the future. In this context, he not only used the term *bangsa* as a "race" but also imagined it as a (potential) political community or "nation" although these two meanings sometimes overlapped considerably. He outlined his expectations:

…but from now on our people will build solidarity of love for the race (*bangsa*). Therefore I believe that 65 million Malay race (*bangsa Melayu*) will rise as a civilized nation (*suatu bangsa yang mempunyai tamadun dan kesopanan*) and that they will at least become a nation which have their homeland (*tanah airnya*) in southern part of the Asian Continent.[38] (*Majlis*, 16 November 1939)

In *Melihat Tanah Air* (1941), Ibrahim clearly presented a territorial stretch of the "Malay world" (*alam Melayu*) as the territories of what we now call Malaysia, Singapore, Indonesia, Brunei, Timor-Leste, and the Philippines.

Where are my people (*orang-orang saya*)? – The "Malay World (*Alam Melayu*)" means the areas inherited by the Malay race (*bangsa Melayu*), includes Sumatra, Java, Celebes, the Borneo Island, the Maluku Islands, the Lesser Sunda Islands and the Philippine Islands. These areas have been renamed as Indonesia. And, surely, the Malay Peninsula is called "Malaya" at the present time. All these areas are referred to as the Malay World.[39] (Ibrahim 1941: 7–8)

Here Ibrahim adopted a broader definition of "Malay" as a race (*bangsa*). In addition, his elaborate description, in the second part of the book, of the people and the land of each state in Malaya clearly demonstrates that he regarded Malay states (*negeri-negeri Melayu*) as basic components of Malaya (*Tanah Melayu*), which in turn is a part of the Malay Archipelago or the Malay world (*alam Melayu*). In the following passages of *Melihat Tanah Melayu*, he articulates his perceptions of the lack of unity in the Malay world.

> *Melayu Raya* consciousness (*Perasaan Melayu Raya*) – I can indeed present my view on *Melayu Raya* consciousness. For these almost five hundred years they [the Malays] have had civil wars (*peperangan saudara*), and, accordingly, the Malay Peninsula was divided into some subgroups that have their own states (*beberapa puak yang bernegeri-negeri*), fighting each other. They now start to want to be allied again, not only among Malay communities (*umat-umat Melayu*) in Malaya, populated by two and half million, but also with Malay communities in Indonesia, populated by 65 million. They intend to become united and co-operate with each other. Yet only this consciousness is new. Most aristocrats and members of royalty steadfastly maintain their old consciousness and strongly resist the new consciousness of seeking the unity of all the Malay communities.[40] (Ibrahim 1941: 12–13)

These passages clearly indicate Ibrahim's dissatisfaction with class distinctions and provincialism among those whom he called "Malay". Being a Malay-educated teacher/journalist from a peasant family of Bugis descent, Ibrahim was not a member of the mainstream elite in colonial Malaya. We can thus consider his advocacy of pan-Malayism as an effort to build a new political community in which he and his comrades could occupy better, more dominant positions.

In search of a nation: Ibrahim in wartime and postwar periods

Collaboration during the Japanese occupation[41]

Just before the Japanese military forces landed on the Malay Peninsula on 8 December 1941, the British authorities arrested Ibrahim and more than one hundred KMM supporters for suspicion of collaborating with Japanese, sending them to jails in Singapore (Cheah 2012 [1983]: 103-104; Nagai 1978:

62). However, some KMM leaders had not been arrested, such as Mustapha and Onan. Onan, who later formed the Barisan Pemuda (Youth Front) in the KMM, asked the Fujiwara Kikan, a Japanese military intelligence unit under Major Fujiwara Iwaichi, for assistance in releasing the imprisoned KMM members and to support the Malay nationalist movement in exchange for the KMM's co-operation with the Japanese (Fujiwara 1966: 168). Mustapha, Onan and other remaining KMM leaders demanded Malaya's independence,[42] but the Japanese rebuffed it (Mustapha 1999: 262–265).

On 16 February 1942, the day after the Japanese occupied Singapore, Ibrahim was released from jail. He met Fujiwara on 18 February. During the meeting, Fujiwara directed that the KMM would no longer be a political organization but a cultural society (Fujiwara 1966: 266–267). After the Fujiwara Kikan was dissolved in March 1942,[43] the Japanese Military Administration assumed direct control of the KMM

From February until June 1942, as an agent for the Japanese Military Administration, the KMM successfully mobilized support from the Malay populace, with its membership reaching ten thousand. Even members of the Malay ruling elite collaborated with the KMM. Ibrahim, however, admitted that most of the supporters had little idea about the KMM's ideology and policy (Agastja 1951: 100). Nevertheless, the Japanese became increasingly concerned about the potential overheating of the Malay political activities, and ordered the KMM to be dissolved in June 1942. After losing his official status as President of the KMM, Ibrahim was asked, or forced, by the Japanese authorities, to accept a post as adviser to the Malayan/Sumatran Military Administration in Singapore (Agastja 1951: 101).

As the tide of war turned against the Japanese around the middle of 1943, the Japanese Military Administration became increasingly aware of the need to garner mass support from the Malays in the form of direct military co-operation with Japanese forces. In December 1943, the Japanese forces established two Malay volunteer forces, namely, the Giyu Gun (Volunteer Army) and the Giyu Tai (Volunteer Corps). The former comprised about 2,000 members around March 1944 and was tasked with the defense of the whole of Malaya. The latter had about 5,000 members assigned to the defense of local administrative units (Boeicho Boeikenshujo Senshishitsu 1976: 169–170). Ibrahim willingly accepted appointment as commander of the Giyu Gun with the rank of Lieutenant Colonel. Expecting to develop the Giyu Gun into a future national army, Ibrahim attempted to strengthen secret relations with the Malayan People's Anti-Japanese Army (MPAJA), a pro-Communist army dominated by non-Malays (Agastja 1951: 106). In July 1943, twenty-five Malays from Malaya and Sumatra left Singapore for a two months' inspection tour of Japan under war conditions. Ibrahim, who led the delegates from Malaya, stated that he intended to "study the conditions of youth education" in Japan (Fortnightly Intelligence Report, Nos. 10, 12 & 13 (CO273/669/50744/7)).

Indonesia Raya as an unsuccessful project

As people in Malaya found everyday life increasingly difficult due to serious shortages of commodities and high inflation, as well as brutal suppression by the Japanese authorities, their distrust of the Japanese Military Administration deepened. Furthermore, the Malays' skepticism of the Japanese authorities was reinforced by the cession of four northern states (Perlis, Kedah, Kelantan and Terengganu) to Thailand in October 1943. Meanwhile, Japan's Prime Minister Koiso Kuniaki promised the former Netherlands East Indies to prepare the independence of Indonesia on 7 September 1944, but there was no such plan announced for Malaya. To mobilize mass support under these unfavorable circumstances, the Japanese Military Administration in Malaya was urged to develop a more positive program for the Malays. Ibrahim grasped this opportunity to advance his idea of incorporating Malaya into *Indonesia Raya* or Greater Indonesia. In May 1945, he was given permission to prepare to establish a Malay nationalist movement named KRIS,[44] with the support of Itagaki Yoichi, the Japanese officer in charge of ethnic affairs (Nagai 1978: 79; Itagaki 1988 [1968]: 161–164).

In the former Netherlands East Indies, the Japanese took concrete steps towards Indonesian independence to ensure that the Koiso Declaration was successfully implemented. In March 1945 the Japanese authorities announced the establishment of Badan Penyelidik Usaha Persiapan Kemerdekaan Indonesia (BPUPKI) (Committee for the Investigation of Preparatory Efforts for Indonesian Independence).[45] Its first session was held on 28 May 1945. The BPUPKI consisted of a Chair (Indonesian), two Vice-Chairs (one from Indonesia and another from Japan), 60 ordinary Indonesian members and seven special Japanese members.

At the second session of the BPUPKI from 10 July 1945, the members discussed several important issues, concerning the framework of a future Indonesian state, such as territory, citizenship, religion, and political structure. On the territory of a future Indonesian state, the following three proposals were submitted: (1) the former territory of the Netherlands East Indies, (2) the former Netherlands East Indies combined with Malaya, northern territories of Borneo (North Borneo, Brunei and Sarawak), New Guinea and Timor, and (3) the former Netherlands East Indies minus New Guinea, combined with Malaya, provided that the Malayan people wanted to join Indonesia. The BPUPKI put the question to vote, with results as follows: 19 for the first proposal, 39 for the second, six for the third, one for another proposal and one blank vote. The second proposal of *Indonesia Raya*, proposed by Muhammad Yamin, received the majority of support including Sukarno.[46] Mohammad Hatta, however, proposed the third idea (Muhammad Yamin 1959: 187–214; Anderson 1961: 29).

At the second session of the BPUPKI, Sukarno disclosed that Ibrahim, referred to as "Lieutenant Colonel Abdullah Ibrahim," had sent a message requesting that Malaya be incorporated into the territory of Indonesia. Sukarno interpreted this to mean that "the Malayan people feel that they belong to the Indonesian nation (*bangsa Indonesia*), have Indonesia as their homeland (*bertanah-air Indonesia*), and are united with us (*bersatu dengan kita*)" (Muhammad Yamin 1959: 206). Furthermore, "though I may be in danger of being labelled as an imperialist," Sukarno dared to say, "Indonesia will not be able to become strong and peaceful unless both sides of the Straits of Melaka are in our hands" (Muhammad Yamin 1959: 206).

As the tide of the war turned against Japan, the Japanese government decided to grant Indonesia independence as soon as possible. On 7 August 1945, the BPUPKI was dissolved into the new Panitia Persiapan Kemerdekaan Indonesia (PPKI) (Committee for the Preparation of Indonesian Independence). Then, on 8 August, an Indonesian delegation including Sukarno, Hatta and Radjiman Wediodiningrat travelled to Saigon to receive the final decision from Field Marshal Terauchi Hisaichi, commander of Japan's Southern Expeditionary Army Group. On 11 August, the delegate met Terauchi in Da Lat, Vietnam, and were told that Indonesia would be granted independence on 24 August, but the territory of the new state would extend only to the former territory of the Netherlands East Indies. Although the Japanese plan fell short of the BPUPKI's proposal to form *Indonesia Raya*, Sukarno accepted the Japanese blueprint (Anderson 1961: 62).

On 12 or 13 August, the Indonesian delegate visited Taiping, Perak, where they met Ibrahim, Itagaki and other Japanese military officials

(Ibrahim 1957: 29; Itagaki 1988 [1968]: 203–205). According to Ibrahim, Sukarno said to him, "let us build one MOTHER state (*satu negara IBU*) for the entire homeland of Indonesia (*seluruh tumpah darah Indonesia*)" (Ibrahim 1957: 29). Ibrahim regarded these words as a promise on the idea of *Indonesia Raya*. Nevertheless, it is questionable whether Sukarno really gave Ibrahim such a promise, considering that Sukarno had already agreed with the Japanese that an independent Indonesia would consist only of the former Netherlands East Indies.

In Malaya, in accordance with Itagaki's proposal, the official inaugural meeting of KRIS was scheduled for 17 and 18 August 1945 in Kuala Lumpur (Itagaki 1988 [1968]: 167–168). The Japanese surrender on 15 August disrupted these plans. Ibrahim called an emergency meeting of KRIS on 15 or 16 August (Cheah 2012 [1983]: 120; Abd. Malek 1975: 313–316). According to Abd. Malek Hj. Md. Hanafiah, one of the decisions made in the meeting was to form the government of *Demokratik Rakyat Malaya* (People's Democratic State of Malaya). Ibrahim personally nominated members of the cabinet of the new government although many of them were neither informed nor consented in advance. The proposed cabinet would include Sultan Abu Bakar of Pahang as President, Sultan Abd. Aziz of Perak, Sultan Musa Uddin of Selangor, five aristocrats such as Onn Jaafar of Johor,[47] and six ex-KMM members, namely, Ibrahim Haji Yaacob, Mustapha Haji Hussain, Hassan Haji Manan, Burhanuddin Al-Helmy, Abd. Karim Rashid and Ishak Haji Muhammad (Abd. Malek 1975: 314–315). The proposed cabinet included not only ex-KMM leaders but also traditional elites such as sultans and aristocrats. Ibrahim, like many leftists with socialist inclinations who supported egalitarian Indonesian nationalism, tended to be critical of the Malay traditional leadership. Yet he realized that they would have to co-operate with the traditional elite because Malay mass support for a radical nationalist movement remained limited, compared to their deep-rooted loyalty to traditional leadership (Stockwell 1979: 13).

On 17 August, instead of the official launch of KRIS, a small unofficial meeting was held in Kuala Lumpur. There were more than ten Malay leaders, including Burhanuddin Al-Helmy and Onn Jaafar, and several Japanese military officials, including Itagaki. Itagaki informed the Malay leaders that while the planned KRIS movement had failed due to the Japanese surrender, the responsibility to achieve Malayan independence still lay on the shoulders of Malay youth. Among the Malay leaders' speeches, Itagaki recalls, Burhanuddin enthusiastically claimed their national right of political independence while Onn declared that the Malays must advance economically before any political independence (Itagaki 1988 [1968]: 172–174).[48] Ibrahim did not attend the meeting on 17 August, having already made arrangements to fly to Jakarta. He argued that he had tried but failed to associate the Giyu Gun with the MPAJA to attain the independence of Malaya together with Indonesia (Ibrahim 1957: 33–34). He left for Jakarta with his wife Mariatun, his brother-in-law Onan, and Hassan Haji Manan on 19 August (Nagai 1978: 81; Itagaki 1988 [1968]: 170–171). Later, Ibrahim claimed that the Japanese authorities had pressured him to move either to Jakarta or Saigon (Nagai 1978: 81). While Ibrahim and some former KMM colleagues argued that he had gone to Indonesia to continue the struggle for *Indonesia Raya*, others accused him of fleeing Malaya due to cowardice (Cheah 2012 [1983]: 123).

On 17 August 1945, Sukarno, accompanied by Hatta and others, proclaimed Indonesian independence, excluding British Malaya and British Borneo. On 18 August, the new Constitution of Indonesia was approved at a session of the PPKI, with modifications to the original draft. Malaya was not incorporated into the territory of Indonesia. According to Nagai's interview with Ibrahim, Sukarno met Ibrahim in Jakarta on 20 August 1945. When Ibrahim asked why Malaya had not been incorporated into Indonesia, Sukarno answered that it was unfavorable for Indonesia to fight against both the Dutch and the British (Nagai 1978: 82). Ibrahim's dream of a pan-Malay/Indonesian nation was thus not realized during his days in Malaya.

Vicissitudes of life in Indonesia

It is difficult to provide details of Ibrahim's life in Indonesia due to the scarcity of sources. In Indonesia Ibrahim was known by his alias, Iskandar Kamel. He was supported by President Sukarno who regarded him as an expert on Malayan affairs. In 1945 he joined Tentara Keamanan Rakyat (TKR) (People's Security Army) and then Tentara Nasional Indonesia (TNI) (Indonesian National Armed Forces) as Lieutenant Colonel in charge of intelligence. After leaving the TNI in 1949 or 1950, he temporarily joined Indonesia's Ministry of Foreign Affairs as an advisor, and subsequently served as an intelligence officer in the Attorney-General's Office (Zulkipli 1979: 138–141; Bachtiar 177; Ramlah 1999: 78–82).

In Java, Ibrahim intended to continue the struggle for the independence of Malaya and its inclusion in *Indonesia Raya*. In Malaya, his former comrades remained active in the pan-Malay nationalist movement. They established the Partai Kebangsaan Melayu Malaya (PKMM) (Malay Nationalist Party of Malaya) in October 1945, holding its inaugural congress from 30 November to 3 December 1945 under the leadership of Mokhtaruddin Lasso (President), Burhanuddin Al-Helmy (Vice President), Dahari Ali (Secretary), Ahmad Boestamam (Head of the Youth Section) and other leaders. After Mokhtaruddin's departure for Indonesia in 1946, the PKMM's leadership was taken over by Burhanuddin (President), Ishak Haji Muhammad (Vice President), and Boestamam (Acting Secretary-General) (Firdaus 1985: 77–78, 81–82).

After fleeing to Indonesia, Ibrahim had little capacity to influence Malayan politics. Ibrahim set up a branch of the PKMM in Yogyakarta in 1946, but remained unable to shape the decision-making of its leaders in Malaya. However, following a British crackdown on the party in Malaya, including the arrest of senior leaders such as Burhanuddin and Taha Kalu, in May 1950 the party gave Ibrahim the imprimatur to continue the struggle from outside Malaya. Around that time, Ibrahim organized the Kesatuan Malaya Merdeka,[49] or, in his own translation, Malaya Independence Movement, to mobilize support in Indonesia for the independence of Malaya as part of *Indonesia Raya* (Ibrahim 1957: 55; Bachtiar 1985: 82–89).[50] Nevertheless, the influence of Ibrahim and his Kesatuan Malaya Merdeka on Malayan politics was quite limited. After the Alliance Party won 51 of the 52 seats contested in the first federal elections of July 1955, Tunku Abdul Rahman, Abdul Razak Hussein and other Malayan leaders visited Indonesia in November 1955 on a goodwill mission. During their stay in Jakarta, Ibrahim had the opportunity to discuss the future independence of Malaya with them (Ibrahim 1957: 56; Bachtiar 1985: 111–115). However, he remained unable to exert any real influence on the process of Malayan decolonization.

At the same time, he was committed to party politics in Indonesia. He was appointed a leader at the Jakarta Raya branch of the Partai Nasional Indonesia (PNI) (Indonesian National Party) (1950–1958) and later joined the Partai Indonesia (Partindo) (Indonesian Party). He also served as a member of the Majelis Permusyawaratan Rakyat (MPR) (People's Consultative Assembly) for the Riau district (1960–1967) (Mss. 176 (3)b; Zulkipli 1979: 138–141; Ramlah 1999: 78–83).

Ibrahim continued to write even after moving to Indonesia. During the period between his flight to Indonesia in 1945 and the independence of the Federation of Malaya in 1957, he published three books. *Sedjarah dan Perdjuangan di Malaya* (History and Struggles in Malaya) (1951), *Nusa dan Bangsa Melayu* (The Malay Archipelago and the Malay Race) (1951) and *Sekitar Malaya Merdeka* (On Free Malaya) (1957). All three can be regarded as political writings in the form of history.

Ibrahim played a considerable role in Indonesia's *Konfrontasi* (Confrontation) with Malaysia from 1963 until 1966. Ibrahim was strongly against the Malaysia proposal by Malaya's Prime Minister Tunku Abdul Rahman in May 1961. For him, the planned merger of Malaya, Singapore and northern Borneo was merely a product of British neo-colonialism, thus totally different from his idea of *Melayu Raya / Indonesia Raya*, although the proposed federation of Malaysia was initially called *Melayu Raya* in Malay. He did exercise some influence on the Indonesian stance towards the Malaysia proposal and co-operated with former PKMM members in Malaya, such as Burhanuddin of the Pan-Malayan Islamic Party (PMIP) and Boestamam of Parti Rakyat (People's Party), in the anti-Malaysia campaign (Poulgrain 1998: 264–266). According to Shamsiah Fakeh, Ibrahim led an organization called Gerakan Kemerdekaan Malaya (The Independence of Malaya Movement), which subsequently formed Badan Kerjasama Untuk Kemerdekaan Sejati Malaya (Cooperative Organization for the True Independence of Malaya) in collaboration with other associations such as Perwakilan Liga Pembebasan Nasional Malaya di Indonesia (The Representative of the National Liberation of Malaya League in Indonesia) and Persatuan Pemuda Malaya di Indonesia (The Association of the Youth of Malaya in Indonesia) (Shamsiah 2004: 103; Hara 2009: 106–108).

Following an attempted coup in 1965 and the downfall of Sukarno, however, Indonesia's confrontation with Malaysia ended in 1966 and Ibrahim's dream of a pan-Malay/Indonesian nation was completely shattered. He retired from politics in the mid-1960s and concentrated on managing the Bank Pertiwi until the late 1970s. The authorities of the colonial/postcolonial state of Malaya/Malaysia blacklisted him as a dangerous radical and a traitor to Malaya/Malaysia. Thus, after fleeing to Java in August 1945, he was unable to return to the Malay Peninsula except for a short visit in 1973. He died in Jakarta on 3 March 1979.

Reconstructing the Malay world

The shifting focus of Ibrahim's argument

The following discussion focuses mainly on Ibrahim's postwar depictions of the Malay world. Of course, fully developing his argument during the Japanese occupation would be very helpful for understanding how his collaboration with the Japanese authorities contributed to his changing position. Unfortunately, it is not possible to reconstruct his thinking during the Japanese occupation because his wartime writings are scarce. Here we are only able to use three articles that Ibrahim published in Singapore-based monthly magazines: two in *Semangat Asia* (Spirit of Asia): "Terbenam 400 Tahun" (Downfall for 400 Years) in the August 1943 issue and "Pendapatan Dari Nippon" (Findings from Japan) in the October-December 1943 issue, and one in *Fajar Asia* (Dawn of Asia): "Sepatah Kata" (A Few Words) in the January 1943 issue. Hence, our discussion here is primarily based on his three postwar books: *Sedjarah dan Perdjuangan di Malaya* (History and Struggle in Malaya) (Agastja 1951), *Nusa dan Bangsa Melayu* (The Malay Archipelago and the Malay Race) (Ibrahim 1951), and *Sekitar Malaya Merdeka* (On Free Malaya) (Ibrahim 1957). These books were written in Malay in the Indonesian spelling system at the time. It is important to note that the main target audience of these three books was Indonesians rather than Malays in Malaya. Though written in the form of history books, they contained a significant amount of political propaganda calling for the formation of *Melayu Raya / Indonesia Raya*.

As mentioned, Ibrahim's prewar writings focused on the following Malay problems: (1) the socio-economic backwardness of the Malays, (2) erosion of Malay rights, and (3) disunity among the Malays. These problems continue to concern him in his postwar writings as well. If we look more closely, though, we find considerable differences between his pre- and postwar interests.

One of the most perceptible shifts occurred in Ibrahim's narrative of British rule. We have already seen that before the war, he had avoided publicly criticizing British businesses while sharply attacking the Chinese and Indians for dominating the Malayan economy. In his wartime and postwar writings, however, he shifted his focus, condemning British economic policy for the socio-economic marginalization of the Malays. Ibrahim now publicly denied the legitimacy of British colonial rule and presented himself as a typical anti-colonial nationalist. He bitterly condemned British "open-door policy" (*dasar/politik pintu terbuka*) as well as their capitalist exploitation (*Semangat Asia*, August 1943: 3; Agastja 1951: 42, 48–52; Ibrahim 1951: 34–35).

Ibrahim then accused the British of usurping the rights of the Malays (Ibrahim 1951: 48–55), no longer seeing them as the protector of Malay rights. Furthermore, he characterized Malay rulers as feudalist (*feodalist*) and blamed them for transferring Malay rights to the British (Agastja 1951: 46). He continued to lament the Chinese and Indian dominance of the economy and rejected their demand to the rights accorded to the Malayan race (*bangsa Malayan*), his focus shifted to what he now considered to lie at the root of these problems, that is, British colonial rule.

Ibrahim also held the British responsible for Malay disunity. During Japanese rule, he had begun to openly accuse the British of introducing a "divide and rule" (*pechah² dan kemudian perentah*) policy, separating the Malay community into different kingdoms (*kerajaan*) and subgroups (*puak²*) (*Semangat Asia*, August 1943: 3). In his later writings, he continued to criticize the British "divide and rule" policy (Ibrahim 1951: 33). He argued that this policy played an important role not only in dividing the society of Malaya but also in promoting the disintegration of the Malay people into smaller segments.

Similarly, a change can be seen in his stance on the Japanese occupation as well. He could not openly criticize the Japanese during the war. In fact, he went the other way, describing in a 1943 article that the Japanese had come to rescue the Malays from drowning under British rule (*Semangat Asia*, August 1943: 3–4). In an essay about his two-month tour of Japan from June 1943, he not only praised Japan's "Greater East Asia" (*Asia Timor Raya*) initiative as an attempt to free the Asian nations (*bangsa-bangsa Asia*) from foreign oppression but also described Japan's industrialization as a model for other Asian countries (*Semangat Asia*, October-December 1943: 9–11). It was only after he fled to Indonesia in 1945 that he began to publicly attack the Japanese occupation of Malaya. He condemned the Japanese as fascist and claimed to have secretly co-operated with the Malayan People's Anti-Japanese Army (MPAJA) during Japanese rule (Agastja 1951: 104–107).

His postwar anti-colonialist stance was finally expressed in his call for the full independence of Malaya and her incorporation into a Greater Malay/Indonesian nation-state, *Melayu Raya / Indonesia Raya*. In postwar writings, Ibrahim preferred the term *Indonesia Raya* to *Melayu Raya*. He explained that the term *Indonesia Raya* could not be embraced in his prewar writings, considering the British fear of Indonesian nationalism spreading to Malaya. He therefore had used *Melayu Raya* as an alternative (Agastja 1951: 132). In the postwar era, Ibrahim tended to use the term *Melayu Raya* to refer to an enlarged community and *Indonesia Raya* to refer to a future state or confederation to be established, as can be seen in a section in *Nusa dan Bangsa Melayu* titled "the desire of *Melayu Raya* for *Indonesia Raya* ([*t*]*jita²* *Melayu-Raya kearah Indonesia-Raya*)" (Ibrahim 1951: 11). Behind the changing terminology, we can see Ibrahim's growing sense of belonging to the Indonesian nation after his flight to Java, although we must also recognize that the concept of *Indonesia Raya* was probably more familiar and acceptable for Indonesian readers, the main audience of his postwar publications.

Links between school textbooks and Ibrahim's books

It is not possible to trace the precise origins of Ibrahim's concepts of *Melayu Raya / Indonesia Raya*. He may have pieced it together from ideas found in wide-range of classical literature, modern novels, non-fiction, school textbooks, academic publications,[51] newspapers and magazines, either in Malay, Indonesian, or English, as well as from oral sources such as conversations and interviews and visual sources such as maps, pictures and photographs. Our focus here is on the interconnections between textbooks on Malay history and geography, which we explored earlier, and Ibrahim's writings. There are two reasons for this method. First, as mentioned, Ibrahim identified the history and geography taught in his Malay primary school and the SITC as significant sources for molding his view of the Malay world. Second, this textual analysis will reveal significant aspects of the process of knowledge transmission and transformation, considering that there was a chain of citations and direct intellectual connections between these textbooks and Ibrahim's writings.

Before addressing the formation of Ibrahim's idea of *Melayu Raya*, let us briefly summarise the findings of our earlier investigation into the four history and geography textbooks written by R.J. Wilkinson, R.O. Winstedt and Abdul Hadi Haji Hasan. Taking a "scientific," positivistic approach, all three authors reconstructed the "Malay world" in terms of community, territory and time. Despite some differences, the four books share several significant factors.

First, they all employed the concept of Malay as a *bangsa*, or race, in contrast to Malay classical literature which presents loyalty to the sultanate or *kerajaan* as the defining characteristic of Malayness. The texts thus played an important role in popularizing new racial classifications that had been introduced through the population censuses, in the process solidifying an image of the Malays as a "mixed race."

Second, the authors shared similar understandings of Malay territoriality, systematically cataloguing geographical data for each political unit in a similar way. This standardized geography and "systematic quantification" served to objectify the territoriality of the Malay community. Embedding the concept of territorial boundary, the authors described three levels of Malay territories: the Malay states (*negeri-negeri Melayu*), Malaya (*Tanah Melayu*), and the Malay world (*alam Melayu*). Furthermore, the authors portrayed Malaya as the focal point of the Malay territories. This Malaya-centric view in turn substantialized the colonial territorial boundary.

Finally, the three authors deployed common conceptions of time. They wrote Malay history according to calendrical time and chronology, from a progressivist historical perspective. They believed in the gradual progression to higher forms of human life and accordingly divided Malay history into distinctive periods on a scale of progress and civilization, from "primitive" to Hindu-Buddhist to Islamic, and then to Portuguese, Dutch and finally British. At the same time, the authors also understood the stratification of Malay history to be visible, with older layers retained as new layers were added on.

Though British colonizers brought a new framework of knowledge into Malay vernacular education, we cannot assume that Malays simply or directly absorbed it. Malays also accommodated modern conceptions of Malayness in their personal transformation and appropriation. We will turn now to Ibrahim's writings to understand his process of reorganizing knowledge of the Malay world.

Ibrahim is connected to Wilkinson, Winstedt and Abdul Hadi through a chain of citations. In *Nusa dan Bangsa Melayu*, he wrote:

> Friends! Looking into the history of [our] homeland (*tanah air*), in fact, history books written by Europeans accept the authenticity of the territorial and racial unity (*kesatuan daerah dan bangsa*) [in the Malay world]. Furthermore, the book *Sedjarah Alam Melayu*, which was officially published for education in government schools as [the Malay School] Series No. 7, explained [the territorial and racial unity in the Malay world]...[52] (Ibrahim 1951: 70)

As we can see, he sought to legitimize his account of a unified Malay world by reference to history books written by Europeans and a history textbook *Sejarah Alam Melayu* which relied heavily on those Europeans' books. In the following sections, we will examine Ibrahim's conceptions of community, space, and time for parallels to our earlier discussion of these school textbooks.

Ibrahim's conception of community

As Milner argues, Ibrahim's concept of Malayness was clearly based on *bangsa* as race. For Ibrahim, neither the sultanate (*kerajaan*) nor the Islamic community (*umat*) should constitute the core of Malayness (Milner 2002 [1995]: 271). As we have seen, since the 1930s, Ibrahim described the Malay community as a large race (*bangsa*) encompassing the Malay world (*alam Melayu*) or the Malay Archipelago. At the same time, however, he deeply lamented that the Malays were yet to develop a broader national consciousness, maintaining a strong sense of belonging to their home states or subgroups. As mentioned earlier, while he continued to use the term *bangsa* to mean "race," he also employed it to connote "nation" as a political community and these two meanings frequently overlapped.

Ibrahim's identification of the Malays as a race (*bangsa*), the same approach adopted by Wilkinson, Winstedt and Abdul Hadi, was also apparent in his postwar publications. In *Sedjarah dan Perdjuangan di Malaya*, he emphasized that the Malays in Malaya, the natives (*bumi putera*) of Malaya, belonged to the Indonesian nation (*bangsa Indonesia*).

> The natives (*bumi putera*) who have the right to inherit Malaya now are the Malays (*orang Melayu*), whose race, language, history, territory and culture are similar to those of the natives of Sumatra, Java, Kalimantan, Sulawesi, the Lesser Sunda and Maluku, who are called the Indonesian nation (*bangsa Indonesia*) today, and are also similar to the Malays called the Filipino nation (*bangsa Filipino*) in the Philippines today. Therefore, the Malays, the natives of Malaya, are of the Indonesian nation (*bangsa Indonesia*).[53] (Agastja 1951: 7–8)

In *Nusa dan Bangsa Melayu*, too, he attempted to show that the Malays in Malaya and the Indonesians constituted one and the same nation. He intended to demonstrate Malay-Indonesian unity in the Malay Archipelago in terms of culture, history, language and geography.

> Friends! Who are the Malays and what is Malaya? It should be made clear. "Due to the break-up for 127 years, the Indonesian nation (*bangsa Indonesia*) has nearly forgotten their siblings (*saudara kandungnja sendiri*) in Malaya." In fact, the Malays are no one but those siblings of the Indonesian race/ nation who are still colonized by the British. I dare say so for sure because according to ethnology, namely, genealogy and life culture, the Malays are similar to the people in Sumatra, Java, Kalimantan, Sulawesi, Maluku, the Lesser Sunda Islands, etc. In particular the history, the language, and the location of the Malay race and Archipelago (*bangsa dan nusa orang Melayu*) prove that Malaya is within the Indonesian circle (*lingkungan Indonesia*).[54] (Ibrahim 1951: 69)

He also presented the Malay as a "mixed race" in a similar way to Wilkinson, Winstedt and Abdul Hadi. This interpretation of the Malays seems to have been useful in establishing the authenticy of Malayness to the Malayo-Muslims of "Indonesian," "Indian," or "Arab" descent and thus in expanding the boundary of Malayness towards *Melayu Raya / Indonesia Raya*. In *Nusa dan Bangsa Melayu*, he wrote:

> Indeed we should not forget that there is no race (*bangsa*) in the world whose blood is pure and immune from the mixture of blood (*pertjampuran darah*) of various races (*berbagai² bangsa*). The Malay race (*ras-Melayu*[55]), which dates from 2500 years ago, was originated from the mixture of Dravidan and Mongolian blood, which was mixed again with the Aryan and Semitic blood flowing into Southeast Asia. This mixture of blood created the Malay stock, which is divided into two nations (*bangsa*) now, namely, Indonesians and Filipinos. In this regard, the Malays in Malaya, Sarawak and Brunei are closer to the Indonesians, and they are one and the same with the Indonesian nation (*bangsa Indonesia*) in all respects.[56] (Ibrahim 1951: 14)

In this way, Ibrahim constructed an argument about the Malays as a race, more particularly as a "mixed race," in order to ensure the unity of the Malays in the Malay Archipelago or the Malay world as well as to justify his advocacy of the independence of Malaya in the scheme of a Greater Malay/Indonesian nation, namely, *Melayu Raya / Indonesia Raya*.

Ibrahim's conception of space

Ibrahim inherited the textbook authors' conceptions of Malay territoriality in three tiers, namely, Malay states (*negeri-negeri Melayu*), Malaya (*Tanah Melayu*) and the Malay world (*alam Melayu*). Though he regarded the natives of the entire Malay Archipelago or Malay world to be Malay, his main prewar concern was with the Malays in Malaya. His prewar writings also paid considerable attention to particular Malay states. His postwar publications, however, paid little attention to them. To legitimize his proposal to incorporate Malaya into *Indonesia Raya*, he focused mainly on Malaya and the Malay Archipelago, or the Malay world. Although his postwar writings continued to focus on the Malays in Malaya, his arguments on the Malays in Malaya were offered in the context of the Malay world outside Malaya. He repeatedly reminded readers that indigenous peoples in Indonesia belonged to the Malay race while also occasionally describing the natives of the Philippines and southern Thailand as Malays. In *Nusa dan Bangsa Melayu*, he again cited Abdul Hadi's history textbook *Sejarah Alam Melayu* on the unity of the Malay world:

> But, the people of the Malay race (*bangsa Melayu*) in Malaya always feel that Indonesians are part of their race (*bangsanja*). In schools, people call the Archipelago the Malay World (*Alam Melayu*) or the Malay Archipelago (*Kepulauan Melayu*). The books on their history were titled *Sedjarah Alam Melayu*, which means Indonesian history (*sedjarah Indonesia*). According to the definition of the Malay race (*bangsa Melayu*) which was used before 1945, "the people of the Malay race (*orang bangsa Melayu*) are the ones who trace their descent from original residents (*penduduk aseli*) in Malay States (Malaya) (*Negeri² Melayu (Malaya)*) and the Malay (Indonesian) Archipelago (*Pulau² Melayu (Indonesia)*) who believe in Islam." They became the subjects (*rakjat*) of the Malay Sultan of the state (*negeri*) where they resided...[57] (Ibrahim 1951: 10)

Ibrahim also invoked geography to support his arguments for the unity of the Malay world. For instance, he provided a map of Southeast Asia to highlight the geographical proximity between Malaya and Indonesia, emphasizing the notion that the territory of Indonesia had the shape of the letter "W."

Malaya and Sarawak/Brunei, which are located between Sumatra and Kalimantan, are situated in the central part of current northern Indonesia. The boundary of northern Indonesia, which should be straight from Sabang to Laut Island to Miangas Island, which is north of Halmahera Island, is forced to make a right-angled turn in the shape of the letter "W" (see the attached map).

Therefore, it is clear that the territories of Malay States (*Negeri² Melayu*) are included in the Indonesian territories and, moreover, are in an important position for Indonesia, particularly in that Malaya occupies part of the Straits of Melaka, which exactly faces a big gateway of Indonesia. In the sense of its location the independence of Indonesia is not complete as long as the right-angled turn which is in the shape of the letter "W" does not disappear from the boundaries of Indonesia. In other words, as long as Malay States are ruled by the foreign force, Indonesia's independence is not complete because [it means that] there are still colonized Indonesian territories.[58] (Ibrahim 1951: 13)

While Ibrahim reproduced his predecessors' conceptions of Malay territoriality in three tiers, his postwar books put greater emphasis on the unity between Malaya and other parts of the Malay world. His studies of Malay history and geography underpinned his argument for the territorial unity of the Malay world and thus was significant in legitimizing his pan-Malayism.

Ibrahim's conception of time

Ibrahim reconstructed Malay history to legitimate his political claim to incorporate Malaya into *Indonesia Raya*. Ibrahim portrayed the history of the Malay world in terms of the rise and fall of *bangsa Melayu* or the Malay race as a potential nation. For him, Malay history should be described as a national history, and no longer as an account of a particular dynasty as seen in classical Malay literature.

Among his postwar publications, *Sedjarah dan Perdjuangan di Malaya* presented the broadest and most detailed account of the history of the Malays in Malaya.[59] In contrast, *Nusa dan Bangsa Melayu* put greater emphasis on the period of the British colonial administration.[60] Finally, *Sekitar Malaya Merdeka*, published in the year of Malayan independence, critically reviewed the Malayan independence movement in early and mid-twentieth-century Malaya.[61] As per the school textbooks, these three books described Malay history chronologically. They divided Malay history into distinctive periods, from "primitive" to Hindu-Buddhist to Islamic, and then to Portuguese to Dutch to British to Japanese, and again to British. In *Nusa dan Bangsa Melayu*, he classifies Malay history into several periods:

> The historical trend of the Malay world (*dunia Melayu,*[62] *Malaynesia*) or Indonesia can be divided into three ages, namely:
>   1. An age of the growth of a race (*Djaman pertumbuhan bangsa*) in Southeast Asia for about one thousand years from B.C. 500 until A.D. 500.
>   2. A brilliant age of expansion and dominance (*Djaman perkembangan dan kekuasaan jang gilang-gemilang*) from A.D. 500 until 1511, namely, from Tarumanegara to Srivijaya to Majapahit and finally to Melaka.
>   3. An age of colonization (*Djaman pendjadjahan*) for four hundred years, namely, "an age of decline" (*Djaman kedjatuhan*).
> Following these three ages, since August 1945 a new page of history has been opened to the history of the race and the Archipelago (*sedjarah bangsa dan nusa*) in Southeast Asia.[63] (Ibrahim 1951: 29)

These passages illustrate that although Ibrahim's historical view was undoubtedly progressivist, it differed significantly from the textbooks' characterization of the distinct periods in Malay history. Ibrahim assessed the progress of Malay history in terms of prosperity and political independence. As per the school textbooks, his postwar publications described Malay history chronologically, dividing Malay history into distinctive periods, from "primitive" to Hindu-Buddhist to Islamic, and then to Portuguese to Dutch to British to Japanese, and again to British. In the same process, he divided Malay history into clear stages, namely, early development (the age of the nascent development of the race), glory (the age of kingdoms), decline (the age of colonization), and revival (the age of independence).[64] His postwar books highlighted the age of colonization, characterizing the periods under Portuguese, Dutch, British and Japanese rule, as "an age of decline" in sharp contrast to the school textbooks. Ibrahim envisaged this age of decline being replaced by the age of independence. Thus his postwar narrative of Malay history appears to be anti-colonialist and pro-independent, which was a distinct departure from both the school textbooks and his prewar writings.

Appropriation of colonial knowledge

Ibrahim's concept of *Melayu Raya* / *Indonesia Raya* incorporated several essential features from his conceptions of community, territory and time. First, while Ibrahim accepted the concept of Malay as a race, more specifically a "mixed race," similar to Wilkinson, Winstedt and Abdul Hadi, he used the concept of race to legitimate his political cause, the pursuit of *Melayu Raya* / *Indonesia Raya,* quite unlike these authors. Second, although Ibrahim and the textbook authors shared conceptions of Malay territoriality in three tiers, Ibrahim put much greater emphasis on the significance of the Malay world as a potential territory of *Melayu Raya* / *Indonesia Raya.* Third, although Ibrahim shared the textbooks' progressivist historical view, he reconceived Malay history to fit his political cause: anti-colonial pan-Malayism.

Let us now position Ibrahim's pan-Malayism in the broader context of the indigenization of colonial knowledge in identity formation. We can separate the process of the localization of colonial knowledge into two aspects: transmission and appropriation. In this context, the first refers to the process by which new conceptualizations of Malay society were disseminated from the British colonizers to the local populace. As we have seen, the two British scholar-administrators (Wilkinson and Winstedt) and the local historian Abdul Hadi shared similar ideas of community, territory and time.

The second aspect refers to the ways in which Malays reorganized the concepts and knowledge that were presented to them and applied it to their own ends. In Ibrahim's case, two points merit our attention. First, Ibrahim drew upon imported knowledge to legitimate his nationalist cause. He repeatedly wrote about the Malay population, the making of the "mixed" Malay race, the geographical proximity of territories in the Malay Archipelago, and a common "national" history of the Malays. In short, he selectively utilized "scientific" knowledge about the Malay race, territories and history, a considerable part of which he had learned via British scholars, to demonstrate the unity and greatness of the Malay world.

Second, Ibrahim also reorganized colonial knowledge for the sake of his advocacy of pan-Malayism. The most remarkable example is his reinterpretation of progressivist views of Malay history. Following the periodization of the textbooks' Malay history, he departed from their characterization of the colonial era as an age of progress, depicting it instead as an age of decline and the pre-colonial period as a golden age. He then anticipated the coming of a new era of independence, an age of rebirth and renewal. In this case study, we can clearly see the transformation of imported knowledge.

To sum up, Ibrahim's appropriation of colonial knowledge helped him invent pan-Malayism. Needless to say, the result was not what British colonizers had intended.

6 *Melayu Raya* and Malaysia: Contested Pan-Malayism

Melayu Raya / Indonesia Raya in postwar Malaya

As discussed, Ibrahim fled to continue campaigning for Malayan independence in the form of *Melayu Raya / Indonesia Raya*. Meanwhile, other former KMM leaders attempted to do the same in Malaya. They established the Partai Kebangsaan Melayu Malaya (PKMM) (Malay Nationalist Party of Malaya) in October 1945 and held its inaugural congress from 30 November to 3 December 1945.[1] The senior leadership of the party consisted of Mokhtaruddin Lasso (President), Burhanuddin Al-Helmy (Vice President), Dahari Ali (Secretary), and others including Ahmad Boestamam (Head of the Youth Section) (Firdaus 1985: 77–78). The President, Mokhtaruddin Lasso, was a former leader of the MPAJA, which had a close relationship with the MCP. Burhanuddin Al-Helmy, Dahari Ali and Ahmad Boestamam were all ex-KMM members. The PKMM's leadership thus comprised two groups, namely, communists led by Mokhtaruddin Lasso and non-communist nationalists represented by Boestamam and Burhanuddin (Stockwell 1979: 45; Ramlah 1996: 34, 36). However, the latter came to dominate after Mokhtaruddin left Malaya for Indonesia.[2] The main posts in the party fell to former KMM leaders including Burhanuddin (President), Ishak Haji Muhammad (Vice President), and Boestamam (Acting Secretary-General) (Firdaus 1985: 81–82).

At the inaugural congress, the PKMM passed four principal resolutions:

1. Malaya is part of *Indonesia Raya.*
2. *Sang Saka Merah Puteh* [The Indonesian national flag in red and white] is the flag as the national symbol (*cogan lambang Kebangsaan*).
3. [We] agree with the Malayan Union (*Kesatuan Malaya*).
4. [We] should be friendly with all the races (*bangsa-bangsa*) in Malaya[3] (Burhanuddin 1980 [1946]: 55).

The PKMM presented eight principles of the party in 1946. Among them were:

1. To unite the nation of Malaya (*bangsa Malaya* [*sic*]),[4] foster the nationalist spirit (*semangat kebangsaan*) in the hearts of the Malays, and aim for uniting Malaya in a big family, that is, *Republic Indonesia Raya*.

   [....]

7. To co-operate with other races (*bangsa*) in the country to live harmoniously and work for the establishment of Malayan United Front in order to make *Malayan Merdeka* [*sic*] prosperous and happy as a part of *Republic Indonesia Raya*.

8. To support the movement of the Indonesian community (*ummat Indonesia*) in the struggle to achieve independence (*Kemerdekaan*).[5] (UMNO/SG No.96/46)

The party constitution also included three strategies to achieve this "independence of nation and homeland (*Kemerdekaan bangsa dan Tanah Ayir*)" namely:

1. To raise the status of the Malay nation (*bangsa Malayu* [*sic*]) to equal that of the other nations (*bangsa*[2]) in the world.
2. To incorporate Malaya into Indonesia.
3. To establish *Republic Malaya* as a part of *Republic Indonesia Raya*.[6] (UMNO/SG No. 96/46)

Although lacking any concrete program, the PKMM obviously embraced the idea of the independence of Malaya as a republic which would form part of a federation or confederation with *Republic Indonesia Raya*.

In Britain, the Secretary of State for Colonies announced the Malayan Union proposal in the House of Commons on 10 October 1945. In the Malayan Union scheme, Malaya would become a unitary colony and a new common Malayan citizenship would be introduced based on *jus soli* regardless of origins. The British government attempted to form the Malayan Union to integrate Chinese and Indian residents into Malayan society as well as to unify and rationalize the complicated colonial administrative structure which comprised nine Malay states consisting of Federated and

Unfederated Malay States; and two of the Straits Settlements. The scheme entailed transferring the formal sovereignty from the rulers of Malay states to the British Crown although the expressed long-term objective is for Malaya to prepare for self-government within the British commonwealth (Ariffin 1993: 45; Liow 2015 [1995]: 243).

It is widely known that the Malayan Union proposal provoked the resistance of Malays who felt that their rights were at stake. The British government's high-handed treatment of Malay rulers strengthened the resistance. The Malay aristocratic elite led the anti-Malayan Union movement primarily to demand the restoration of the sovereignty of Malay rulers and resist the idea of common citizenship. Most of them were more interested in restoring the prewar status quo than in gaining immediate political independence. Meanwhile, at the initial stage, the PKMM supported the Malayan Union proposal "with its principles of self-determination and its promises of independence – as a steppingstone towards the ideal of *Indonesia Raya*" (Stockwell 1979: 47). When the Pan-Malayan Malay Congress was held in Kuala Lumpur in March 1946, however, the party formally changed its position and joined the anti-Malayan Union movement, claiming that the British had forced Malay rulers to accept the proposal. It was also a response to the PKMM's initial stance having been criticized as "anti-Malay" by supporters of the anti-Malayan Union campaign (Ariffin 1993: 55, 58). Forty-one Malay associations sent delegates to the congress to oppose the Malayan Union scheme. During the congress, the PKMM supported the proposal to establish the United Malays National Organisation (UMNO) as a united force to oppose the scheme.

At the same time, however, the differences in political positions and views between the PKMM and the mainstream of the UMNO was clear. Conservative and aristocratic UMNO leaders were disturbed by the radical and egalitarian PKMM's challenge to the traditional order and structure. The PKMM's *Indonesia Raya*-oriented political inclinations also led to friction with other groups at the congress. For instance, there was conflict between Ahmad Boestamam of the PKMM and Onn Jaafar, the then chairman of the congress. Boestamam advocated the early independence of Malaya as part of *Indonesia Raya*. Onn, however, believed that achieving personal and economic independence for Malays should supersede political independence, and that the anti-Malayan Union movement should be regarded as a matter of the highest priority, rather than the establishment of an unrealistic *Indonesia Raya* (Ramlah 1994: 114–122; Stockwell 1979: 68–69). Only two months after UMNO was established in May 1946, the PKMM broke away.

As Donna J. Amoroso argues, the conservative UMNO aristocrats attempted to preserve and strengthen their political ascendancy by incorporating the politics of nationalism into traditionalism and vice versa (Amoroso 2014: chaps. 5–6). Their efforts were successful. The UMNO successfully pressured the British to replace the Malayan Union with the Federation of Malaya on 1 February 1948, which gave more substantial power to sultans than the Malayan Union would have, and tightened conditions for non-Malays to acquire citizenship. The definition of "Malay" based on "the Muslim religion," "the Malay language" and "Malay customs" that was introduced in the Federation of Malaya Agreement, carried through to the current Federal Constitution (The Federation of Malaya Agreement 1948: Clause 124).

After breaking away from the UMNO, the PKMM formed the Pusat Tenaga Rakyat (PUTERA) (Centre of People's Power) with two other leftist organizations: the Angkatan Pemuda Insaf (API) (Movement of Aware Youth) and the Angkatan Wanita Sedar (AWAS) (Movement of Aware Women). These two organizations had originally been established as the PKMM's youth and women's movements, respectively. The PUTERA then worked with the non-Malay based All-Malaya Council of Joint Action (AMCJA) to oppose the Federation of Malaya scheme, which had been proposed in December 1946 by the Anglo-Malay Constitutional Working Committee, made up of four sultans' representatives, two UMNO representatives and six British. The PUTERA-AMCJA drafted "The People's Constitutional Proposals for Malaya" in July and August 1947. The proposal suggested that Malaya should include Singapore as a territory of the Federation (Section 1). Section 2 read:

> There shall be established a citizenship of Malaya. This citizenship shall be a nationality, to be termed "Melayu" and shall carry with it the duty of allegiance to the Federation of Malaya.
>
> NOTE – The term "Melayu" shall have no religious implications whatever.
>
> (PUTERA-AMCJA 1947: 11 (Section 2))

Although the Working Committee did not adopt this proposal, it is interesting to note the difference between the People's Constitutional Proposal and the PKMM's party constitution. First, the People's Constitutional Proposal defined nine Malay States and three Straits Settlements as the territory of the Federation and made no mention of joining Indonesia, unlike the PKMM's constitution. Second, the Proposal adopted the nationality of "Melayu" as one which would include the non-Muslim Chinese or Indian populations of Malaya. This interpretation seems to have been a compromise between the PKMM and PUTERA aspiration for a Malay nation-state and the AMCJA's desire for citizenship by birth (*jus soli*).

The communist revolt and the declaration of the Emergency in June 1948 undermined the basis of the radical Malay nationalist movement. Several leaders of the PKMM, such as Ishak Haji Muhammad and Ahmad Boestamam, were arrested and accused of collaborating with the communists. The PKMM was finally dissolved in April 1950 (Firdaus 1985: 102–103).

In the early 1950s a multi-ethnic coalition was formed in response to the newly introduced electoral politics in Malaya. The first Malayan election was held for the Georgetown Municipal Council in December 1951. In the election of the Kuala Lumpur Municipal Council in February 1952, the UMNO formed a coalition with the Malayan Chinese Association (MCA). They won 9 of 12 seats. Between 1952 and 1954, the UMNO-MCA Alliance gained 226 of 268 municipal and town council seats (Andaya and Andaya 2017 [1982]: 280). The Malayan Indian Congress (MIC) joined the Alliance before the election of Federal Council scheduled for July 1955. The UMNO-MCA-MIC won 51 of the 52 contested seats in the Federal Council election. Tunku Abdul Rahman, President of the UMNO, became Chief Minister of the Federation of Malaya.

While drafting a constitution between 1956 and 1957, a "social contract" or "bargain" was made between the parties of the Alliance. Due to its overwhelming electoral success, the UMNO-MCA-MIC Alliance was able to take the initiative in the Reid Commission, which was established by the British in 1956 to prepare a constitution for an independent Malaya. During negotiations between leaders of the Alliance Party, citizenship and Malay privileges were among the hot issues. The MCA and the MIC asked the UMNO to accept open citizenship based on the principle of *jus soli*. The Reid Commission accepted the UMNO's compromise proposal that all those born on and after independence should become citizens of the country, rather than the MCA's demand that all those born before, on and after Malaya's independence should become Malayan citizens. The UMNO in turn successfully asked the MCA and the MIC to agree to the special position of the Malays, Malay as the national language, Islam as the religion of Federation, and Malay rulers as constitutional monarchs (Cheah 2002: 37). The Federation of Malaya achieved independence on 31 August 1957 and Tunku Abdul Rahman became its first Prime Minister.

Formation of the concept of Malaysia

Nearly four years after Malaya's independence, Prime Minister Tunku Abdul Rahman[7] officially proposed the formation of Malaysia on 27 May 1961 as a plan to bring together the territories of the Federation of Malaya, Singapore, North Borneo (Sabah), Brunei and Sarawak through political and economic co-operation. The formation of Malaysia was finally achieved on 16 September 1963 although Brunei did not join the new federation. Singapore left the federation less than two years later, on 9 August 1965. The political formation of Malaysia must be understood in the context of international relations, particularly between Britain, the United States, Japan, Indonesia, the Philippines, Malaya, Singapore and the Borneo territories (Sarawak, North Borneo and Brunei), and the internal power struggles in these countries and territories.[8] However, these power relations are beyond the scope of this study. The following discussion concentrates on the contested ideas of Malayness which underlie the conceptualization of Malaysia. More specifically, it focuses on debates among Malay political leaders in Malaya, and does not address disputes over the Malaysia plan in Singapore and the Borneo territories.

As far as Tunku Abdul Rahman and other UMNO leaders were concerned, there were at least two primary reasons for the formation of Malaysia. First, they were persuaded to accept that a merger between the Federation of Malaya and Singapore was necessary to obstruct the communist attempts for political dominance in Singapore and reduce their threat to security in Malaya and Southeast Asia. Second, incorporating the Borneo states into the new federation was seen as necessary to maintain the "Malayness" of the federation. Without the Borneo states, a merger between the Federation of Malaya and the non-Malay dominated Singapore would create a new federation in which Malays were outnumbered by non-Malays.

Although the first reason seems to have had more direct influence, the second one might have been as important in legitimizing the idea of Malaysia. The second reason was based on the presumption of the Tunku and other UMNO leaders that the natives of Borneo, regardless of religion or belief, language and custom, could be considered "Malay" in a broad sense. This somewhat broad interpretation of "Malayness" is quite interesting in view of the Federal Constitution officially defining a "Malay" as "a person who professes the Muslim religion, habitually speaks the Malay language, conforms to Malay customs..." (Federation of Malaya 1962a: 124 (Article 160)).

In fact, we can trace the origins of the concept of Malaysia to long before 1961. According to Mohamed Noordin Sopiee, the first to suggest uniting the Malaysia region appears to have been Lord Brassey, a director of the British North Borneo Company, in 1887 (Mohamed Noordin 1973: 720; 1974: 127). Half a century later, in mid-1942, just after the Japanese invasion of Malaya, the British Colonial Office and the Foreign Office jointly suggested a "Malayan Union" including Malaya, Singapore, North Borneo, Sarawak and Brunei (CO 825/35/4 in (Stockwell 1995: 18–25)]. Later, a plan named the "Dominion of Southeast Asia" covering the entire Malaysia region was embraced by Malcolm MacDonald, Commissioner-General for the United Kingdom in South-East Asia from 1948 to 1955 (Ranjit Singh 1998; Suzuki 1998).

Some Malay leaders in Malaya had also formed ideas about the unification of the Malaysia region before 1961.[9] For instance, Muhammad Ghazali Shafie, one of the key proponents for the formation of Malaysia, claims that he began thinking of "a greater union comprising the States of the Federation of Malaya, Singapore, Sarawak, Brunei and North Borneo" while studying law at the University College of Wales during the late 1940s. In 1954, he wrote a letter to *The Straits Times* to advance his concept of a "Commonwealth of Southeast Asia," outlining the economic, political, cultural, strategic, and administrative merits (Muhammad Ghazali 1998a: 15–17; Mohamed Noordin 1973: 723).

Tunku Abdul Rahman expressed his desire to unite the Malaysia region on 26 December 1955, at the UMNO General Assembly. The Tunku pointed out the difficulty Singapore faced in becoming independent alone and continued:

> We understand what Chief Minister of Singapore said. [He said,] Singapore is a small island and therefore is surely not qualified to become independent separately. If so, we consider that it would be better for Singapore to demand to join the Federation of Malaya and to become a territory of the Federation as other states are. Likewise, if Brunei, Sarawak and other colonies in Borneo would like to join the Federation, it would be very nice.[10] (Tunku Abdul Rahman Putra 1997 [1955]: 265)

At this stage, however, he seems to have voiced a long-term aspiration with neither a specific scheme nor a concrete action plan.

For a long time the term "Malaysia" had been used to refer to the whole territory of the Malay Archipelago or Maritime Southeast Asia.[11] It is not obvious when the term "Malaysia" was used for the first time to mean all the territories of the (former) British colonies and protectorates in Maritime Southeast Asia. Mohamed Noordin Sopiee informs us of an interesting dispute among UMNO members over the name before its independence in 1957. According to him, in August 1956, the UMNO officially chose the name "Malaysia" over three other proposals: "Tanah Melayu," "Semenanjung Tanah Melayu" and "Persekutuan Tanah Melayu." The UMNO-MCA-MIC Alliance subsequently adopted "Malaysia" to suggest to the Reid Commission. Mohd. Khir Johari claimed that "Malaysia" had been chosen in order "to give room" to other territories, especially of Borneo, to join it later (Mohamed Noordin 1973: 726). It is interesting to note that the UMNO, the largest Malay political party in Malaya, was prepared to accept a larger federation. Additionally, in 1956 Onn Jaafar, the first President of the UMNO and the then President of the Parti Negara, also advocated the name "Malaysia" for a new independent country with due regard to future political unification between the Federation of Malaya, Singapore, North Borneo (Sabah), Sarawak and Brunei (Ramlah 1992: 342–343).

Moreover, it is worth briefly surveying Ibrahim Haji Yaacob's concept of "Malaysia." In *Sedjarah dan Perdjuangan di Malaya*, written in 1948 and published in 1951, Ibrahim used the term "Malaysia" as equivalent to "the Malay world" or "the Malay Archipelago." For instance, he wrote, "Melayu-Polynesian is abbreviated to Malaysian" or "seventy million *bangsa*

Indonesia (Malaysia)" (Agastja 1951: 9, 53). Nevertheless, in his *Sekitar Malaya Merdeka*, published in 1957, he wrote:

> Thus, our people's desire to incorporate Singapore, Brunei and Sarawak in North Kalimantan to create *Persatuan Negara Malaysia* has not been achieved yet. On the contrary, [the Malaysia region] has been disintegrated by the British.[12] (Ibrahim 1957: 11)

> ...the struggle of the people of Malaya reached the first step of independence. [But] there are still many other people of Malaysia (*anak*[2] *Malaysia*) – including Singapore, which is still colonized, and other Malaysia regions, namely, Brunei, Sabah (British North Borneo) and Sarawak, which are still under a colonial power...[13] (Ibrahim 1957: 15)

It seems that the term "Malaysia" in his 1957 book no longer meant "the Malay Archipelago" as a whole. Instead, it implied the whole territories of the (former) British colonies and protectorates in the Malay Archipelago, matching the Tunku's conception.

It is worth emphasizing two points. First, on the eve of independence, both conservative and radical Malay leaders had already argued about the future expansion of the territory to include the entirety of the (former) British colonies and protectorates in the insular Southeast Asia. Second, the term "Malaysia," originally equivalent to "the Malay Archipelago," had acquired another meaning. Before the independence of the Federation of Malaya in 1957, some Malay leaders had started to use "Malaysia" to refer to the territories of the (former) British colonies and protectorates in Insular Southeast Asia.

The concept of Malayness in the Malaysia proposal

For Malay political leaders in Malaya, one of the main motives for the incorporation of the Borneo territories was to ensure "Malays" constituted the majority population of the new federation. However, it seems that most indigenous people in the Borneo territories did not meet the official definition of a Malay as "a person who professes the Muslim religion, habitually speaks the Malay language, conforms to Malay customs..." (Federation of Malaya 1962a: 124 (Article 160)). We must therefore examine why the Tunku and other Malay leaders considered that the dominance of the Malays would be ensured by incorporating the Borneo territories.

In July 1961, Tunku Abdul Rahman and others went to the Borneo territories on a tour of inspection. The Tunku faced strong opposition to the Malaysia proposal from local leaders in the Borneo territories such as Stephen Kalong Ningkan and Ong Kee Hui of Sarawak, A.M. Azahari of Brunei, and Donald Stephens of Sabah (Mohamed Noordin 1974: 141–142). At the same time, the Tunku widened his view of Malayness on this tour. Muhammad Ghazali Shafie, who accompanied the Tunku on the tour as the Permanent Secretary, Ministry of External Affairs, recalls that "he was much impressed by the similarity between the Iban and the Malay in look and language even if the pronunciation of certain words were different" (Muhammad Ghazali 1998b: 51). According to Ghazali, the Tunku considered all indigenous groups in the Borneo territories to be "Malay".[14]

On 16 October 1961, about four and half months after announcing the Malaysia proposal, the Tunku explained the proposal to the Dewan Rakyat (House of Representatives). As well as similarities between the Federation and the Borneo territories in customs, current problems, administrative system, language and ruling system, the Tunku pointed out their similarity of "race."

> From the Federation's point of view, we are linked to the Borneo territories not only by proximity and close association but also because the Borneo territories have the same types of culture and racial origin as the Malayans... The territories, like the Federation, have a diversity of races. There are Chinese there just as there are here and also there are others, but the other races are of the same ethnic stock as the Malays.[15] (PDDR, Vol. III, No. 16, 16 October 1961: Cols. 1604–1605)

Here the Tunku pronounced that all indigenous ethnic groups in the Borneo territories "are of the same stock as the Malays."

To the delegates of the UMNO members as well, the Tunku emphasized not only Malaya's geographical proximity to the Borneo territories but also an affinity between the Malays in Malaya and the indigenous people in the Borneo territories from the perspective of ethnic origins. He attempted to keep his audience's attention on the ethno-cultural or "primordial" ties between the Malays in Malaya and the indigenous people of the Borneo territories without touching on their meaningful differences, for instance, their religious differences. In his speech at the Special Assembly of the UMNO on 4 November 1961, the Tunku claimed that:

> Gentlemen, you can see the geographical arrangement of the States of Malaya (*Negeri-negeri Tanah Melayu*), Brunei, Sarawak and Sabah as a crescent. So, it makes sense that Malaya (*Tanah Melayu*) and the states of Borneo are symbolized as a new moon in the world. Thus, our proposed Malaysia is located in the world like the symbol of the moon, which is the single symbol of the greatness of Islam.
>
> From a different point of view as well, the entry of the states (*negeri-negeri*) of Singapore and Borneo is surely proper and reasonable because our state (*negeri kita*) and these states have common residents (*penduduk-penduduk yang sama*) – they are the family of the same blood and descent with us (*saudara sedarah daging dan seketurunan dengan kita*). They use the same administrative system with ours and they use the same *ringgit* with ours. In short, there is no difference between us and these states.[16] (Tunku Abdul Rahman Putra 1997 [1961]: 395–396)

At the outset, the Tunku's proposed federation was referred to by several names, including "Malaysia," "Greater Malaysia," "Federation of Malaysia" and "Greater Malaya." "*Melayu Raya*" was also often used as the Malay equivalent of these English names. At the Special Assembly of the UMNO on 4 November 1961, the Tunku explained his plan as follows:

> As I said in Parliament, our aim and desire is to establish an association or a merger of states (*persatuan atau gabungan negeri-negeri*), named *Persekutuan Melayu Raya* or *Malaysia Raya*, that is, [to make] the states which are now in the Federation of Malaya (*Persekutuan Tanah Melayu*) and the states in Borneo merge into a Federation with equal status.
>
> Under the concept of Malaysia, any state will no longer be a colony. The current Federation of Malaya, too, will be extinguished because the territory will be taken over by the state of Free *Melayu Raya* or Malaysia.[17] (Tunku Abdul Rahman Putra 1997 [1961]: 397])

The use of *Melayu Raya* to refer to the new federation seems to have reflected the Tunku's perception of a Greater Malay federation. Later, however, *Melayu Raya* was withdrawn with consideration due to the anxieties of non-Malays and non-Muslims in the Borneo territories that they would be positioned as inferior to the Malay Muslims (Federation of Malaya 1962b: para. 148 (d)). The name "Malaysia" thus became generally used, whether in English or Malay.

Anthony Milner argues that the confrontations surrounding the formation "Malaysia" should be seen as a process of defining and redefining "Malayness." He suggests that the Tunku's Malaysia proposal hijacked or reformulated the idea of *Melayu Raya*, originally proposed by leftists like Ibrahim Haji Yaacob, Burhanuddin Al-Helmy and Ahmad Boestamam (Milner 1992). As we have seen, there is little doubt that the Tunku's concept of Malaysia beared similarities to Ibrahim's postwar idea of *Melayu Raya / Indonesia Raya*. They shared a wide definition of Malayness, based on ethno-cultural and geo-historical affinity.

Yet there were also several significant differences between the Tunku's idea of Malaysia and Ibrahim's *Melayu Raya / Indonesia Raya*. First, we note the difference in territorial reach. While the Tunku's proposed Malaysia was limited to the (former) British colonies and protectorates in the Malay Archipelago, Ibrahim's *Melayu Raya / Indonesia Raya* included the entirety of the Archipelago, irrespective of colonial heritage. Second, their ideological orientations were also different. On the one hand, the Tunku's concept of Malaysia basically inherited the idea of Malaya's existing constitutional monarchy as a federation of traditional Malay states (*negeri*). On the other hand, Ibrahim's idea of *Melayu Raya / Indonesia Raya* reflected his socialist inclination, strongly influenced by radical nationalism in Indonesia, though he did not categorically deny the legitimacy of Malay rulers and their states (*negeri*). Third, we can also distinguish between Ibrahim's and the Tunku's attitudes towards the British. Britain was among the parties involved in formulating the Malaysia proposal, and the proposal therefore presumed a continuing British presence in trade, industry, defense, etc. In contrast, Ibrahim's postwar idea of *Melayu Raya / Indonesia Raya* was basically anti-British.

A more basic difference lay in their visions of nation and state. The Tunku's Malaysia proposal was formulated as a viable response to the pressing need for the decolonization of Singapore and the Borneo territories. The proposed "Malaysia" was thus essentially a state (*negara*) with a vaguely defined nation (*bangsa*). In contrast, when Ibrahim proposed *Melayu Raya / Indonesia Raya*, he did not have a clear conception of what the state should be like. *Melayu Raya / Indonesia Raya* was essentially a vision of nation (*bangsa*) with only a hazy idea of state (*negara*). At risk of oversimplifying, nation followed state in one case while state followed nation in the other.

Final call for *Melayu Raya*

It seems that advocates of *Melayu Raya / Indonesia Raya* in Malaya were rather perplexed by the Malaysia proposal. Let us take two of Ibrahim's former comrades as examples: Burhanuddin Al-Helmy and Ahmad Boestamam.

Burhanuddin Al-Helmy,[18] who had attended Malay, Islamic (Arabic) and English schools in Malaya and India, taught Arabic and practiced as a homeopath in Singapore. He was a former member of the KMM and worked with the Japanese military administration during the Japanese occupation. After the war, he took part in the establishment of the PKMM as vice-president and later became its second president. In 1956 he joined the Pan-Malayan Islamic Party (PMIP) or Persatuan Islam Se-Malaya (PAS) as president. He was elected as a Member of Parliament from Besut, Terengganu, in 1959.

Burhanuddin was one of the leading supporters of the idea of *Melayu Raya / Indonesia Raya.*[19] His discourse on Malayness had a lot in common with Ibrahim's pan-Malayism. Like Ibrahim, Burhanuddin also justified the unity of the Malay race (*bangsa*), geographical unity of the Malay World (*Alam Melayu*) and the common history of the Malay World through "scientific evidence" in geography and geopolitics (*ilmu geography dan geopolitic*), geology (*ilmu bumi*), history (*ilmu tawarikh/sejarah*), anthropology (*ilmu antropologi*) and ethnology (*ilmu rupa bangsa, ilmu etnologi*). It should be added, however, that with his deep knowledge of Islam and Arabic, Burhanuddin also attempted to legitimate Malay nationalism with Islamic teaching (Burhanuddin 1980 [1954]).

Burhanuddin's response to the Tunku's Malaysia proposal was complex. On 16 October 1961, as a Member of Parliament from the PAS,

Burhanuddin initially responded positively to the Tunku's motion named "Malaysia" in the House of Representatives.

> Mr. Speaker, I am really glad about the motion which was brought forward by our Honorable Prime Minister during a debate on the motion named *Melayu Raya*. I am glad because actually I have struggled for *Melayu Raya* for a long time – and [the proposal of *Melayu Raya*] has just started to be debated openly and extensively.[20] (PDDR, Vol. III, No. 16, 16 October 1961, Col. 1631)

While Burhanuddin appeared to welcome the Tunku's proposal of Malaysia or *Melayu Raya*, he argued that he could not agree with a number of points in the motion, especially about the suggestion that the territories of *Melayu Raya* or Malaysia would be confined to Malaya (*Tanah Melayu*), Singapore, North Borneo (Sabah), Sarawak and Brunei. He proposed amending the motion to include Indonesia, the Philippines, and other parts of the Malay Archipelago. His amended motion read:

> That this House agrees, in principle, to the proposal to build *Melayu Raya* including eleven states in the Federation of Malaya (*Persekutuan Tanah Melayu*), Singapore, Brunei, North Borneo, Sarawak, the Republic of Indonesia, the Philippines and other parts of the Malay Archipelago (*gugusan Pulau² Melayu*), and demand that the Government endeavor to take action for the attainment of this purpose and that the Honorable Prime Minister inform the House of whatever action taken from time to time.[21] (PDDR, Vol. III, No. 16, 16 October 1961: Cols. 1638–1639)

After the House of Representatives passed the Tunku's motion, Burhanuddin put forward a motion named "*Melayu Raya*" (not "Malaysia") to the Parliament on 1 May 1962. He moved:

> That this House adopts the resolution that as *Melayu Raya* is, in principle, the Malay Archipelago (*Gugusan Pulau² Melayu*), territories of Indonesia and the Philippines should be incorporated into the scheme of *Melayu Raya* and that the Prime Minister should conduct preliminary negotiations with the authorities of Indonesia and the Philippines to form *Kesatuan Melayu Raya* (Greater Malay Union).[22] (PDDR, Vol. IV, No. 5, 1 May 1962: Col. 632)

Burhanuddin supported his motion by referring to the *Indonesia Raya* movement in Indonesia and Jose Rizal's movement for Malay unity in the Philippines, Western knowledge about the geographical affinity of the Malay Archipelago, and common historical experiences in the area where there had previously been several large kingdoms such as Srivijaya, Majapahit, and Melaka (PDDR, Vol. IV, No. 5, 1 May 1962: Cols. 635–637, 642–643).

Although it remains unclear what form of government was envisaged in his plan for *Melayu Raya*, he was attracted to an idea of confederation, namely "Maphilindo" coined by Indonesia's Foreign Minister Subandrio in June 1963 and put forward by the Philippines' President Macapagal as a plan for a confederation among the three nations of "Malay stock," namely Malaya, the Philippines and Indonesia (Mackie 1974: 9, 53). Burhanuddin maintained close relationships with various Indonesian political leaders and officials, which resulted in his detention by the Malaysian government in 1965.

Ahmad Boestamam[23] was another leading supporter of the idea of *Melayu Raya*. He was a former leader of the KMM and the PKMM, and founded PKMM's youth wing, Angkatan Pemuda Insaf (API) in 1946. After he was detained by the colonial government for seven years (from 1948 to 1955), he founded the Partai Rakyat Malaya (PRM) (People's Party of Malaya) in 1955 and took office as president. He was elected to Parliament in 1959 from Setapak, Selangor, as a member of the Socialist Front (SF), an opposition coalition between the PRM and the Labour Party of Malaya.

Boestamam declared that he would accept the planned "Malaysia," which differed from his concept of *Melayu Raya*, only if the former was the first step on the way to the latter. In his remark on the Tunku's motion "Malaysia" in Parliament on 17 October 1961, he stated:

> Mr. Speaker, from my viewpoint, the Malaysia proposed by Tunku Abdul Rahman is not *Melayu Raya*... *Melayu Raya* [should] include all the states (*negeri*) of the Malay Archipelago (*Gugusan Pulau² Melayu*). So, it would be wrong if I say that Malaysia is equivalent to *Melayu Raya*. Malaysia is Malaysia, and *Melayu Raya* is different. If the Malaysia plan put forward by the Honorable Prime Minister, which we would like to accept in principle, is the way to *Melayu Raya*, or the way to *Malaysia Raya*, I will support it.[24] (PDDR, Vol. III, No. 17, 17 October 1961: Col. 1792)

Mr. Speaker, if Malaysia is the first step on the way to *Malaysia Raya*, I, Mr. Speaker, will give full support for the plan. But, if Malaysia aims to compete with Indonesia and to become a tool for the interests of the British, we, Mr. Speaker, cannot help opposing the plan.[25] (PDDR, Vol. III, No. 17, 17 October 1961: Cols. 1795-1796)

He also demanded self-determination for the Borneo territories, observing that "what has been remarked by the people of the three territories is that they want to have the right to determine their own future at an earlier stage" (PDDR, Vol. III, No. 17, 17 October 1961: Cols. 1794–1795). The right to self-determination of the Borneo territories was supported at the Malaysian Socialist Conference in January 1962.

Yet the Malayan government brought an end to Boestamam's involvement in the *Melayu Raya* movement. In February 1963, about two months after the Brunei Revolt, which was led by the Partai Rakyat Brunei (PRB) (Brunei People's Party), Boestamam was arrested on suspicion of being in contact with the Partai Komunis Indonesia (PKI) (Communist Party of Indonesia), alleged to be his underground movement for subversive purposes during the conflict between Malaya and Indonesia, and his connection with A.M. Azahari, the founder of the PRB and the leader of the Brunei Revolt, as well as for his use of the PRM to support the revolt (Ramlah 1994: 337–338, Mackie 1974: 52).

The Federation of Malaya, Singapore, Sarawak and Sabah officially formed Malaysia on 16 September 1963, but the Philippines and Indonesia did not recognize the new federation. The Philippines had a claim to Sabah, arguing that a British commercial syndicate had obtained a concession from the Sultan of Sulu by agreement in 1878 (Stockwell 1998: 142–143). When the Tunku announced the Malaysia proposal in 1961, the Indonesian government was not immediately opposed. Even the PKI did not strenuously object until December 1961, when the party publicly denounced the proposed Malaysia as a product of British neo-colonialism. In January 1963, however, Subandrio, the Indonesian Foreign Minister, openly attacked the planned formation of Malaysia and declared *Konfrontasi* (Confrontation). An aggressive campaign against Malaysia started in September 1963 when Sukarno announced that Indonesia would *ganyang* (crush) Malaysia, borrowing the slogan from the PKI (Mackie 1974: 104, 125, 154, 156, 200). Sukarno attacked Malaysia "on the grounds that it perpetuated British power in Southeast Asia and divided the Malay world of Indonesia, the Philippines, and Malaya" (Stockwell 1998: 143). There is no doubt that the British attempted to protect their economic and military interests in their former colonies and protectorates in Southeast Asia. However, as British power declined in Southeast Asia, the British made considerable compromises with local leaders in Malaya, Singapore, and the Borneo territories in negotiations over the formation of Malaysia (Stockwell 1998).

In Malaysia, the Alliance government successfully capitalized on the Indonesian confrontation with Malaysia to win a landslide victory in the general election of 1964, winning 89 of 104 parliamentary seats. During the campaign, the PMIP (PAS) and the SF, the two major opposition parties which had advocated for *Melayu Raya* instead of the newly-formed Malaysia, were accused of being Indonesian agents disloyal to the Malaysian state (Ratnam and Milne 1967: 110–120). The PMIP had its number of parliamentary seats reduced from 13 to 9. The SF suffered more heavily, with their parliamentary seats reduced from 8 to 2. Boestamam was still detained during the election while Burhanuddin could not stand because he was facing charges of being involved in prohibited commercial activities before the election (Ramlah 1996: 200).

In the election's aftermath, various major events suddenly changed the political climate in Southeast Asia. Indonesia experienced drastic political changes when the military seized power after a failed coup in October 1965. Major General Suharto took power from President Sukarno in 1966. Under Suharto's leadership, Indonesia ended the confrontation with Malaysia in 1966 and re-established formal diplomatic relations in 1967. The election of Ferdinand Marcos as President of the Philippines in 1965 changed the Philippines' policy towards Malaysia. President Marcos sought reconciliation with Malaysia and formally recognized Malaysia's sovereignty in 1966, although the Philippines' claim to Sabah was not completely withdrawn. In short, neighboring countries ended their open opposition to Malaysia in the mid-1960s, but advocates of *Melayu Raya* could no longer expect to find support for their vision of a pan-Malay nation among their neighboring countries.

The political movement for *Melayu Raya / Indonesia Raya* thus died away in the mid-1960s. Nevertheless, as Milner argues, the confrontations over the formation of Malaysia can be seen as a process of defining and redefining "Malayness" (Milner 1992). There was indeed open conflict between the Tunku and Malay leftists in real politics as well as significant differences between the former's Malaysia proposal and the latter's idea of *Melayu Raya* in ideological orientation, assumptions about the territorial reach of the state, etc. Yet, the concepts of Malaysia and *Melayu Raya* were strikingly similar in their assumptions that a broader definition of "Malay" could be justified on the basis of ethno-cultural and geo-historical affinity.

7 Conclusion

In the previous chapters, we have discussed the indigenization of colonial knowledge and the quest for pan-Malay identity in Malaya. Let us briefly summarize our findings. British education policy towards the Malays, outlined in the Winstedt report of 1917, reflected a compromise between two contradictory orientations: conservation and innovation. On the one hand, the common Malay people were expected to preserve their "Malayness" or "Malay character," which was associated with peasantry. On the other hand, they were also advised to master more "rational" and "practical" ways of thinking.

We have seen that the SITC, as a fully residential teacher training college, provided all-round education, providing various opportunities for students to accumulate knowledge and experience. The college was tasked by the colonial authorities to (re)produce ethnicity (Malayness), class (peasantry) and gender (masculinity). SITC teachers and students, however, did not necessarily or unquestioningly accept what the British attempted to communicate. Rather, they selectively reconstituted their received knowledge and applied it to their own ends.

To examine the transmission of colonial knowledge, we conducted a comparative analysis of history and geography textbooks about the Malay world. Our analysis revealed that not only British scholars (R.J. Wilkinson and R.O. Winstedt) but also a Malay teacher (Abdul Hadi Haji Hasan) reconstituted the Malay world using the methods of modern historiography and geography. There were striking similarities in their conceptions of community, space and time. They conceptualized the Malay community as a race, more specifically a mixed race. Their conceptions of Malay territoriality were three-tiered, made up of Malay states (*negeri-negeri Melayu*), Malaya (*Tanah Melayu*) and the Malay world (*alam Melayu*). While Malaya was always the focal point of their argument, Abdul Hadi's textbook paid more attention to the Malay world outside Malaya than Wilkinson and Winstedt. The three authors shared similar perceptions of the past as well. Malay history was traced according to calendrical time and chronology. Their historical views were basically progressivist.

We then proceeded to investigate the utilization of colonial knowledge, via a case study of Ibrahim Haji Yaacob's identification of *Melayu Raya / Indonesia Raya*. Ibrahim's concept of pan-Malay/Indonesian unity had the following basic characteristics in respect of his conceptions of community, space and time. First, while Ibrahim accepted the concept of Malay as a race, or a mixed race, similar to the textbook authors, he deployed this concept of race for his own political objectives, namely, to advocate pan-Malay/Indonesian nationalism. Second, although Ibrahim shared the authors' conceptualization of Malay territoriality in three tiers, he put much greater stress on the importance of the Malay world as the potential territory for his imagined pan-Malay/Indonesian nation. Third, although Ibrahim shared a progressivist historical perspective, he sought to reconstitute Malay history to fit his political cause.

Finally, we briefly discussed the postwar development of pan-Malayism and the formation and confrontations of Malaysia in the 1960s. There were considerable differences between the Malaysia proposal and the idea of *Melayu Raya*. Yet the advocates of both positions adopted similar justifications based on ethno-cultural and geo-historical affinity. Both Malaysia and *Melayu Raya* were based on knowledge about the history, geography and ethnology of the Malay world. The marginalization of Malay leftists in Malaysian politics in the mid-1960s and the diplomatic recognition of Malaysia by Indonesia and the Philippines in the late-1960s marked the end of the advocacy of a pan-Malay/Indonesian nation, called *Melayu Raya / Indonesia Raya*.

To sum up, although British colonizers imposed new forms of knowledge about the Malay world on the local "Malay" populace in colonial Malaya, it was not uncommon for the locals, evidenced by Ibrahim, to appropriate and reorganize colonial knowledge for their own claims, even for anti-colonial and trans-colonial pan-Malayism. While nationalist thinking and action in other countries, especially in the Netherlands East Indies or Indonesia, were important influences in formulating pan-Malayism in British Malaya, British colonialism played an equally important, if unintended, role in the formation of pan-Malay identity.

Finally, let us briefly touch on the contemporary relevance of pan-Malayism. There are no longer political leaders in Malaysia who advocate a pan-Malay/Indonesian nation, but this does not render pan-Malay identity in Malaysia irrelevant. One can find its legacy in current Malaysia.

First, since the 1970s, pan-Malayism has been continuously expressed as a form of transnational regionalism, which can be defined as the expression of pride in a particular region across national boundaries. There are some pan-Malay oriented associations and institutes, and international organizations.[1] One example is Majlis Bahasa Brunei Darussalam-Indonesia-Malaysia (MABBIM) (Language Council of Brunei Darussalam-Indonesia-Malaysia), a regional language organization which consists of three Malay-speaking countries: Brunei, Indonesia and Malaysia.[2] The council was originally formed as Majlis Bahasa Indonesia-Malaysia (MBIM) (Language Council of Indonesia-Malaysia) in 1972 and was subsequently renamed Majlis Bahasa Brunei Darussalam-Indonesia-Malaysia (MABBIM) when Brunei joined in 1985. The council aims to plan and monitor the development of the Malay/Indonesian language in the region.

In Malaysia the *Dunia Melayu* (Malay World) movement has been led by Gabungan Persatuan Penulis Nasional Malaysia (GAPENA) (Federation of National Writers' Associations of Malaysia), which was established in 1969 as an umbrella organization for various writers' associations in Malaysia.[3] The GAPENA started the *Dunia Melayu* movement in the 1980s under the leadership of Ismail Hussein, a scholar of Malay literature. Abdul Latiff Abu Bakar, a scholar of Malay history, culture and media, also played a significant part in the association's leadership. The association held a series of symposiums on the Malay world and diaspora Malays and has advocated pan-Malay identity (Tomizawa 2010). In Malaysian academia, research and educational institutes such as Universiti Kebangsaan Malaysia's Institut Alam dan Tamadun Melayu (ATMA) (Institute of the Malay World and Civilisation) and Universiti Malaya's Akademi Pengajian Melayu (APM) (Academy of Malay Studies) have promoted studies of the Malay world based on broad definitions of Malayness.[4]

More recently, the Dunia Melayu Dunia Islam (DMDI) (Malay and Islamic World) movement was inaugurated by the state government of Melaka in 2000. The former Chief Minister of Melaka, Mohd. Ali Rustam, initiated the organization of DMDI. Abdul Latiff Abu Bakar played a crucial role in the DMDI's formation and became Chairman of its Socio-Cultural Bureau.[5] It is not surprising, therefore, that the DMDI inherited the broad concept of Malayness from the GAPENA, although with greater emphasis on Islam. The DMDI tries "to generate commitment among the Muslim-Malay ummah all over the world to unite and to excel in the major fields, i.e. Economics, Information Technology, Culture, Education, Women and Youth for the freedom and well-being of the people of the world" (Sekretariat Dunia Melayu Dunia Islam n.d.: 3). For this purpose, the DMDI attempted to form cultural and business networks among a number of "Malay" political leaders from across the "Malay and Islamic world," including Indonesia, Singapore, the Philippines, Brunei, Thailand, Sri Lanka, South Africa, as well as Malaysia. According to Minako Sakai, the movement played a considerable role in reviving Malay ethnicity in various parts of Sumatra in post-Suharto Indonesia (Sakai 2009; 2010). After Mohd. Ali stepped down as the Chief Minister of Melaka in 2013, he continued to head the DMDI. The regime change in Malaysia in May 2018, however, may be unfavorable to the movement.

In short, contemporary pan-Malayism is substantially different from the earlier idea of *Melayu Raya / Indonesia Raya*. Current pan-Malayism no longer aims to challenge the political boundaries between Malaysia, Singapore, Brunei, Indonesia and the Philippines. Today's pan-Malay oriented organizations seek solidarity and cooperation between governments, organizations and businesses in the Malay world. They tend to be more interested in socio-cultural and economic spheres than in explicitly political matters. It is also noteworthy that pan-Malay oriented movements in the early twenty-first century are no longer characterized by leftist or socialist inclinations, such as those that propelled *Melayu Raya / Indonesia Raya*.

Second, the current Malaysian concept of *bumiputera*, which literally means "sons of the soil," seems to have inherited a broader definition of "Malay" from pan-Malayism. It is true that the *bumiputera* now officially refers to indigenous peoples in any nation-state like Malaysia or Brunei, unlike the idea of *Melayu Raya / Indonesia Raya*, which transcended political boundaries. Nevertheless, there are similarities between these two concepts in that both are founded on indigeneity and ethno-cultural affinity in the Malay world.

It is not clear when the term *bumiputera* first appeared in the Malay Peninsula, but the word *bumiputera* (*bumi putera*) or *putera bumi* was in use during the early twentieth century (Abdul Rahman Haji Ismail 2003: 111–112). Malay textbooks on the history and geography of the Malay world employed the term *bumi-putera* to refer to the natives as well as local inhabitants. Ibrahim Haji Yaacob also used the term *bumiputera* (*bumi putera*) in the 1930s to refer to the native population of Malaya, particularly Malays. A Malay periodical titled *Bumiputera* was published in Penang from 1933 until 1936.

The word *bumiputera* became more popular after the formation of Malaysia in 1963. The incorporation of Sabah and Sarawak into the new federation significantly increased the indigenous population that did not fit the constitutional definition of "Malay" based on Islam, the Malay language and Malay customs. The term *bumiputera* thus began to be used as a concept referring to all indigenous peoples (Malays, the Orang Asli, and natives of Sabah and Sarawak).[6] To improve the economic status of Malays and other indigenous groups in Malaysia, the first Kongres Ekonomi Bumiputera (Bumiputera Economic Congress) was held in 1965, followed by a second congress in 1968 (Ariffin 2003: 20).[7] *Bumiputera* as a social category became more important after the New Economic Policy (NEP) was introduced in 1971 "to eradicate poverty among all Malaysians, irrespective of race, and to restructure Malaysian society in order to correct racial imbalance, in the context of an expanding economy, leading towards the creation of a dynamic and just society" (Malaysia 1971: 1). Since the 1970s, the distinction between *Bumiputera* and non-*Bumiputera* became increasingly significant in the public life of Malaysia because the government gave, and still gives, preferential treatment to *Bumiputera* in the socio-economic domain.

While the concept of *bumiputera*, which is closely related to pan-Malay identity, has developed a more inclusive sense of belonging than the concept of "Malay" as defined in the Federal Constitution of Malaysia, it has limitations for creating an all-encompassing national identity in Malaysia. First, the preferential policy could perpetuate the rift between *Bumiputera* and non-*Bumiputera* citizens. There is no doubt that the NEP-like *Bumiputera* policy has succeeded in reducing the socio-economic imbalance between ethnic groups and has thus enhanced social and political stability in Malaysia. Apparently, the majority of the *Bumiputera* continue to support the special treatment they receive, based on the historical "social contract" which provides non-Malay/*Bumiputera* residents with citizenship, in return for granting a "special position" to Malays and other *Bumiputera* groups. At the same time, though, many non-*Bumiputera* Malaysians appear to be increasingly frustrated by the continuing preferential treatment for the *Bumiputera*. Even some

Malay/*Bumiputera* people recognize the need to overcome the existing *Bumiputera* policy's inefficiency and cronyism.

Furthermore, the *Bumiputera* do not necessarily share a strong sense of belonging to a single community. One could easily find various divisions among the *Bumiputera* in Malaysia, such as between Malays and "other" *Bumiputera*, between Muslim and non-Muslim *Bumiputera*, and between Peninsular, Sabahan and Sarawakian *Bumiputera*. For instance, strong advocacy of Malay and Islamic supremacy may arouse anxiety among non-Malay or non-Muslim *Bumiputera*. Meanwhile, growing demands for state rights and autonomy in Sabah and Sarawak can perplex the *Bumiputera* of Peninsular Malaysia.

Discussions of ethnic and national identity in Malaysia remain open-ended.[8] The end of the NEP in 1990 prompted government leaders to seek a new grand design for Malaysia. In 1991 Mahathir Mohamed, the then prime minister, introduced a national vision popularly known as *Wawasan 2020*, or Vision 2020, which aimed to make Malaysia a fully developed country by the year 2020. The first of the nine strategic challenges to create a fully developed Malaysia was

> the challenge of establishing a united Malaysian nation with a sense of common and shared destiny. This must be a nation at peace with itself, territorially and ethnically integrated, living in harmony and full and fair partnership, made up of one *Bangsa Malaysia* with political loyalty and dedication to the nation. (Mahathir 1993 [1991]: 404)

Wawasan 2020 thus encouraged the Malaysian people to identify as belonging to one united nation, named *Bangsa Malaysia*, without either denying people's right to embrace their distinctive customs, cultures and religions or questioning the legitimacy of existing affirmative action for the *Bumiputera*. The coining of the term *Bangsa Malaysia* might be viewed as an innovation in political vocabulary in Malaysia in view of the fact that the word *bangsa* had conventionally been used primarily to refer to each distinct ethnic group, for instance, *bangsa Melayu, bangsa Cina, bangsa Iban*, etc., rather than to indicate the Malaysian people as a whole, unlike the term *bangsa Indonesia*, or the Indonesian nation, which has long been common in Indonesia.

Around the same time, another concept *Melayu Baru*, or New Malays, was also popularized by Mahathir as a vital component of *Bangsa*

Malaysia described in *Wawasan 2020*. He defined *Bangsa Melayu Baru* and *Bumiputera Baru* as a new Malay and *Bumiputera* which "possesses a culture suitable to the modern period, capable of meeting all challenges, able to compete without assistance, learned and knowledgeable, sophisticated, honest, disciplined, trustworthy and competent" (Mahathir 1997 [1991]: 524; Khoo Boo Teik 1995: 335). The target audience for the *Melayu Baru* identity was new Malay capitalist and middle classes while peasants, workers, aristocrats and civil servants were not treated so favorably (Khoo Boo Teik 1995: 336–338). Abdul Rahman Embong explains that

> the *Melayu Baru* is a project directed to the transformation and modernization of the Malay society, with its emphasis currently on the creation and expansion of the Malay capitalist and the new middle classes, and the development of a work culture and ethics in keeping with the demands of the work regime of a rapidly industrializing society. (Abdul Rahman Embong 2002: 169)

Again, we should not overestimate the effect of these official visions and concepts in the formation of ethnic and national identity. Political and economic change can profoundly influence the reception of official concepts. For instance, the serious losses incurred by many of Malay entrepreneurs and businessmen following the financial and economic crisis of 1997 revealed the vulnerability of *Melayu Baru*, and substantially hurt its credibility. Since the change of leadership from Mahathir to Abdullah Ahmad Badawi in 2003, *Bangsa Malaysia* and *Melayu Baru* has been mentioned less frequently. In its place, Abdullah attempted to propagate the concept of *Islam Hadhari* (Civilizational Islam). This slogan, however, was not embraced by his successor Mohd. Najib Abdul Razak, who took office in 2009.

Najib tried to popularize a new concept of "1Malaysia," which encapsulated the idea of "unity in diversity" in a multiethnic society.[9] The "1Malaysia" concept was supposedly based on the Federal Constitution and earlier government efforts to promote national unity including *Wawasan 2020*. In the early stages of his premiership, Najib expressed an intention to reduce ethnically based preferential treatment and to address the needs of the people irrespective of ethnicity, as can be seen in government programs such as the New Economic Model (NEM). This seemingly liberal approach was, however, not welcomed by some sections of the Malay community, represented by right-wing Malay NGOs such as

Pertubuhan Pribumi Perkasa (PERKASA) (Mighty Native Organisation). Milner and Ting argue that Najib's "1Malaysia" program was not sufficient to displace the race paradigm, which had long been deeply embedded in Malaysian politics (Milner and Ting 2014: 43–46). Especially after the 2013 general elections, which resulted in a reduced majority for the ruling coalition Barisan Nasional (BN) (National Front), Najib shifted focus to the ethnically based Malay and *Bumiputera* agenda to secure support from Malay and other *Bumiputera* communities. While Najib continued to advocate the "1Malaysia" concept, he no longer referenced *Wawasan 2020* as frequently, probably due to growing conflict with Mahathir, who strongly criticized the Najib administration, especially after the 1Malaysia Development Berhad (1MDB) scandal was reported in the press in 2015. In the end, Najib launched a new long-term development program, *Transformasi Nasional 2050* (National Transformation 2050) in 2017.

The 14th General Election held in May 2018 changed Malaysia's political landscape. Opposition coalition Pakatan Harapan (PH) (the Alliance of Hope), led by former Prime Minister Mahathir Mohamad, won a majority of lower house seats in the general election, paving the way for the country's first change of power since the independence of the Federation of Malaya in 1957. Mahathir, serving as the Prime Minister of Malaysia for the second time, instructed all ministries to stop using the "1Malaysia" slogan. He has not, however, reverted to the *Wawasan 2020* agenda that he conceptualized in 1991. Instead, he introduced another national vision *Wawasan Kemakmuran Bersama 2030* (Shared Prosperity Vision 2030) in October 2019.

It remains questionable the extent and way in which the Malaysian people internalize and appropriate such concepts promoted "from above".[10] We must therefore continue to analyze not only the production of new concepts and forms of knowledge but also their transmission, localization, transformation, reproduction and reconstruction.

Appendix

Educational Systems in the Federated Malay States during the 1930s

Primary education　　　Secondary education　　　Higher education

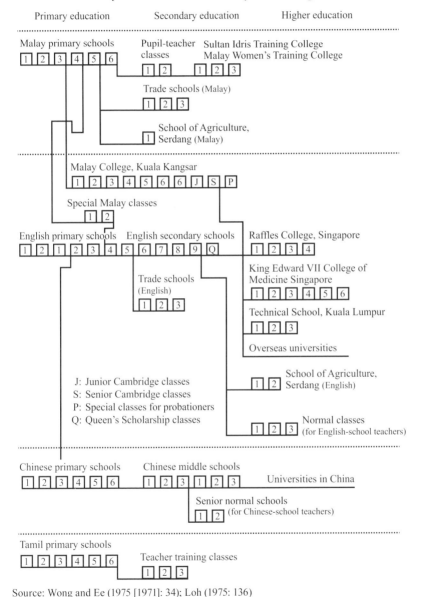

Source: Wong and Ee (1975 [1971]: 34); Loh (1975: 136)

Notes

Chapter 1

1 Ibrahim used both terms *Melayu Raya* and *Indonesia Raya* in his writings. According to Cheah Boon Kheng, "'Melayu Raya' is a term more commonly used by Malays, and 'Indonesia Raya' by Indonesians. However, one does come across Indonesian-influenced Malays preferring the term 'Indonesia Raya' or using both terms interchangeably" (Cheah 2012 [1983]: 11). I contend that while Ibrahim used both terms, he used *Melayu Raya* more frequently in his writings before the Pacific War, and he preferred *Indonesia Raya* in his postwar writings. For more detailed account of the usage of the terms, see the discussion in chapters 5 and 6 below.
2 Rustam A. Sani is the first scholar who characterized *Melayu Raya* as a Malay "nation-of-intent" (Rustam 1986 [1976]; 2008). Shamsul A.B. has elaborated the concept to apply it beyond the Malay left context. According to Shamsul, "nation-of-intent" means "a more or less precisely defined idea of the form of a nation, i.e. its territory, population, language, culture, symbols and institutions" (Shamsul 1996c: 328).
3 Donna J. Amoroso explains convincingly how the Malay ruling class established and preserved their ascendancy in colonial Malaya by incorporating nationalism into traditionalism and vice versa (Amoroso 2014).
4 See Milner (2002 [1995]).
5 See Roff (1994 [1967]), Cheah (1979; 1992; 2012 [1983]), Ahmat (2013), Liow (2005) and Roslan (2009).
6 See Roff (1994 [1967]) and Firdaus (1985).
7 See Akashi (1976).
8 Some of his unpublished private papers, written in the postwar era, are deposited in the Perpustakaan Peringatan Za'ba (Za'ba Memorial Library), University of Malaya.

Chapter 2

1 For a detailed account of the history of Malaya, see for instance Andaya and Andaya (2017 [1982]).
2 When the British took control of the possessions of the Dutch East India Company (VOC) in the Malay Archipelago in 1795, Melaka came under British rule. The British returned Melaka to the Dutch in 1818.

3 Major categories in the 1891 census were "Europeans and Americans," "Eurasians," "Chinese," "Malays & Other Natives of the Archipelago," "Tamils & Other Natives of India," and "Other Nationalities."

4 A *surau* is a small building used mainly for religious purposes such as prayers and teaching.

5 A *pondok* is made up of several small huts surrounding the religious teacher's residence or a one-room premise. Unlike the *pondok*, which has neither fixed school hours nor curriculum, the *madrasah* is a religious school following the organization and design of the modern school.

6 The exceptional case was the Malay College, Kuala Kangsar, founded mainly for Malay boys of privileged background. After completing three standards at Malay schools, they could directly enter the Malay College without attending the Special Malay Class.

7 King Edward VII College of Medicine was originally established in Singapore in 1905 as the Straits Settlements and Federated Malay States Government Medical School. The school was renamed King Edward VII Medical School in 1913 and later King Edward VII College of Medicine in 1921.

8 Raffles College was established in Singapore in 1928. It was the nucleus of the future University of Malaya, established in Singapore in 1949, into which the Medical College was incorporated.

9 Technical School was opened in Kuala Lumpur in 1904 to train apprentices in engineering from various government departments. Though it was closed in 1915, it was reopened in 1926.

10 School of Agriculture was established in Serdang in 1931 to train government apprentices in the Department of Agriculture.

11 A full discussion of training college for Malay-school teachers will be provided in the following parts of this study.

12 For a detailed account of the Malay Training College, Melaka, see Ramlah (1991).

13 Even as late as 1930s, Raja Chulan, the Raja di-Hilir Perak and a son of ex-Sultan Abdullah, displayed his reluctance to the idea of extending English schools to Malay rural areas. "History has taught us," he said, "that under-education is not so serious an evil as over-education…" (Roff 1994 [1967]: 201).

14 It should be noted, as Shamsul explains, that each of the eleven states in Malaya offered a different definition of a "Malay," who was entitled to own Malay reserve land (Shamsul 2004: 141).

15 Richard Olof Winstedt was born in 1878 at Oxford, England. His father was a naturalized Swede and his mother was an Englishwoman. He was educated at New College, Oxford, and joined the Malayan Civil Service in 1902 as a cadet. Between 1906 and 1912, he served at various district offices in the Federated Malay States. He was Secretary, Committee for Malay Studies in 1913 and was appointed District Officer, Kuala Pilah, from 1913 to 1915. In 1916 he became Assistant Director of Education in charge of Malay schools. He was also appointed Acting Director of Education in the Straits Settlements and the Federated Malay States in 1920 and in 1923. Between 1924 and 1931 he served as Director of Education in the Straits Settlements and the Federated Malay States. He was also the Principal of Raffles College, Singapore, from 1921 to 1931. He was a member of the Legislative Council of the Straits Settlements (1924–1927), and of the

Federal Council of the Federated Malay States (1927–1931). In 1931 he moved to Johor as Acting General Adviser and remained there until 1935 when he retired. After his return to England, he was offered posts at the School of Oriental and African Studies, University of London. He was elected a Fellow of the British Academy in 1945. He died in 1966. For details of his career, see AREFMS (various years), Winstedt (1969), Bastin (1964), Roff (1994 [1967]: 137–142) and Yeo (1982: 358–359).

16 "Report by Mr. R.O. Winstedt, Asst. Director of Education S.S. and F.M.S., on Vernacular and Industrial Education in the Netherlands East Indies and the Philippines" (Council Paper, Legislative Council, Straits Settlements, No. 22 of 1917).

17 The textbook was often referred to simply as *Tawarikh Melayu* (Malay History).

18 In Chapter 4 I examine these textbooks within the context of conceptualizations of Malayness. See also Zainal Abidin (1940; 1941a), Khoo Kay Kim (1979a), Maier (1988), Cheah (1997), Gullick (1998) and Milner (2005).

Chapter 3

1 Although it was a Malay-medium training college, the SITC's official name was in English. In 1959, however, it was renamed as Maktab Perguruan Sultan Idris (MPSI) in Malay. It was upgraded to Institut Perguruan Sultan Idris (IPSI) (Sultan Idris Training Institute) in 1987 and subsequently was accorded university status as Universiti Pendidikan Sultan Idris (UPSI) (Sultan Idris Education University) in 1997.

2 For a detailed account of public schools in England and Wales, see Walford (1986).

3 For a detailed history of the MCKK before World War II, see Khasnor (1996). Khasnor (2005) also briefly discusses the prewar history of the MCKK while mainly discussing its postwar development.

4 For his biographical details, see Abdullah (1982).

5 In first and second years, each student was given an individual plot, divided into three ridges. On each of these three ridges he had to plant a different crop. As he had at least two crop changes per year, he was expected to acquire a general knowledge about the growth and habits of at least six different crops. Each student was required to record his daily work in his notebook and card-index. Third-year students were given practice in teaching in the vernacular school attached to the SITC. There were different duties in school gardening, (i) care of orchard, planting new fruit trees, pruning and manuring where necessary, (ii) care of large communal plots (maize, sweet potato, ground-nut, tomato, lettuce, Lima bean, long bean, French bean, etc.), (iii) care of the grounds under economic crops (pine-apples, tea, bemban, mengkuang and coffee), (iv) supervision of the plots of first and second year students, and (v) ornamental work and care of flowers in college grounds, (vi) nurseries, (vii) manuring, (viii) raising seed foreign to Malaya, and (ix) pests. In each year there were five classes. Each class had to undertake one of the duties in rotation (Bretherton 1931: 10–13).

6 Religious teachers at Malay schools were not trained at the SITC but at religious schools.
7 "Kulit dan tubuh badannya orang Putih (Inggeris) tetapi hatinya Melayu."
8 Other than English schools, clubs such as Selangor Club, Teluk Anson Club, Tanjung Malim Club and the YMCA also competed against the SITC (Buyong 1956: 16; *Chenderamata,* April 1928: 17–18).
9 In 1930, 209 students joined the MVI while 199 became Scouts (AREFMS 1930: 26).
10 Khasnor (1996: chap. 9) examines some aspects of the MCKK as a "royal" school.
11 For detailed accounts of the development of the history curriculum in the English schools of Malaya, see Blackburn and Wu (2019).
12 Tennikoit is a game played with a rubber ring on a tennis-style court.

Chapter 4

1 To observe the development of Malaysian historiography, see Stockwell (1976), Khoo Kay Kim (1979a), Cheah (1997; 2003), Gullick (1998), Shamsul (2004), Milner (2005) and Blackburn and Wu (2019). For a more general discussion about the role of modern history and geography in the identification of nationhood, see Reid and Marr (1979), Chatterjee (1993) and Thongchai (1994).
2 According to Kato Tsuyoshi, a geography textbook of the Netherlands East Indies had been published in Malay by the late nineteenth century [Kato 2017: 267].
3 Richard James Wilkinson was born in 1867 at Salonika (Thessaloniki), Greece, where his father, R. Wilkinson, served as British Consul. After living on the continent in his childhood, he was educated at Trinity College, Cambridge. As well as English, he knew various European languages such as French, German, Greek, Italian and Spanish. After joining the Straits Settlements Civil Service as a cadet in 1889, he qualified in Malay and in Hokkien. In 1896 he was appointed Acting Director of Education in Penang. He was Acting Inspector of Schools, Straits Settlements, from 1898 to 1900. Between 1903 and 1906, he acted as Inspector of Schools for the Federated Malay States. In 1906 he was appointed Secretary General to Resident, Perak. In 1910 he was Resident, Negeri Sembilan and the following year became Colonial Secretary in the Straits Settlements. In 1916 he went to Sierra Leone and served as Governor until 1922 when he retired. He died in 1941. For details of his career, see Burns (1971: 1), Winstedt (1947), Heussler (1981:132–134), Roff (1994 [1967]: 130–135) and Gullick (1992: 370–371).
4 For a detailed account of the Orang Asli, see for instance Nicholas (2000) and Nobuta (2009).
5 For this study I use Wilkinson (1971 [1923]; 1975 [1923]), both of which are reprints of the third edition.
6 For a detailed account of Winstedt's career, see Chapter 2, footnote 15.
7 An apparent inconsistency in his rural-oriented suggestions was the proposal to introduce English-language instruction into Malay vernacular education. He suggested that English should be taught in Malay schools and training colleges while also proposing that classes in Malay for Malay boys might be attached to

some of the English schools. Neither proposal was implemented. O.T. Dussek, the first principal of SITC, seems to have played an important role in the monolingual policies of both the SITC and the Malay schools (Loh 1975: 87).

8 For a bibliography of his writings, see Bastin (1964).

9 For instance, in the preface to the second edition of *A History of Malaya* (1961), Winstedt claims that "[t]he history is written largely from a Malay angle" (Winstedt 1968: v–vi).

10 Although the first edition of this book was written in Jawi or Arabic script, the Romanized version became available the following year.

11 Anthony Milner points out that at least sixty years earlier, some Malay students had already been brought into contact with "scientific" knowledge about "Malay" through the empirical Malay geography textbook, *Hikayat Dunia* (Milner 2002 [1995]: 66). Hendrik M.J. Maier rejects Za'ba's claim about the usage of *tawarikh* by showing that the term had been used to refer to "history" long before 1918. Nevertheless, "Winstedt's authority accelerated the spread of the term and its content, so different from the prescripts of the heritage" (Maier 1988: 147–148).

12 For this study I use the 1927 edition.

13 For this study, I use the 1926 edition.

14 Abdul Hadi Haji Hasan was born in 1900 at Batang Tiga, Melaka. After completing his primary education at Malay School, Batang Tiga, he became a probationary teacher at a Malay school in Melaka in 1913. In 1917 he entered the Malay Training College, Melaka, and studied there until 1919. Having taught at Malay schools for two years, he became a teacher at the Malay Training College, Melaka, in 1921 and taught history and the Malay language. He was transferred to the SITC in 1922 and remained there until 1929 when he was appointed Inspector of Schools, Kelantan. He retired from the post in 1933 due to illness and died in 1937. For details of his career, see *Ensiklopedia Sejarah dan Kebudayaan Melayu* (1999: vol. 1, 31–33), Muhammad Yusuf (1982) and Ramlah (1991:82–87).

15 It was used in Malay schools until the early 1950s (Khoo Kay Kim 1979a: 305n). For this study I use the 1928 reprint of the first and second volumes and the 1930 reprint of the third volume.

16 "Al-kesah, maka ada-lah pada zaman perba kala, bahawa Tanah Melayu kita ini telah di-diami oleh orang bangsa liar sahaja ia-itu orang Semang dan orang Sakai: maka tetkala datang orang kita Melayu, akan bangsa-bangsa itu pun undor-lah ka-darat dan ka-gunong-gunong."

17 "Maka sunggoh pun ada hikayat mencheritakan hal zaman purba kala itu, tetapi tiada-lah berapa guna-nya; kerana segala yang di-riwayatkan dari hal dewa-dewa dan orang kesaktian yang tersebut kesah-nya di-dalam hikayat-hikayat itu sa-mata-mata-lah nampak-nya cherita menyedapkan telinga sahaja, bukan-nya dari-pada perkara yang di-terima dan di-hargakan pada nilayan tawarikh."

18 "Dan apa saksi-nya ia-itu berhubong? Maka nyata-lah salah-nya cherita yang terkarang di-dalam *Sejarah Melayu* itu!"

19 "Dalam pada itu pun tiada-lah boleh kita berpegang pada-nya, kerana kebanyakan tiada munasabah pada akal kita."

20 "Akan tetapi dalam pada itu pun, chetera di-dalam *Hikayat Marong Mahawangsa* ini belum-lah di-peroleh apa-apa keterangan atau saksi hendak meyakinkan benar-nya."

21 "Bahawa ada pun *Tawarikh Melayu* ini telah terkarang dengan membandingkan beberapa hikayat Melayu serta kitab-kitab Arab dan babad Jawa, serta tawarikh China dan hikayat Portugis dan hikayat Belanda. Maka yang terutama di-dapati nukil-nya ia-lah dari-pada kitab Inggeris bagi cherita tawarikh orang-orang Melayu Semenanjong ini yang di-karangkan oleh Tuan R.J. Wilkinson, C.M.G., dalam bahasa Inggeris."

22 While "Manilamen" was included in the category "Malays & other Native of the Archipelago" in censuses of the Straits Settlements in 1891 and 1901 and of the Federated Malay States in 1901, "Manilamen" was replaced by the term "Filipino(s)" or "Philipino" and was dropped from the comprehensive Malay category in census taken after 1911. They became categorized as "Other(s)".

23 "Ada pun isi negeri Selangor itu menurut banchi pada T.M. 1921 ia-itu di-dapati lebih 40 laksa ramai-nya, ia-itu orang China sahaja 17 laksa, orang Hindi 13 laksa, dan orang Melayu 9 laksa… Maka akan orang Biduanda atau Mantera, ia-itu bangsa Melayu asli, ada-lah pula sa-ribu orang; demikian jua banyak-nya orang Besisi, ia-itu bangsa kachokan dari-pada Melayu asli berkhamir dengan bangsa Sakai."

24 "Shahadan ada-lah bangsa Jakun yang tersebut di-atas ini, makin lama sa-makin berkurangan-lah mereka itu. Maka boleh-lah di-katakan hampir-hampir luput bangsa-nya itu; bahkan, di-dalam negeri Pahang telah di-dapati kenyataan daripada pembanchi-pembanchi (T.M. 1921), ada-lah bangsa itu sa-banyak 50 orang sahaja tinggal-nya lagi…."

25 "Sa-sunggoh-nya ada-lah sakalian mereka yang tersebut itu Melayu belaka asal daging darah-nya; tetapi sudah mereka itu berbahasa sendiri dan beradat sendiri lain daripada bahasa dan adat Melayu, kerana tersangat-lah mereka berchampor dengan bangsa-bangsa asing iaitu Hindi, dan lain-lain. Maka pada masa sekarang telah meriak-riak-lah bangsa mereka itu pada sa-luroh Alam Melayu dan Pulau-Pulau Melayu: ia-itu di-Semenanjong Tanah Melayu, Pulau Percha, Tanah Jawa, Pulau-Pulau Sunda Kechil, pantai Tanah Bugis, pantai Pulau Berunai dan Pulau-Pulau Filipina pun juga."

26 "Bermula, ada pun di-Pulau Percha itu baharu-lah sahaja menjadi-nya bangsa Melayu yang ada sekarang ini; dan tersangat-lah pula mereka berdamping dengan lain-lain bangsa, ia-itu bangsa Hindu dan bangsa-bangsa yang terdahulu mendiami Pulau Sumatera dan Pulau Berunai serta pulau yang lain-lain juga. Bahkan bangsa Melayu itu dari zaman purba kala pun sudah menjadi bangsa champoran, ia-itu sama sa-olah-olah-nya saperti orang Inggeris juga."

27 "Sa-sunggoh-nya daripada perchamporan lain-lain bangsa (terutama orang Hindu) dengan beneh pancharan nenek moyang orang Melayu itu-lah telah jadi-nya bangsa Melayu yang ada sekarang ini, ia-itu yang memenohi jadi pendudok-pendudok merata-rata Alam Melayu."

28 I am indebted to James T. Collins for his explanation about the different meanings of the terms *alam* and *dunia*.

29 For his discussion of the role of the Spanish in the formation of the concept of the Malay world, Ismail largely depends on the work of Zeus A. Salazar, a pan-Malayist Filipino scholar. See Salazar [1998], a collection of his early writings on pan-Malay unity.

30 Interestingly, the British Borneo territories of Brunei, Sarawak and Sabah were described in this chapter along with the Dutch-ruled southern part of Borneo

Island (*Pulau Borneo*) (Winstedt 1926 [1918]: 174–180), although the table of
contents lists these states in the eleventh chapter.

31 For discussion of the British origins of the Peninsula-centric view, see Reid (2004).

32 Sultan Iskandar Dzu'l-Karnain's visit to Hindustan (B.C. 327); the birth of the
Prophet Isa (A.D. 1); the birth of the Prophet Muhammad (569); the passing away
of the Prophet Muhammad (632); the establishment of a Buddhist chandi by the
Maharaja of Palembang (775); Khalifah Harun a'r-Rashid's reign in Baghdad
(786-809); Ibn Khordadzbeh's visit to Kedah state (846); the tribute by the Raja of
Palembang to the Emperor of China (905); the passing away of the Raja of Pasai,
the first Malay king who converted to Islam (1297); the ascendancy of Majapahit
in most areas of the Malay Archipelago (1350?);the establishment of the Kingdom
of Melaka and the conversion of the Raja to Islam in the following years (1400); the
making of gravestones in Pasai, Gerisik and Beruas by craftsmen from Hindustan
(1409); the invention of type printing in Europe (1450); the Turkish conquest of
the eastern Roman Empire (1453); the defeat of Majapahit by a Muslim kingdom
in Java (1478); the coming of the Portuguese to Melaka (1509); the Portuguese
conquest of Melaka (1511); the coming of the British to Penang (1591); the coming
of the Dutch to Java (1596); the establishment of the British East India Company
(1600); the production of *Sulalatu's-Salatin* or *Sejarah Melayu* (1612); the Dutch
East India Company's conquest of Melaka from the Portuguese (1641); the end
of the royal lineage of Melaka as a result of the assassination of Sultan Mahmud
Shah II (1699); the instalment of Raja Melewar as Yang di-Pertuan of Negeri
Sembilan (1773); the lease of Penang from the Sultan of Kedah by the British
East India Company (1786); the cession of Singapore to the British East India
Company (1819); the first railway transport in Britain and the first voyage with a
steamship to Hindustan (1825); and the opening of Suez Canal (1869) (Winstedt
1927: 122–137).

33 Anderson borrows this idea of "homogeneous, empty time" from Walter Benjamin.

34 "Maka sebab pun di-katakan mereka itu-lah yang asli mendiami Tanah (dan juga
Pulau-Pulau) Melayu ini, ia-lah kerana jikalau sa-kira-nya orang Melayu telah
sedia ada mendiami di-sini terdahulu dari-pada mereka itu, betapa pula dapat
dan boleh di-datangi kemudian oleh bangsa-bangsa yang lemah lagi bebal itu?
Kerana orang Melayu ini tentu-lah terlebeh cherdek dan maju serta terlebeh
pandai berikhtiar melawan serangan musoh dari-pada orang bangsa Semang yang
liar dan sentiasa takut akan manusia itu."

35 "Maka tiada-lah pernah orang-orang liar itu berkampong kekal, atau berumah
yang tetap, dan tiada-lah ia tahu mengorek tali ayer dan berbuat sawah padi saperti
manusia yang telah keluar dari-pada sempadan keliaran, ada-nya."

36 "Sunggoh pun demikian jika kita tilek pada beberapa keadaan dan susok baka
mereka itu, ada-lah berlainan juga daripada Orang Liar yang telah lalu kesah-nya
itu. Kerana sa-sunggoh-nya ada-lah nenek moyang orang Melayu itu berusaha
pada membuat kampong halaman dan bersawah padi serta tahu bertukang besi."

37 "Maka bangsa Jakun yang tersebut ini sa-bangsa-lah dengan orang Kubu dalam
Pulau Percha, orang Kalang di-Tanah Jawa, orang Bajau yang mendiami pada
sa-genap telok dan suak Pulau Berunai; dan dengan orang yang mendiami di-
Pulau Filipina ia-itu orang Bontok dan Igorot (Melayu Liar) serta orang Tagalog,
Pampango dan Bisaya (Melayu Jinak) ada-nya."

38 For Tylor's contribution to evolutionary anthropology, see Stocking (1982: chaps. 4 & 5).

39 Both spellings "civilization" and "civilisation" are used in the 1923 edition of the book.

40 The thirteen chapters in the 1923 edition of *A History of the Peninsular Malays with Chapters on Perak & Selangor* are titled: 1. The Peninsular Aborigines; 2. The Proto-Malay; 3. Early Peninsular Civilization; 4. The Coming of the Malays; 5. The Malacca Sultanate; 6. The Portuguese Ascendancy; 7. The Dutch Ascendancy; 8. Singapore, Johore and Muar; 9. Early Perak History; 10. Larut; 11. The Pangkor Treaty; 12. The Perak War and 13. Selangor.

41 *Kitab Tawarikh Melayu* has eight chapters: 1. The Orang Asli living in Malaya, namely, the Orang Liar (*Orang Asli Mendiami Tanah Melayu, iaitu Orang Liar*); 2. The Proto Malays (*Orang Melayu yang Asli*); 3. The Coming of the Sumatrans (*Kedatang[an] Orang Sumatera*); 4. The Conversion of the Malays to Islam (*Orang Melayu Masok Ugama Islam*); 5. The Malay Kingdom in Melaka (*Kerajaan Melayu di Melaka*); 6. The Coming of the Portuguese (*Kedatangan Orang Portugis*); 7. The Coming of the Dutch (*Kedatangan Orang Belanda*) and 8. The Coming of the British (*Kedatangan Orang Inggeris*). The book also contains two appendices, "Conversion between the Muslim Year and the Gregorian Year" (*Menukar-nukarkan Tahun Hijrat dan Tahun Masehi*) and "Chronological Table" (*Daftar Tawarikh*). The coming of Indian civilization is discussed in chapter 2.

42 The three volumes of Abdul Hadi's *Sejarah Alam Melayu* have twelve chapters: Volume I – 1. The Orang Liar or the Orang Asli, that is, the Semang and the Sakai: the Original Inhabitants in Malaya (*Orang Liar atau Orang Asli ia-itu Semang dan Sakai, ia-lah Pendudok yang asli di-Tanah Melayu*); 2. The Proto Malays: Ancestors of the Malays *(Orang Melayu Asli, ia-lah Nenek Moyong Orang Melayu)*; 3. The Influx of the Sumatrans into Malaya (*Tumpuan Orang Sumatera ka-Tanah Melayu*) and 4. The Influx of Hindus into the Malay World and the Power of Hindu Kingdoms in Java (*Tumpuan Orang-orang Hindu ka-Alam Melayu, dan Kuasa Kerajaan Hindu di-Tanah Jawa*). Volume II – 5. The Coming of Hinduism to the Malay World (*Kedatangan Ugama Hindu ka-Alam Melayu*); 6. The Coming of Islam to the Malay World (*Kedatangan Ugama Islam ka-Alam Melayu*); 7. The Siamese Settling Down and Holding Power in Malaya (*Orang-orang Siam Mendudoki dan Berkuasa di-Tanah Melayu*) and 8. Malay Sultanates in Malaya: (1) Singapore, (2) Melaka, and (3) Johor (*Kerajaan-kerajaan Melayu di-Tanah Melayu, ia-itu (1) Singapura, (2) Melaka, (3) Johor*). Volume III – 9. The Influx of the Chinese into the Malay World (*Tumpuan Orang Cina ka-Alam Melayu*); 10. The Coming of the Portuguese to the Malay World (*Kedatangan Orang-orang Portugis ka-Alam Melayu*); 11. The Coming of the Dutch to the Malay World (*Kedatangan Orang Belanda ka-Alam Melayu*) and 12. The Coming of the British to the Malay World (*Kedatangan Orang Inggeris ka-Alam Melayu*).

43 "Maka guru yang mula-mula datang memberi tiruan atau tuladan ka-pada orang Melayu berkenaan dengan perkara-perkara kemajuan dan tamaddun dan fikir-fikiran baharu yang tiada pada orang Melayu zaman itu ia-lah orang Hindu; khabar-nya mereka mulai datang itu pada kurun Masehi yang kedua (T.M. 200), tatkala Tanah Jawa sudah di-dudoki oleh orang Hindu itu."

44 "Maka ada pun orang Portugis itu sudah menjadi resmi bagi kaum-nya terlalu suka sa-kali pada mengembangkan ugama-nya (Masehi), dan menasihatkan orang-orang lain ugama dan lain-lain kaum supaya masok ka-pada ugama-nya: maka dengan sebab itu tersangat-lah menjadi kebenchian ka-pada orang-orang Islam akan dia."

45 "Maka bertambah-tambah pula bangat jatoh-nya kekuasa[a]n Portugis itu oleh sebab zalim dan bi'adab kelakuan segala jeragan dan kapitan-kapitan-nya, ia-itu hampir-hampir saperti perompak lanun dan penyamun...."

46 "Akan tetapi sa-kira-nya tiada di-dahului oleh ugama Islam kapada kebanyakan negeri-negeri Melayu, barangkali harus sakalian pendudok-pendudok yang di-Alam Melayu kita ini telah tertarek kapada ugama Nasrani (Keristian) ia-lah sa-umpama anak-anak negeri Filipina yang telah di-bawa oleh orang-orang Sepanyol kapada ugama Nasrani itu... Bahkan sa-sunggoh-nya ugama Islam itu-lah yang menjadi suatu galangan besar kapada orang-orang Portugis hendak menanam dan mengembangkan ugama Nasrani kapada anak-anak Melayu."

47 "Ada pun tujuan Kompeni Belanda itu pada mula-mula-nya bukan-lah saperti niat dan chita-chita orang Portugis dan orang Sepanyol; kerana Kompeni Belanda itu tiada-lah berhajat dari mula-mula-nya hendak mena'alokkan negeri dan mamashhorkan ugama Masehi, melainkan ia-nya perchuma hendak berniaga sahaja. Akan tetapi tentang perkara negeri-negeri Melayu kerap kali juga Kompeni Belanda itu kena menchampori; kerana raja-raja negeri itu ada yang menyekat dan ada yang meluluskan hasrat Kompeni itu."

48 "Maka sekarang tatkala orang-orang Jawa itu sudah beroleh kesenangan, mulai-lah berkurangan sudah kerajaan Belanda dari-pada menjalankan ikhtiar yang keras itu; dan perentah-nya pun lebeh kurang sama-lah dengan perentahan orang Inggeris juga, ada-nya."

49 For instance, he pointed out the weakness of the British East India Company in the seventeenth century compared with the Dutch East India Company (Abdul Hadi 1930 [1929]: 259–260, 270–272).

Chapter 5

1 According to Bachtiar Djamily's biography of Ibrahim, Ibrahim was not two years old but one year old when his parents divorced (Bachtiar 1985: 31–32).

2 "Guru saya mengajarkan semua wilayah dalam peta Gugusan Pulau Melayu itu adalah tanah air orang Melayu yang telah terbagi dibawah kekuasaan penjajah orang Putih..."

3 "Sehubungan dengan pelajaran ilmu alam/bumi inilah saya dan kawan saya sekolah berpendapat Peta Gugusan Pulau[2] Melayu itu adalah peta Tanah Ayer orang Melayu, yang dirasakan nama Melayu itu sebagai nama bangsa saya. Tambahan pula di dalam buku sejarah yang bernama Tawarikh Melayu, menjelaskan Kerajaan [*sic*] Melayu Sri Vidjaya dan kemudian jadi daerah Keradjaan Melaya [*sic*, Melayu?] Djawa Madjapahit."

4 *Cikgu* is Malay for "teacher".

5 His correct name is Abdul Rahman bin Mahyuddin.

6 "...maka saya sebagai seorang pelajar yang baru mengenal dan merasakan rasa kebangsaan setelah mendengar syarahan² yang diberikan oleh guru² Sejarah (Cik Gu [*sic*] Abdul Hadi bin Haji Hassan [*sic*], Cikgu Buyong bin Adil) dan Guru Ilmu Alam Cik Gu [*sic*] Abdul Rahman bin Haji Sahabuddin, Guru Ilmu Pertanian Cikgu Nordin bin Haji Harun dan syarahan² dari Cikgu Harun bin Mohd Amin, dan terutamanya syarahan daripada Cikgu Zainal Abidin bin Ahmad (Za'aba [*sic*])...."

7 "Pendek kata Tuan Dussek sebagai berbelah dua badannya iaitu sebelah Inggeris dan sebelah Melayu. Sebab itu beliau tak lupa daripada menanamkan perasaan yang elok-elok pada penuntut Melayu, menyuruh orang Melayu kasih sayang akan bangsa, tanah air dan rajanya."

8 "Demikian juga dalam pelajaran Sejarah, kami mempelajari dari buku Tawarikh Melayu dan buku Sejarah Alam Melayu, selanjutnya di SITC Tanjung Malim yang menjadi pelajaran sejarah pokok ialah mengenai sejarah Alam Melayu iaitu sejarah² yang berkenaan dengan zaman Sri Vijaya, Majapahit, dan perkembangan ugama Islam keseluruh Gugusan Pulau² Melayu (Malay Archipelago) yakni Sumatera, Jawa, Borneo (Kalimantan), Celebes (Sulawesi), Kepulauan Maluku sampai ke Papua, Kepulauan Sunda Kecil serta Kepulauan Filipina."

9 According to William R. Roff, in 1930, a society named Belia Malaya (Young Malaya) was formed by Ibrahim and other SITC students (Roff 1994 (1967): 222, 225). The relationship between Belia Malaya and Ikatan Semenanjung/Borneo is not clear.

10 Note that "Malays" of non-Peninsular origin could be found not only among radical nationalists but also among traditional leaders such as sultans and aristocrats.

11 Due to the absence of documents about the KMM, Abd. Malek's argument is primarily based on in-depth interviews with former KMM members. My account of the KMM is indebted to his academic exercise.

12 Ramlah Adam, however, questions the credibility of Abd. Malek's accounts, arguing that he depends too much on weak oral evidence about what happened thirty years ago (Ramlah 2004a: 17).

13 According to Ibrahim, the second part of the book was seized by the Criminal Intelligence Department in Singapore and thus could not be published (Ibrahim 1975[1941]: 12). I am sincerely grateful to Cheah Boon Kheng for making the first edition of the book available to me.

14 Ibrahim referred to the role of Sutan Djenain, a former Partai Komunis Indonesia (PKI) (Communist Party of Indonesia) and an active MCP member, to relate the KMM to the MCP (Ibrahim 1957: 25–26). Moreover, in an interview with Nagai Shin'ichi, Ibrahim claimed to be acquainted with some Malay communists including Musa Ahmad, Abdullah C. D., Rashid Maidin, Shamsiah Fakeh and Mokhtaruddin Lasso (Nagai 1978: 59). But, it should be added that before the Pacific War, some of them, like Abdullah C.D. and Shamsiah Fakeh, were still teenagers and were not members of the MCP (Abdullah 2005; Shamsiah 2004).

15 For further details about his connection with the Japanese before the Pacific War, see Cheah (1979: 91–98) and Nagai (1978: 59–69).

16 According to Tsurumi Ken, however, he was not involved in this financial assistance. His guess is that a Japanese major, disguised as a consular officer, may have been made the transaction (Tsurumi 1981: 292)

17 The Japanese Army established the Fujiwara Kikan, or F Kikan in 1941 to contact and collaborate with local independence movements in Southeast Asia.

18 Milner points out that the word *sedar* is used constantly in Ibrahim's book *Melihat Tanah Air* (Milner 2002 [1995]: 264).

19 "Akan tetapi pihak bangsa-bangsa Melayu ia-itu anak bumi putera apa? Medan perniagaan-nya sa-makin halus hingga ta'kelihatan lagi di-dunia sekarang."

20 "Hai bangsa-ku majukan-lah perniagaan dan perusahaan bangsa sendiri buang-lah sifat malu membeli di-kedai-kedai bangsa sendiri walau pun sa-suku sen pertolongan yang sadikit amat berfaedah."

21 "Sebab-sebab menjadikan orang-orang saya berkeadaan tanah air ada serupa tidak, ialah oleh kerana kehidupannya terdesak. Maka yang mendesaknya itu ialah: (1) modal luar, (2) buruh daripada luar dengan bawaan modal luar, dan (3) barang-barang luar dengan bawaan modal dan buruh (kaum pekerja) daripada luar, iaitu untuk membuka negeri ini dengan seluas-luasnya dengan tidak menghiraukan hal kehidupan orang-orang saya (Melayu)."

22 Ibrahim pointed out that Malays tended to afford too much respect to Arabs, particularly those who had the title of "Syed." He suggested that Malays should regard Arabs on equal terms (*Majlis*, 14 April 1937). Though he categorized Arabs as an "other race" in his prewar articles, he does not seem to have rejected incorporating Arab and Indian Muslims into the category of "Malay" as did Abdul Rahim Kajai.

23 In prewar Malaya, the Malays, both radicals and conservatives, tented to regard "Malayan" as a term which referred only to "non-Malay" (Ariffin 1993: 98, 113, 194–196; Yamamoto 2006: 56).

24 "Pelajaran anak-anak Melayu umum tersangatlah rendahnya. Tamatnya dari sekolah Melayu tatkala berumur setinggi-tinggi empat belas tahun dan pada biasanya dua belas tahun. Fikirannya belum sempurna. Sebab itu sudah lepas daripada sekolah, baliklah ia semula seperti lama dengan berharapkan tanggungan ibu bapanya dan membiasakan malas...

25 "Saya sangat dukacita mendengarkan ada di antara orang-orang Melayu berkata, 'orang Melayu tak boleh maju kalau berugama Islam' ... Islam sekali-kali tidak menyekat kemajuan. Islam menyeru kepada kemajuan..."

26 The Malayan Civil Service started recruiting a limited number of qualified Malays in 1921. Only ten posts for Malays were created in the following decade (Roff 1994 [1967]: 109).

27 The term *dagang* means "trade" and "business" as well.

28 "Malaya ini sekarang sudah jadi rebutan benar di antara bangsa anak negeri (orang Melayu) dengan bangsa timur asing (iaitu Cina dan India), lima enam tahun ini tidak berputus-putusnya suara bangsa asing itu meminta hak seolah-olah tidak puas hati dengan pemerintah British yang selama-lamanya setia dengan raja-raja Melayu tetapi bangsa dagang yang tak bermalu dan tamak itu tidak jua mengerti terus menerus jua ... meminta pada barang yang tak patut bagi mereka."

29 "1. Supaya disamakan hak mereka dengan anak negeri di dalam bahagian pemerintahan. 2. Mereka hendak menjadikan bangsa Malayan di Malaya seolah-olah Melayu itu mahu dihapuskan. 3. Meminta tanah sawah. 4. Meminta buang tulisan Jawi. 5. Meminta sekolah-sekolah rendah di dalam bahasa mereka itu dengan belanja kerajaan."

30 Ramlah Adam also observes that Ibrahim did not express anti-colonial sentiments in his prewar works (Ramlah 1999: 46).

31 "…tetapi jangan lupa mestilah menghadapkan perasaan kasih sayang kita pada pemerintah agung iaitu British iaitu sebagai bapa angkat kita yang tempat kita sangat bermanja."

32 "Melayu Wajib Mempertahankan British Empayar"

33 The first State Council was established in Perak in 1877.

34 "1. Adakah ahli-ahli mesyuarat itu dipilih dengan menggunakan persetujuan undi rakyat umum? 2. Adakah sebenar-benarnya ahli mesyuarat itu orang yang tidak bersangkut paut dengan jawatan kerajaan? 3. Adakah sebenar-benar [*sic*] ahli mesyuarat itu daripada orang kebanyakan?"

35 On the changing status of "immigrant Malays" in Malaya, see Kahn (2006) and Tsuboi (2004).

36 "Orang-orang Melayu mempunyai semangat kebangsaan tetapi perasaan-perasaan itu telah menjadi berpecah belah oleh sebab ketiadaan anjuran dan ketiadaan urusan yang tertentu.

Sesungguhnya kita bolehlah mimpikan pada masa ini semangat kebangsaan Melayu itu masih kuat terpaku di dalam hati orang-orang kita, akan tetapi keadaan berpecah dan masih sempit, sebahagian daripadanya masih bernegeri-negerian, seumpama berperakan, berterengganuan, berkelantanan, bersumateraan, berjawaan, dan sebagainya."

37 "Sanya lebih dua milion orang-orang kita di Tanah Melayu. Lebih 60 milion lagi orang-orang kita Melayu di seluruh Gugusan Pulau-Pulau Melayu dan lebih dua milion orang-orang kita yang merantau di India, Ceylon, Afrika Selatan, China, Jepun, Siam dan lain-lainnya. Maka nyatalah bangsa kita Melayu tidak kurang daripada 65 milion jiwa maka nyatalah kita suatu bangsa yang ramai tetapi oleh lemah semangat kebangsaan, lemah pengalaman, lemah di atas serba serbinya bangsa Melayu telah menjadi satu bangsa yang corot dan berpecah belah kerana kebanyakan orang-orang kita hanyalah berkasih kepada puak-puak tidaklah kasih kepada bangsa…"

38 "…akan tetapi mulai sekarang orang-orang kita telah memulakan ikatan kasih kepada bangsa oleh itu dipercayai 65 milion bangsa Melayu akan bangun, iaitu bangun sebagai satu bangsa yang mempunyai tamadun dan kesopanan sekurang-kurangnya akan menjadi satu bangsa yang hidup di selatan Benua Asia hidup dengan tanah airnya."

39 "Di mana orang-orang saya – 'Alam Melayu' ertinya kawasan-kawasan pusaka bagi bangsa Melayu ialah Sumatera, Jawa, Selebes, Pulau Berunai, kumpulan Pulau Maluku, kumpulan Pulau Sunda Kecil dan kumpulan Pulau Filipina. Kawasan-kawasan ini telah ditukar dengan nama Indonesia. Dan Semenanjung Tanah Melayu telah digelar memang 'Malaya' pada masa ini. Maka semua tempat-tempat itulah yang dikatakan Alam Melayu."

40 "Perasaan Melayu Raya – sesungguhnya saya bolehlah memberi pandangan berkenaan dengan perasaan Melayu Raya. Pada masa yang akhir ini iaitu lepas daripada hampir-hampir lima ratus tahun lamanya mereka mengadap peperangan saudara hingga Semenanjung Tanah Melayu ini terbahagi kepada beberapa puak yang bernegeri-negeri dan berlawanan di antaranya sama sendiri, maka pada masa ini mulailah datang cita-cita hendak bersekutu semula. Bukannya sahaja

di antara umat-umat Melayu dua million setengah di Tanah Melayu ini, akan tetapi dengan umat-umat Melayu di Indonesia seramai 65 million itu. Mereka telah ingin hendak bersatu bekerjasama-sama. Tetapinya hal ini hanyalah satu perasaan sahaja baharukan dan sebahagian ramai daripada pihak kaum pertuanan dan darah-darah raja yang masih memegang teguh dengan perasaan lamanya itu tersangat-sangat menentang akan perasaan-perasaan baharu hendak mempersatukan umat-umat Melayu seumumnya itu."

41 A more detailed investigation of Ibrahim's thought and behavior during the Japanese occupation can be found in the work of Cheah Boon Kheng (1979; 2012 [1983]: chap. 4) and Nagai Shin'ichi (1978: chap. 2).

42 Ibrahim argued that they had demanded to build *Republik Malaya* (Republic of Malaya) (Agastja 1951: 95).

43 The Fujiwara Kikan was dissolved into the Iwakuro Kikan, headed by Colonel Iwakuro Hideo, which focused on liaising with Indian independence movements in Southeast Asia.

44 Itagaki refers to KRIS as "Kekuatan Rakyat Istimewa (The Special Strength of the People)" (Itagaki 1988 (1968): 163). Ibrahim, however, called it "Kesatuan Rakjat Indonesia Semenandjung (The Union of the Peninsular Indonesian People)" (Ibrahim 1957: 28). See also Cheah (1979: 111) and Nagai (1978: 79).

45 For details about the BPUPKI, see Muhammad Yamin (1959: Bahagian Kedua) and Anderson (1961: 16–32).

46 In Indonesia, the idea of greater Malay/Indonesian nation was always called *Indonesia Raya*, not *Melayu Raya*. For an examination of the conceptualization of *Indonesia Raya* in Indonesia, see McIntyre (1973) and Ahmat (2013: chap. 5).

47 The other nominees were Abd. Rahman of Johor, Abu Samah and Hussein Mohd. Taib of Pahang, and Raja Kamarulzaman of Perak.

48 Itagaki Yoichi stressed this point when I interviewed him in Tokyo on 26 April 1998.

49 The Kesatuan Malaya Merdeka and the Kesatuan Melayu Muda, which was formed by Ibahim and his friends in 1938, had the same initials "KMM."

50 In *Sekitar Malaya Merdeka*, Ibrahim noted that the Kesatuan Malaya Merdeka was established on 27 June 1950 (Ibrahim 1957: 55). However, he had referred to it in the Forward (*Pendahuluan*) of *Sedjarah dan Perdjuangan di Malaya*, which was dated 25 November 1948, although the book was not published until 1951 (Agastja 1951: 3).

51 A. Samad Ahmad notes that Rupert Emerson's *Malaysia: A Study of Direct and Indirect Rule* was one of the most important sources of Ibrahim's ideas (A. Samad Ahmad 1981: 111–112). Emerson used the term "Malaysia" as "a somewhat unfamiliar term embracing British Malaya and the Netherlands Indies, which are also known as Indonesia" (Emerson 1964 [1937]: 9), a formulation with obvious similarities to Ibrahim's *Melayu Raya* or *Indonesia Raya*. Emerson's *Malaysia* was cited in the political writing of another proponent of pan-Malay nationalism, Burhanuddin Al-Helmy (Burhanuddin 1980 [1946]: 46, 56).

52 "Saudara²! Menindjau kepada sedjarah tanah air, sesungguhnja sedjarah jang ditulis oleh orang² Eropah sendiri, mengaku akan kebenaran kesatuan daerah dan bangsa ini, bahkan didalam kitab Sedjarah Alam Melayu jang dikeluarkan

dengan resmi untuk peladjaran disekolah[2] pemerintah di Malaya Serie No.7 telah mendjelaskan, jaitu…"

53 "Adapun bumi putera jang berhak mewarisi Malaya itu sekarang ini ialah orang Melayu jang sama–bangsanja, bahasanja, sedjarahnja, daerahnja, dan kebudajaannja dengan bumi-putera Sumatera, Djawa, Kalimantan, Sulawesi, Sunda Ketjil, dan Maluku jang disebut bangsa Indonesia sekarang, dan sama pula dengan orang Melayu jang disebut bangsa Filipino jang menduduki Philippine sekarang, djadinja orang Melayu (Malays) bumi putera Malaya itu adalah bangsa Indonesia…"

54 "Saudara[2]! Siapakah orang Melayu dan apakah Malaya itu? Ini perlu didjelaskan, 'Perpisahan selama 127 tahun inilah jang menjebabkan bangsa Indonesia hampir lupa kepada saudara kandungnja sendiri di Malaya.' Sesungguhnja orang Melayu itu tidaklah lain daripada segerombolan saudara kandung bangsa Indonesia jang masih didjadjah oleh Inggeris. Sebabnja saja berani mengatakan begitu tepat; ialah karena Rupa bangsa (Ethnology) jakni keturunan darah dan kebudajaan hidup orang Melayu adalah bersamaan dengan orang[2] di Sumatera, Djawa, Kalimantan, Sulawesi, Maluku, Sunda Ketjil, dan lain[2]-nja itu, istimewa pula sedjarah, bahasa, kedudukan daerah bangsa dan nusa orang Melayu itu telah menentukan sendiri Malaya masuk kepada lingkungan Indonesia."

55 Although infrequently, Ibrahim used the term *ras* in his postwar writings published in Indonesia, where the term *ras* was more commonly used to mean "race" than in Malaya. This does not mean, however, that he no longer used the term *bangsa* to mean "race."

56 "Sesungguhnja kita tidak lupa, bahwa tidak ada bangsa didalam dunia ini jang bersih darahnja dari pertjampuran darah dari berbagai[2] bangsa. Bahkan asal timbulnja ras-Melayu sedjak 2500 tahun dahulu, adalah dari pertjampuran darah Dravida dan Mongol, kemudian bertjampur[2] lagi dengan darah orang Aria (Aryan) dan Semite jang datang ke Asia Tenggara ini, pertjampuran darah inilah jang melahirkan Malay-stock sekarang djadi dua bangsa, jaitu Indonesia dan Filipino, dalam hal ini orang[2] Melayu di Malaya dan Serawak [*sic*]/Brunei ada lebih hampir kepada Indonesia, dan mereka satu dengan bangsa Indonesia dalam segala hal."

57 "Tetapi, bagi bangsa Melayu di Malaya tetap merasa, Indonesia adalah sebahagian daripada bangsanja, disekolah[2] rakjat menjebut Kepulauan ini dengan nama Alam Melayu atau Kepulauan Melayu (Malay-Archipelago), buku[2] Sedjarahnja disebut 'Sedjarah Alam Melayu' artinja sedjarah Indonesia. Dan didalam définisi bangsa Melayu jang dipakai di Malaya sebelum tahun 1945 dahulu ialah: 'Orang bangsa Melayu itu ialah orang[2] berasal keturunan penduduk aseli di Negeri[2] Melayu (Malaya) dan Pulau[2] Melayu (Indonesia) jang beragama Islam.' Orang ini mendjadi rakjat kepada Sultan Melayu dinegeri mana orang itu bertempat tinggal…"

58 "Malaya dan Serawak [*sic*]/Brunei jang berkedudukan diantara Sumatera dengan Kalimantan; adalah merupakan duduk ditengah[2] bahagian utara Indonesia sekarang, hingga garis perbatasan utara Indonesia jang seharusnja lurus dari Sabang ke Pulau Laut terus ke Pulau Miangas di utara Pulau Halmahera itu terpaksa djadi bersiku[2] merupakan satu huruf 'W' digaris perbatasan Indonesia (Lihat peta jang terlampir).

Dari itu njatalah bahwa daerah Negeri[2] Melayu itu masuk kepada daerah Indonesia, bahkan kedudukan jang sangat penting bagi Indonesia, terutamanja

Malaya jang memliki sebahagian dari Selat Malaka jang duduknja betul[2] dimuka pintu besar Indonesia, hingga dalam arti kedudukan alamnja; belumlah sempurna kemerdekaan Indonesia, selama siku[2] huruf 'W' itu tidak dihapuskan dari garis perbatasannja, jakni selama Negeri[2] Melayu itu dikuasai oleh kuasa asing, berartilah belum sempurna kemerdekaannja, karena masih ada daerah Indonesia jang didjadjah."

59 The book has six chapters: 1. Malaya in previous centuries; 2. British despotism in Malaya; 3. Malay nationalist movement; 4. Malaya during the Japanese Occupation; 5. The British return to Malaya; and 6. The incorporation of Malaya into *Indonesia Raya*.

60 The book contains eight chapters: 1. The desire of the Malay race; 2. History of the relation of the homeland and the race; 3. History of the split between the Malay states; 4. The oppression by the British colonizers; 5. The national rights of the Malays were divided; 6. The Malays defended their national rights; 7. Towards the unity of the race; and 8. Malaya as an important corner of Asia.

61 The four chapters of the book are: 1. At a stage of independence; 2. Malayan independence movement (1); 3. Malayan independence movement (2); and 4. Malaya: today and future.

62 As noted in chapter 4, both terms *alam* and *dunia* can be translated as "the world" in English, but *dunia*, which originally means "the present world" (as an antonym of *akhirat*, or "the next world"), connotes "the human world" while *alam* implies the "natural" or "geographical" world.

63 "Adapun aliran Sedjarah dunia-Melayu (Malaynesia) atau Indonesia ini, dapat dibahagikan kepada tiga Djaman, jaitu:

    1. Djaman pertumbuhan bangsa di Asia Tenggara mulai 500 B.M. sampai tahun 500 M. mengambil k.l. 1000 tahun.

    2. Djaman perkembangan dan kekuasaan jang gilang-gemilang diantara tahun 500 M. mulai dari Tarumanagara; ke Sri-Vidjaja; masuk ke Madjapahit, berachir dengan Melaka tahun 1511 M.

    3. Djaman Pendjadjahan jang sudah masuk kepada 4 abad lamanja ini; jaitu 'Djaman kedjatuhan.'

    Setelah melewati tiga djaman tersebut, maka mulai bulan Agustus 1945, Lampiran Sedjarah baru mulai dibuka untuk Sedjarah bangsa dan nusa di Asia Tenggara ini."

64 A similar periodization can be found in Burhanuddin Al Helmy's writing on Malay history (Burhanuddin 1980 [1946]; Ariffin 1993: 41).

Chapter 6

1 On thoughts and behavior of the leaders of the PKMM in general, see Ariffin (1993), Firdaus (1985), Ramlah (1994, 1996, 2004a), Stockwell (1979), and Aljunied (2015).

2 According to Stockwell, Mokhtaruddin withdrew to Indonesia because he had been suspected of Trotskyite inclinations. After his resignation, the leading Stalinists including Rashid Maidin, Abdullah C. D. and Wahi Anwar remained (Stockwell 1979: 137).

3 " 1. Malaya adalah sebahagian dari Indonesia.
  2. Sang Saka Merah Puteh jadi cogan lambang Kebangsaan.
  3. Bersetuju kepada sebuah Kesatuan Malaya.
  4. Berbaik-baik dengan segala bangsa-bangsa yang tinggal di Malaya. "

4 It is not clear why they chose the term *bangsa Malaya*, rather than *bangsa Melayu* or *bangsa Malayu*. Ariffin Omar and Firdaus Abdullah translate it as "the *bangsa Melayu* (Malay race)" and "the Malay nation (*bangsa Melayu*)" respectively (Ariffin 1993: 38; Firdaus 1985: 79). They may consider that the term was misspelled. Khoo Kay Kim, however, translates the same term as "the Malayan races" (Khoo Kay Kim 1991: 268). He regards the *bangsa* as plural. Ramlah Adam interprets it not as a misspelling but as one of the signs which reveals that the PKMM was no longer a party for Malays but for the *bangsa Malayan* under the influence of the Malayan Communist Party (MCP) (Ramlah 1994: 79–83). Nevertheless, we should be cautious about equating the term *bangsa Malaya* with *bangsa Malayan*, recalling that the latter term referred mainly to non-Malay residents in Malaya, and had negative connotations for Malay nationalists like Burhanuddin (Burhanuddin 1980 [1954]: 105–109).

5 " 1. Mempersatu padukan [*sic*] bangsa Malaya [*sic*] menanamkan semangat kebangsaan dalam sonubari [*sic*] orang[2] Malayu [*sic*] dan bertujuan untuk menytukan [*sic*] Malaya, di dalam kaluarga [*sic*] yang besar yaitu Republic Indonesia Raya.
  [...]
  7. Party [*sic*] Kebangsaan Malayu handak [*sic*] bekerja sama dengan lain[2] bangsa yang tingal [*sic*] dalam nagrinya [*sic*] ini hidup dengan berbaik[2] dan bekerja untok mendirikan perpaduan pendudok[2] Malaya (Malayan United Front) bagai menjadikan Malayan Merdeka makmor dan bahagia sebagai satu anggota Republic Indonesia Raya.
  8. Menyokong gerakan ummat Indonesia dalam perjuangan mereka merebot kemerdekaan."

6 "I. Meninggikan tarap [*sic*] bangsa Malayu sehingga setarap dengan bangsa[2] lain di dunia.
  II. Menggabongkan Malaya dengan Indonesia.
  III. Mendirikan Republic Malaya sebagai satu anggota dari pada [*sic*] Republic Indonesia Raya."

7 Tunku Abdul Rahman was born in 1903 in Alor Setar, Kedah. The Tunku was the twentieth child of Sultan Abdul Hamid Halim Shah of Kedah. He was educated at a Malay school and an English school in Kedah before being sent to Bangkok to further his studies. After returning to Malaya in 1915, he continued his studies at Penang Free School. He went to England in 1920, where he earned a Bachelor of Arts degree from St. Catherine's College, University of Cambridge in 1925. After a short stay in Kedah, he returned to England in 1926 to study Law at the Inner Temple. After failing the Bar examination in London he returned to Kedah in 1931, where he joined the Kedah Civil Service. During the Japanese occupation, he served as District Officer and later as Superintendent of Education. After the war, he returned to the Inner Temple and passed the Bar examination. Returning to Malaya in 1949, he was appointed Deputy Public Prosecutor in Kuala Lumpur and later President of the Selangor Sessions Court. After accepting the chairmanship

of the Kedah branch of the UMNO, he was elected as the second president of the party in 1951. He became the Chief Minister of the Federation of Malaya in 1955 and then the first Prime Minister of the Federation when the country became independent on 31 August 1957. The May 13 riots in 1969 made the Tunku's position untenable and he resigned his post in 1970 in favor of the then Deputy Prime Minister, Abdul Razak Hussein. During the 1970s, he served as head of the Islamic Secretariat in Saudi Arabia. He later entered journalism and became a major critic of the Mahathir administration in the 1980s. He died in 1990. For more details on his career, see Gill (1990), Sheppard (1995) and Ramlah (2004b).

8 There are many works dealing with the politics surrounding the formation of Malaysia. See, for instance, Simandjuntak (1969), Mohamed Noordin (1974), Mackie (1974), Ongkili (1985), Poulgrain (1998), Jones (2002), Tan (2008), and Suzuki (2017; 2018).

9 Before 1961, the proposals for political unification in the Malaysia region were also championed by some political leaders outside the Federation of Malaya, such as A.M. Azahari of Brunei, the Progressive Party of Singapore, and so on (Mohamed Noordin 1973: 722–725). Nevertheless, this study is necessarily limited to the proposals made by Malay leaders within the Federation of Malaya.

10 "Kita faham apa yang Ketua Menteri Singapura katakan itu, iaitu Singapura adalah sebuah pulau yang kecil, dari itu tentulah tidak layak hendak merdeka sendiri. Kiranya begitu, kita nampak lebih baik bagi Singapura minta masuk dalam Persekutuan Tanah Melayu menjadi sebuah kawasan dalam Persekutuan sebagaimana negeri-negeri yang lain. Begitu juga Brunei, Sarawak dan lain-lain jajahan dalam Borneo kiranya suka bercantum dengan Federation sangatlah baik."

11 According to the Oxford English Dictionary (second edition), the use of the term "Malaysian" as of "or belonging to Malaysia" could be traced to 1883 and its use as "[a] native or inhabitant of the Malay archipelago or of Malaysia" could be traced to 1625 (Simpson and Weiner 1989, vol. 10: 258). I acknowledge my debt to James T. Collins for his information on the origins of the term "Malaysia" and "Malaysian."

12 "Djadinja keinginan rakjat supaja mempersatukan Singapura dan bersatu dengan Brunei serta Serawak [*sic*] di Kalimantan Utara untuk melahirkan Persatuan Negara Malaysia belum tertjapai, malahan di-petjah[2] oleh Inggeris."

13 "…perdjuangan rakjat Malaya sampai kepada *satu anak tangga* kemerdekaan jang masih banjak anak[2] Malaysia – termasuk Singapura jang masih didjadjah, begitu pula wilajah[2] Malaysia jang lain[2], jaitu Brunei, Babah [*sic*, Sabah] (British North Borneo), dan Serawak [*sic*] masih dibawah kekuasaan pendjadjah…" [Original Italics].

14 My interview with Muhammad Ghazali Shafie on 23 October 1998 in Kuala Lumpur.

15 In the 1960s, members of Parliament were permitted to speak either Malay or English during parliamentary debates. Tunku Abdul Rahman spoke English during debates on the Malaysia proposal.

16 "Kedudukan alam Negeri-negeri Tanah Melayu, Brunei, Sarawak dan Sabah itu tuan-tuan akan dapat lihat seperti bulan sabit atau *crescent*, jadi sangatlah munasabahnya Tanah Melayu dan negeri-negeri Borneo itu disifatkan sebagai bulan yang baharu timbul dalam alam dunia ini, maka jadilah kelak Malaysia

yang kita cadangkan itu berbentuk pada segi alamnya seperti lambang bulan, iaitu satu-satunya lambang keagungan Islam.

Dari segi yang lain pula, percantuman negeri-negeri Singapura dan Borneo itu memanglah patut dan munasabah kerana negeri kita dan negeri-negeri yang tersebut itu mempunyai penduduk-penduduk yang sama – mereka adalah saudara sedarah daging dan seketurunan dengan kita. Mereka menggunakan sistem atau cara pemerintahan yang sama dengan kita, dan mereka menggunakan wang ringgit yang sama dengan kita. Pendek kata, tidaklah ada perkara yang berlainan di antara kita dengan negeri-negeri itu."

17 "Sebagaimana yang telah saya katakan dalam parlimen, tujuan dan cita-cita kita ialah hendak mengadakan persatuan atau gabungan negeri-negeri yang dinamakan Persekutuan Melayu Raya atau Malaysia Raya, iaitu negeri-negeri yang sekarang dalam Persekutuan Tanah Melayu dan negeri-negeri di Borneo bercantum dalam satu Persekutuan yang sama taraf.

Di bawah konsep Malaysia ini, tidak ada negeri yang menjadi tanah jajahan, dan Persekutuan Tanah Melayu yang ada sekarang ini pun akan hilang kerana tempatnya digantikan dengan sebuah negera Melayu Raya atau Malaysia Merdeka."

18 Burhanuddin Al-Helmy, whose real name was Burhanuddin Haji Mohammad Noor, was born in Kampung Cangkat Tualang, Perak, in 1911. His father, an Islamic religious teacher, was of Minangkabau origin while his mother was of Arab descent. Burhanuddin was educated at several Malay schools in Perak and Madrasah al-Mashoor, Penang, as well as at an English school. He later studied philosophy and literature at Aligarh University in Northern India. He also earned a degree in homeopathy from the Ismaileah Medical College at Hyderabad, India. He taught Arabic at Madrasah al-Junid in Singapore, worked as a journalist, and practiced as a homoeopath. He was a leader of the KMM in Singapore. He was detained by the British just before the outbreak of the Pacific War in 1941 on suspicion of pro-Japanese activities. During the Japanese occupation, he served as an advisor on Malay customs and culture to the Japanese Command Centre in Taiping, Perak, and later assumed leadership of the KRIS. In 1946 he became the second president of the PKMM and encouraged the AMCJA-PUTERA coalition. He was detained by the British in 1950 for his involvement in the Nadrah (Maria Hertogh) affair. He supported the establishment of the Partai Rakyat Malaya (PRM) in 1955 though he did not become a member of the party. Later he joined the PAS, becoming president in 1956, and was elected to parliament in 1959. In 1964 he was condemned for involvement in prohibited commercial activities and, as a result, lost his seat in parliament. He was detained again in 1965 on a charge of collaboration with the Indonesian authorities. He died in 1969. For a more detailed account of Burhanuddin Al-Helmy, see Ramlah (1996) and Farish (2004, vol. 1).

19 While Burhanuddin used both terms *Melayu Raya* and *Indonesia Raya* to mean the Malay Archipelago in his writing of 1946, he referred to the same territory only as *Melayu Raya* in his book published in 1954. As previously dsicussed, the PKMM officially promoted the idea of *Indonesia Raya* in 1946. Using the term *Indonesia Raya* in 1954, however, would have resulted in his being labelled as anti-British and "pro-Indonesian."

20 "Dato' Yang di-Pertua, saya sukachita benar dengan usul yang dibawa oleh Yang Teramat Mulia Perdana Menteri kita dalam membahathkan usul nama Melayu Raya. Saya sukachita ia-lah kerana yang sa-benar-nya saya telah lama memperjuangkan Melayu Raya ini—dan sekarang baharu timbul di-bahathkan dengan chara terbuka dan berbesar²an."

21 "Bahawa Majlis ini dengan bersetuju pada dasar-nya dengan chadangan hendak menubohkan Melayu Raya mengandongi sabelas negeri dalam Persekutuan Tanah Melayu, Singapura dan Brunai [*sic*] dan Borneo Utara dan Sarawak, dan Negera Republik Indonesia dan Filipina serta gugusan Pulau² Melayu yang lain, dan menuntut supaya Kerajaan berusaha pada menjalankan langkah² untok menchapai tujuan ini, dan sa-banyak mana telah di-jalankan langkah itu akan di-ma'alumkan kapada Majlis ini oleh Yang Berhormat Perdana Menteri dari satu masa ka-satu masa."

22 "Bahawa Dewan ini mengambil ketetapan oleh kerana Melayu Raya itu pada dasar-nya ia-lah Gugusan Pulau² Melayu, hendak-lah di-masokkan di-dalam Ranchangan Melayu Raya itu, daerah² Indonesia dan Pilipina dan hendak-lah Perdana Menteri membuat rundingan² awal dengan pehak² negara² Indonesia dan Pilipina bagi mengujudkan Kesatuan Melayu Raya itu."

23 Ahmad Boestamam, whose real name was Abdullah Thani (Abdullah Sani) Raja Kechil, was born in Kampung Behrang Ulu, Tanjung Malim, Perak, in 1920. His father was of Minangkabau origin. Boestamam attended a Malay school and then the English-medium Anderson School, Ipoh, Perak. Before the war, he worked as a journalist for several Malay newspapers and joined the KMM as Assistant Secretary-General. He was detained by the British in 1941 for alleged involvement in a pro-Japanese youth movement. During the Japanese occupation, he worked as a censorship officer in the Propaganda Department (*Sendenka*) in Ipoh. After the war, he became a founding member of the PKMM in 1945 and established its youth wing, API, the following year. He was detained by the British again from 1948 to 1955 on suspicion of his connection with the Malayan Communist Party. He founded the Partai Rakyat Malaya (PRM) and became its president in 1955. He led the Socialist Front (SF), a coalition between the PRM and the Labour Party of Malaya, in the general election of 1959 and was elected as a Member of Parliament from Setapak, Selangor. During the Indonesian Confrontation with Malaysia, he was detained by the Malayan government in 1963 for alleged subversive activities. After release from detention, he resigned from the PRM and established a new party, Parti Marhaen, which later merged with the Parti Keadilan Masyarakat (PEKEMAS). He retired from party politics in 1978 and died in 1983. For his biographical details, see Ramlah (1994) and Ahmad Boestamam (2004 [1972]; 2004 [1983]).

24 "Tuan Yang di-Pertua, menurut anggapan saya Malaysia yang dichadangkan oleh Tunku Abdul Rahman itu bukan Melayu Raya…. Melayu Raya meliputi seluroh negeri dalam Gugusan Pulau² Melayu. Jadi, salah kalau kita mengatakan Malaysia sa-rupa dengan Melayu Raya. Malaysia ada-lah Malaysia, dan Melayu Raya ada-lah lain. Kalau ranchangan Malaysia yang di-bawa oleh Yang Berhormat Perdana Menteri, dan yang hendak kita terima pada prinsip-nya ini, satu jalan menuju kapada Melayu Raya, satu jalan menuju kapada Malaysia Raya, saya menyokong."

25 "Tuan Yang di-Pertua, kalau Malaysia merupakan langkah pertama menuju kapada Malaysia Raya, saya, Tuan Yang di-Pertua, memberi sokongan yang sa-penoh-nya kapada ranchangan ini. Akan tetapi, kalau Malaysia mempunyai tujuan hendak bersaing dengan Indonesia, hendak menjadi alat kapada kepentingan[2] Inggeris di-daerah itu, maka kami, Tuan Yang di-Pertua, terpaksa menentang chadangan ini."

Chapter 7

1 For details on cultural forms of pan-Malayism, see Roslan (2009: chap. 6).
2 Singapore is a non-member observer.
3 For a detailed analysis of GAPENA's *Dunia Melayu* movement, see Tomizawa (2010).
4 Both Ismail Hussein and Abdul Latiff Abu Bakar taught at the Universiti Malaya's Jabatan Pengajian Melayu (Department of Malay Studies), which was incorporated into Akademi Pengajian Melayu (APM) in 1995. Between 1987 and 1993, Ismail was the Director of Institut Bahasa, Kesusasteraan dan Kebudayaan Melayu (IBKKM) (Institute of the Malay Language, Literature and Culture), which became Institut Alam dan Tamadun Melayu (ATMA) in 1993.
5 My interview with Abdul Latiff Abu Bakar on 18 November 2016 in Melaka.
6 Malays and natives of Sabah and Sarawak are granted special status in the Federal Constitution of Malaysia.
7 As early as March 1947, Persidangan Agung Ekonomi-Agama Se-Malaya (All-Malaya Grand Conference on Economics and Religion) was held at a religious school Maahad Il Ihya Assyarif Gunung Semanggol (MIAGUS) on the initiative of the PKMM. During the conference, Pusat Perekonomian Melayu Se-Malaya (PEPERMAS) (All-Malaya Malay Economic Bureau) was established. This conference can be seen as a predecessor to the Kongres Ekonomi Bumiputera in the 1960s. For details of the conference, see Nabir (1976: 110–129), Firdaus (1985: 36–47) and Hara (1997).
8 For more detailed discussion of ethnic and national identity in contemporary Malaysia, see Shamsul (1996a; 1996b; 1996c; 1999; 2004), Ariffin (2011), Milner and Ting (2014), and Ting (2014b).
9 For a detailed and insightful discussion on the "1Malaysia" concept, see Milner and Ting (2014).
10 Abdul Rahman Embong analyzes the perceptions and interpretations of *Melayu Baru*, as understood and defined by a small sample of Malay middle-class informants that he interviewed (Abdul Rahman Embong 2002: chap. 9).

Bibliography

Unpublished Official Records

CO 273 Straits Settlements: Original Correspondence (microfilm copy).
    CO 273/671/50790 Malayan Campaign: Malayan Campaign: Attitude of Local Population (Fifth Column Allegations), 1943.
    CO 273/669/50774/7 War – Japan: Conditions in the Enemy Occupied Malayan Territory, 1942–1943.
CO 537 Colonies (General): Supplementary Original Correspondence (microfilm copy)
    CO 537/4742 Malay Nationalist Party, 1948–1949.
CO 717 Federated Malay States Original Correspondence (microfilm copy).
    CO 717/53 Education in Malaya, 1926–1927.

(The Colonial Office records above were collected in the Arkib Negara Malaysia, Kuala Lumpur, the Universiti Kebangsaan Malaysia Library, Bangi, and the National University of Singapore Library, Singapore. They are also available on microfilm.)

Published Official Records

AREFMS *Annual Reports on Education in the Federated Malay States*, 1901–1903, 1905–1908, 1911, 1920–1938.
ARFMS. *Annual Reports, Federated Malay States*, 1921–1932.
Bretherton, E.H.S. 1931. *Memorandum on the Sultan Idris Training College and Malay Vernacular Education*. Singapore: Printers Limited.
Cmd. 3235 of 1928–1929. *Report by The Right Honourable W.G.A. Ormsby Gore, M.P. (Parliamentary Under-Secretary of State for the Colonies) on His Visit to Malaya, Ceylon, and Java during the Year 1928*. Parliamentary Papers, Great Britain.
Colonial Office. 1939. *Higher Education in Malaya: Report of the Commission appointed by the Secretary of State for the Colonies*. London: His Majesty's Stationery Office.
Education Code V, Regulations for the Malay Vernacular Schools in the Straits Settlements and Federated Malay States and for the Sultan Idris Training College, 1927. Singapore: Government Printing Office, 1927.
Education Code, Part V, Regulations for Malay Vernacular Education in the Straits

Settlements and Federated Malay States, 1936, second and revised edition. Singapore: Government Printing Office, 1937.

The Federation of Malaya Agreement 1948. 1948.

Federation of Malaya. 1962a. *Malayan Constitutional Documents,* second edition, volume one. Kuala Lumpur: The Government Press.

Federation of Malaya. 1962b. *Report of the Commission of Enquiry, North Borneo and Sarawak.*

Malaysia. 1963a. *Malaya/Indonesia Relations, 31ˢᵗ August 1957 to 15ᵗʰ September 1963.* Kuala Lumpur: Jataban Cetak Kerajaan.

Malaysia. 1963b. *Malaya/Philippine Relations, 31ˢᵗ August 1957 to 15ᵗʰ September 1963.* Kuala Lumpur: Jataban Cetak Kerajaan.

Malaysia. 1965. *A Plot Exposed.* Kuala Lumpur: Jabatan Cetak Kerajaan.

Malaysia. 1971. *Second Malaysia Plan, 1971–1975.* Kuala Lumpur: The Government Press.

Nathan, J.E. 1922. *The Census of British Malaya, 1921.* London: Waterlow & Sons.

No. 22 of 1917. *Report by R.O. Winstedt, Asst. Director of Education S.S. and F.M.S. on Vernacular and Industrial Education in the Netherlands East Indies and the Philippines.* (Council Papers, Legislative Council, Straits Settlements)

PDDR. *Parliamentary Debates Dewan Ra'ayat,* 1961–1963.

Pountney, A.M. 1911 *The Census of the Federated Malay States, 1911.* London: Darling & Son.

Republic of Indonesia. n.d. *The Era of Confrontation.* Jakarta: Department of Information, Republic of Indonesia.

Republic of Indonesia. n.d. *The Malaysia Issue: Background and Documents.* Jakarta: Department of Information, Republic of Indonesia.

Vlieland, C.A. 1932 *British Malaya, A Report on the 1931 Census and on Certain Problems of Vital Statistics.* Westminster: The Crown Agents for the Colonies.

Wong, Francis H.K.; and Gwee Yee Hean, eds. 1980 *Official Reports on Education: Straits Settlements and the Federated Malay States, 1870–1939.* Singapore: Pan Pacific Book Distributors (S).

Unpublished Private Papers

Malaysia (Arkib Negara Malaysia, Kuala Lumpur)

UMNO/SG (UMNO/Secretary General)
   UMNO/SG No. 96/46

Malaysia (Perpustakaan Peringatan Za'ba, Universiti Malaya, Kuala Lumpur)

Ahmad Abdullah (Ahmad Bakhtiar). 1956. "Kenang²an di College Tanjong Malim." Typescript dated 1956.

Dussek, O.T. 1939. "Growing Points in Native Education: The Sultan Idris Training College." Typescript dated May 1939.

Mss. 176. Koleksi Ibrahim Yakob (The Ibrahim Yaacob Collection)

Mss. 176 (1). IBHY (Ibrahim Haji Yaacob). "Cherita Saya (Kesah Saya)." Typescript dated 19 August 1974.

Mss. 176 (2). Drs. Iskandar Kamel (IBHY). "Lambaian Merah Putih." Typescript (n.d., 1976 or 1977?).

Mss. 176 (3) a. Drs. Iskandar Kamel (IBHY). "Mengikuti Perjuangan Indonesia-Raya Merdeka: Sekitar Gema Cita-Cita Indonesia-Raya." Typescript dated 19 August 1971.

Mss. 176 (3) b. A letter from Drs. Iskandar Kamel (IBHY) to En. Mustapha Hussain, dated 20 May 1975.

Mss. 176 (3) c. "Takrif Melayu." Typescript (n.d.).

Mss. 176 (16). A letter from Drs. Iskandar Kamel [@ Ibrahim Haji Yaacob] to Asraf dated 5 December 1977.

Newspapers and Periodicals

Chenderamata, Tanjung Malim, 1928–1930.
Fajar Asia, Singapore, 1943.
Majallah Guru, Seremban, 1931.
Majlis, Kuala Lumpur, 1932–1939.
Semangat Asia, Singapore, 1943.
Warta Ahad, Singapore, 1936.
Warta Jenaka, Singapore, 1937.
Warta Negeri, Kuala Lumpur, 1930.

Books, Articles and Theses

English and Malay Sources

A. Samad Ahmad. 1981. *Sejambak Kenangan (Sebuah Autobiografi).* Kuala Lumpur: Dewan Bahasa dan Pustaka.

A. Samad Ismail. 1993. *Memoir A. Samad Ismail di Singapura.* Bangi: Penerbit Universiti Kebangsaan Malaysia.

Abd. Malek Hj. Md. Hanafiah. 1975. Sejarah Perjuangan Kesatuan Melayu Muda, 1937–1945. B.A. academic exercise, Universiti Kebangsaan Malaysia.

Abdul Hadi Haji Hasan. 1928a [1925]. *Sejarah Alam Melayu, penggal I.* Singapore: Fraser & Neave, Limited, Printers.

Abdul Hadi Haji Hasan. 1928b [1926]. *Sejarah Alam Melayu, penggal II.* Singapore: Fraser & Neave, Limited, Printers.

Abdul Hadi Haji Hasan. 1930 [1929]. *Sejarah Alam Melayu, penggal III.* Singapore: Printers Limited.

Abdul Latiff Abu Bakar. 1977. *Ishak Haji Muhammad: Penulis dan Ahli Politik sehingga 1948.* Kuala Lumpur: Penerbit Universiti Malaya.

Abdul Latiff Abu Bakar. 1981. Ibrahim Haji Yaacob: Kegelisahan dan Impian seorang Pejuang Melayu. In *Imej dan Cita-Cita: Kertas Kerja Hari Sastera 1980,* pp. 212–237. Kuala Lumpur: Dewan Bahasa dan Pustaka.

Abdul Latiff Abu Bakar. 1984. *Abdul Rahim Kajai: Wartawan dan Sasterawan Melayu*. Kuala Lumpur: Dewan Bahasa dan Pustaka.

Abdul Rahman Embong. 2002. *State-led Modernization and the New Middle Class in Malaysia*. Basingstoke and New York: Palgrave.

Abdul Rahman Embong. 2006 [2000]. *Negara Bangsa: Proses dan Perbahasan*, second edition. Bangi: Penerbit Universiti Kebangsaan Malaysia.

Abdul Rahman Haji Ismail. 1985. Takkan Melayu Hilang di Dunia: Suatu Sorotan Tentang Nasionalisme Melayu. In *Nasionalisme: Satu Tinjauan Sejarah*, edited by R. Suntharalingam and Abdul Rahman Haji Ismail, pp. 36–63. Petaling Jaya: Penerbit Fajar Bakti.

Abdul Rahman Haji Ismail. 1995. Nasionalisme Melayu dan Nasionalisme Melayu Setanah Melayu: Satu Perbincangan tentang Soal Pemulaannya. In *Isu-Isu Pensejarahan: Esei Penghargaan kepada Dr. R. Suntharalingam*, edited by Abu Talib Ahmad and Cheah Boon Kheng, pp. 163–192. Penang: Penerbit Universiti Sains Malaysia.

Abdul Rahman Haji Ismail. 2003. *Bumiputera*, Malays and Islam: A Historical Overview. *Kajian Malaysia* 21 (1&2): 105–121.

Abdul Rahman Haji Ismail. 2006. Bangsa: Ke Arah Ketepatan Makna dalam Membicarakan Nasionalisme Melayu. In *Nasionalisme dan Revolusi di Malaysia dan Indonesia: Pengamatan Sejarah*, edited by Abdul Rahman Haji Ismail, Azmi Ariffin and Nazarudin Zainun, pp. 1–14. Penang: Penerbit Universiti Sains Malaysia.

Abdul Rahman Haji Ismail and Badriyah Haji Salleh. 2003. History through the Eyes of the Malays: Changing Perspectives of Malaysia's Past. In *New Terrains in Southeast Asian History*, edited by Abu Talib Ahmad and Tan Liok Ee, pp. 168–198. Singapore: Singapore University Press.

Abdullah C.D. 2005. *Memoir Abdullah C.D.: Zaman Pergerakan sehingga 1948*. Petaling Jaya: Strategic Information Research Development.

Abdullah C.D. 2007. *Memoir Abdullah C.D. (Bahagian Kedua): Penaja dan Pemimpin Regimen Ke-10*. Petaling Jaya: Strategic Information Research Development.

Abdullah Hussain. 1982. *Harun Aminurrashid: Pembangkit Semangat Kebangsaan*. Kuala Lumpur: Dewan Bahasa dan Pustaka.

Abdullah Sanusi. 1966. *Peranan Pejabat Karang Mengarang: Dalam Bidang² Pelajaran Sekolah² Melayu dan Kesusasteraan Di-kalangan Orang Ramai*. Kuala Lumpur: Dewan Bahasa dan Pustaka.

Abu Talib Ahmad. 2003. *The Malay Muslims, Islam and the Rising Sun: 1941–1945*. Kuala Lumpur: Malaysian Branch of the Royal Asiatic Society.

Adnan Hj. Nawang. 1998. *Za'ba dan Melayu*, Kuala Lumpur: Berita Publishing.

Agastja, I.K. (pseudonym for Ibrahim Haji Yaacob). 1951. *Sedjarah dan Perdjuangan di Malaya*. Jogjakarta: Penerbit Nusantara.

Ahmad Boestamam. 1946. *Testament Politik A.P.I.* Kuala Lumpur: L.T. A.P.I. Malaya.

Ahmad Boestamam. 1972. *Dr. Burhanuddin: Putera Setia Melayu Raya*. Kuala Lumpur: Penerbitan Pustaka Kejora.

Ahmad Boestamam. 2004 [1972]. Merintis Jalan ke Puncak. In his *Memoir Ahmad Boestamam: Merdeka dengan Darah dalam Api*, pp. 113–249. Bangi: Penerbit Universiti Kebangsaan Malaysia.

Ahmad Boestamam. 2004 [1983]. Lambaian dari Puncak. In his *Memoir Ahmad*

Boestamam: Merdeka dengan Darah dalam Api, pp. 37–111. Bangi: Penerbit Universiti Kebangsaan Malaysia.

Ahmad Fauzi Abdul Hamid. 2011. Malay Racialism and the Sufi Alternative. In *Melayu: The Politics, Poetics and Paradoxes of Malayness*, edited by Maznah Mohamed and Syed Muhd. Khairudin Aljunied, pp. 68–100. Singapore: NUS Press.

Ahmat Adam. 2013. *Melayu, Nasionalisme Radikal dan Pembinaan Bangsa.* Kuala Lumpur: Penerbit Universiti Malaya.

Akashi, Yoji. 1969. Japanese Military Administration in Malaya: Its Formation and Evolution in Reference to Sultans, the Islamic Religion, and the Moslem-Malays, 1941–1945. *Asian Studies* 7(1): 81–110.

Akashi, Yoji. 1976. Education and Indoctrination Policy in Malaya and Singapore under the Japanese Rule, 1942–1945. *Malaysian Journal of Education* 13 (1/2): 1–46.

Akashi, Yoji. 1980. The Japanese Occupation of Malaya: Interruption or Transformation? In *Southeast Asia under Japanese Rule*, edited by Alfred McCoy, pp. 65–90. New Haven: Yale University Press.

Alatas, Syed Hussein. 1977. *The Myth of the Lazy Native: A Study of the Image of the Malays, Filipinos and Javanese from the 16th to 20th Century and Its Function in the Ideology of Colonial Capitalism.* London: Frank Cass.

Aljunied, Syed Muhd. Khairudin. 2009. British Discourses and Malay Identity in Colonial Singapore. *Indonesia and the Malay World* 37 (107): 1–22.

Aljunied, Syed Muhd. Khairudin. 2011. A Theory of Colonialism in the Malay World. *Postcolonial Studies* 14(1): 7–21.

Aljunied, Syed Muhd. Khairudin. 2015. *Radicals: Resistance and Protest in Colonial Malaya.* DeKalb: Northern Illinois University Press.

Amoroso, Donna J. 2014. *Traditionalism and the Ascendancy of the Malay Ruling Class in Colonial Malaya.* Petaling Jaya: Strategic Information and Research Development Centre.

Andaya, Leonard Y. 2004. The Search for the "Origins" of Melayu. In *Contesting Malayness: Malay Identity Across Boundaries*, edited by Timothy P. Barnard, pp. 56–75. Singapore: Singapore University Press.

Andaya, Leonard Y. 2008. *Leaves of the Same Tree: Trade and Ethnicity in the Straits of Malacca.* Honolulu: University of Hawai'i Press.

Andaya, Barbara Watson, and Andaya, Leonard Y. 2017 [1982]. *A History of Malaysia*, third edition. London: Palgrave.

Anderson, Benedict R. O'G. 1961. *Some Aspects of Indonesian Politics under the Japanese Occupation: 1944–1945.* Interim Report Series, Modern Indonesian Project, Southeast Asian Program, Department of Far Eastern Studies, Cornell University, Ithaca, New York.

Anderson, Benedict R. O'G. 1991 [1983]. *Imagined Communities: Reflections on the Origins and Spread of Nationalism*, second edition. London: Verso.

Arba'iyah Mohd Noor. 2009. Perkembangan Pendidikan Sejarah di Malaysia dari Zaman Tradisional ke Zaman Moden. *Sejarah* 17: 45–61.

Ariffin Omar. 1993. *Bangsa Melayu: Malay Concepts of Democracy and Community, 1945–1950.* Kuala Lumpur: Oxford University Press.

Ariffin Omar. 2003. Origins and Development of the Affirmative Policy in Malaya and Malaysia: A Historical Overview. *Kajian Malaysia* 21 (1&2): 13–29.

Athi Sivan Mariappan. 2005. Proses Pembentukan Bangsa Melayu: Beberapa Perbahasan dan Permasalahan. M.A. thesis, Universiti Kebangsaan Malaysia.

Awang Had Salleh. 1974. *Pelajaran dan Perguruan Melayu di Malaya Zaman British*. Kuala Lumpur: Dewan Bahasa dan Pustaka.

Awang Had Salleh. 1979 *Malay Secular Education and Teacher Training in British Malaya*. Kuala Lumpur: Dewan Bahasa dan Pustaka.

Azman Mamat. 1995. Ibrahim Yaakub dan Idea Kebangsaannya: Kajian terhadap Tulisan-Tulisannya dalam Akhbar Majlis. B.A. academic exercise, Universiti Kebangsaan Malaysia.

Bachtiar Djamily. 1985. *Ibrahim Yaacob: Pahlawan Nusantara*. Kuala Lumpur: Pustaka Budiman.

Bachtiar, Harsja Wardhana. 1981. Muhammad Yamin: Dari Desa ke Indonesia Raya. In *Imej dan Cita-Cita: Kertas Kerja Hari Sastera 1980,* pp. 191–211. Kuala Lumpur: Dewan Bahasa dan Pustaka.

Barlow, H.S. 1995. *Swettenham*. Kuala Lumpur: Southdene.

Barthes, Roland. 1988 [1968]. The Death of the Author. In *Modern Criticism and Theory: A Reader,* edited by David Lodge, pp. 167–172. London: Longman.

Bastin, John. 1964. Introduction: Sir Richard Winstedt and His Writings. In *Malayan and Indonesian Studies: Essays Presented to Sir Richard Winstedt on His Eighty-Fifth Birthday*, edited by John Bastin and R. Roolvink, pp. 1–23. London: Oxford University Press.

Blackburn, Kevin and Zong Lun Wu. 2019. *Decolonizing the History Curriculum in Malaysia and Singapore*. London and New York: Routledge.

Bourdieu, Pierre. 1977. Cultural Reproduction and Social Reproduction. In *Power and Ideology in Education*, edited by J. Karabel and A.H. Hasley, pp. 487–511. New York: Oxford University Press.

Bourdieu, Pierre, and Passeron, Jean Claude. 1990 [1977]. *Reproduction in Education, Society and Culture*. London: Sage Publications.

Burhanuddin Al Helmy. 1980 [1946]. Perjuangan Kita. In *Dr. Burhanuddin Al Helmy: Politik Melayu dan Islam*, edited by Kamarudin Jaffar, pp. 29–60. Kuala Lumpur: Yayasan Anda.

Burhanuddin Al Helmy. 1980 [1954]. Falsafah Kebangsaan Melayu. In *Dr. Burhanuddin Al Helmy: Politik Melayu dan Islam*, edited by Kamarudin Jaffar, pp. 65–122. Kuala Lumpur: Yayasan Anda.

Burns, P.L. 1971. Introduction. In *Papers on Malay Subjects*, edited by R. J. Wilkinson, selected and introduced by P. L. Burns, pp. 1–10. Kuala Lumpur: Oxford University Press.

Buyong Adil. 1951 [1934]. *Sejarah Alam Melayu, penggal IV*. Singapore: Malaya Publishing House, Limited.

Buyong Adil. 1952 [1940]. *Sejarah Alam Melayu, penggal V*. Kuala Lumpur: Di-Caxton Press, Limited.

Buyong Adil. 1956. Kenangan kepada Sultan Idris Training College. In *Album Kenangan 1955–56, Sultan Idris Training College*, pp. 12–17. Tanjung Malim: Sultan Idris Training College.

Buyong Adil. 1983. *Perjuganan Orang Melayu Menentang Penjajahan: Abad 15–19.* Kuala Lumpur: Dewan Bahasa dan Pustaka.

Chatterjee, Partha. 1986. *Nationalist Thought and the Colonial World: A Derivative Discourse?* London: Zed Books.

Chatterjee, Partha. 1993. *The Nation and Its Fragments: Colonial and Postcolonial Histories.* Princeton: Princeton University Press.

Cheah Boon Kheng. 1979. The Japanese Occupation of Malaya, 1941–1945: Ibrahim Yaacob and the Struggle for Indonesia Raya. *Indonesia* 28: 85–120.

Cheah Boon Kheng. 1992. *From PKI to the Comintern, 1924–1941: The Apprenticeship of the Malayan Communist Party.* Ithaca: Southeast Asia Program, Cornell University.

Cheah Boon Kheng. 1997. Writing Indigenous History in Malaysia: A Survey on Approaches and Problems. *Crossroads: An Interdisciplinary Journal of Southeast Asian Studies* 10 (2): 33–81.

Cheah Boon Kheng. 2002. *Malaysia: The Making of a Nation.* Singapore: Institute of Southeast Asian Studies.

Cheah Boon Kheng. 2003. Ethnicity, Politics, and History Textbook Controversies in Malaysia. *American Asian Review* 21 (4): 229–252.

Cheah Boon Kheng. 2007. New Theories and Challenges in Malaysian History. In *New Perspectives and Research on Malaysian History*, edited by Cheah Boon Kheng, pp. 119–145. Kuala Lumpur: The Malaysian Branch of Royal Asiatic Society.

Cheah Boon Kheng. 2012 [1983] *Red Star over Malaya: Resistance and Social Conflict during and after the Japanese Occupation, 1941–1946*, fourth edition. Singapore: NUS Press.

Chelliah, D.D. 1960 [1947]. *A History of the Educational Policy of the Straits Settlements with Recommendations for a New System Based on Vernaculars.* Singapore: G. H. Kiat.

Choy Chee Meh nee Lum et al. 1995. History of the Malaysian Branch of the Royal Asiatic Society, based on an academic thesis by Choy Chee Meh nee Lum, 1984, edited and updated by others. *Journal of the Malaysian Branch of the Royal Asiatic Society* 68 (2): 81–148.

Cohn, Bernard S. 1996. *Colonialism and Its Forms of Knowledge: The British in India.* Princeton: Princeton University Press.

Collins, James T. 2018 [1996]. *Malay, World Language: A Short History*, third edition. Kuala Lumpur: Dewan Bahasa dan Pustaka.

Crawfurd, John. 1967 [1820]. *History of the Indian Archipelago: Containing an Account of the Manners, Arts, Languages, Religions, Institutions, and Commerce of Its Inhabitants*, 3 vols. London: Frank Cass.

Dussek, O.T. 1948 [1930]. The Preparation and Work of Rural School Teachers in Malaya. In *Education in Malaya: Being Articles Reprinted from "Oversea Education" (published by The Colonial Office), 1930–1942, and 1946*, pp. 19–23. Kuala Lumpur: The Government Press.

Emmanuel, Mark. 2010. Viewspapers: The Malay Press of the 1930s. *Journal of Southeast Asian Studies* 41 (1):1–20.

Emerson, Rupert. 1964 [1937]. *Malaysia: A Study of Direct and Indirect Rule.* Kuala Lumpur: University of Malaya Press.

Ensiklopedia Sejarah dan Kebudayaan Melayu, second edition, 4 vols. 1999. Kuala Lumpur: Dewan Bahasa dan Pustaka.

Farish A. Noor. 2002. *The Other Malaysia: Writings on Malaysia's Subaltern History*. Kuala Lumpur: Silverfish Books.

Farish A. Noor. 2004. *Islam Embedded: The Historical Development of the Pan-Malaysian Islamic Party PAS (1951–2003)*, 2 vols. Kuala Lumpur: Malaysian Sociological Research Institute.

Fernandez, Callistus. 1999. Colonial Knowledge, Invention and Reinvention of Malay Identity in Pre-Independence Malaya: A Retrospect. *Akademika* 55: 39–59.

Firdaus Haji Abdullah. 1985. *Radical Malay Politics: Its Origins and Early Development*. Petaling Jaya: Pelanduk Publications.

Freedman, Maurice. 1988. Evolution, Social and Cultural. In *The Fontana Dictionary of Modern Thought*, edited by Alan Bullock and Oliver Stallybrass, p. 292. London: Fontana.

Funston, N.J. 1980. *Malay Politics in Malaysia: A Study of the United Malays National Organisation and Party Islam*. Kuala Lumpur: Heinemann Educational Books (Asia).

Gill, Ranjit. 1990. *Of Political Bondage: An Authorized Biography of Tunku Abdul Rahman, Malaysia's First Prime Minister and His Continuing Participation in Contemporary Politics*. Singapore: Sterling Corporate Services.

Goffman, Erving. 1961. *Asylums: Essays on the Social Situation of Mental Patients and Other Inmates*. New York: Anchor Books.

Gopinathan, S. 1989. University Education in Singapore: The Making of a National University. In *From Dependence to Autonomy: The Development of Asian Universities*, edited by Philip G. Altbach and Viswanathan Selvaratnam, pp. 207–224. Dordrecht: Kluwer Academic Press.

Gullick, J.M. 1967. *Malaysia and Its Neighbours*. London: Routledge & Kegan Paul.

Gullick, J.M. 1992. *Rulers and Residents: Influence and Power in the Malay States, 1870–1920*. Singapore: Oxford University Press.

Gullick, J.M. 1998. A History of Malayan History (to 1939). *Journal of the Malaysian Branch of the Royal Asiatic Society* 71 (2): 91–102.

Harper, T.N. 1999. *The End of Empire and the Making of Malaya*. Cambridge: Cambridge University Press.

Heussler, Robert. 1981. *British Rule in Malaya: The Malayan Civil Service and Its Predecessors, 1867–1942*. Westport, Connecticut: Greenwood Press.

Hirschman, Charles. 1986. The Making of Race in Colonial Malaya: Political Economy and Racial Ideology. *Sociological Forum* 1 (2): 330–361.

Hirschman, Charles. 1987. The Meaning and Measurement of Ethnicity in Malaysia: An Analysis of Census Classifications. *The Journal of Asian Studies* 46 (3): 555–581.

Hirschman, Charles. 2004. The Origins and Demise of the Concept of Race. *Population and Development Review* 30 (3): 385–415.

Hooker, Virginia Matheson. 2000. *Writing a New Society: Social Change through the Novel in Malay*. Honolulu: University of Hawai'i Press.

Ibrahim Haji Yaacob. 1941. *Melihat Tanah Air*. Kota Bharu: Matbaah Al-Ismailiah.

Ibrahim Haji Yaacob. 1951. *Nusa dan Bangsa Melayu*. Djakarta (?): N. V. Alma'arif.

Ibrahim Yaacob. 1957. *Sekitar Malaya Merdeka*. Jakarta: Kesatuan Malaya Merdeka, Bhg. Penerangan.

Ibrahim Haji Yaakub. 1975 [1941]. *Melihat Tanah Air*, second edition. Kuantan: Percetakan Timur.

Iguchi Yufu. 2001. The Colonial Look in the Papers on Malay Subjects. *Gengo Chiiki Bunka Kenkyu* (Tokyo University of Foreign Studies) 7: 39–49.

Ishak Haji Muhammad. 1997. *Memoir Pak Sako: Putera Gunung Tahan*. Bangi: Penerbit Universiti Kebangsaan Malaysia.

Ishak Saat. 2011. *Radikalisme Melayu Perak 1945–1970*. Penang: Penerbit Universiti Sains Malaysia.

Ishikawa Noboru. 2010. *Between Frontiers: Nation and Identity in a Southeast Asian Borderland*. Singapore: NUS Press; and Athens: Ohio University Press.

Ismail Hussein. 1993. *Antara Dunia Melayu dengan Dunia Kebangsaan*. Bangi: Penerbit Universiti Kebangsaan Malaysia.

Itagaki Yoichi. 1962. Some Aspects of the Japanese Policy for Malaya under the Occupation with Special Reference to Nationalism. In *Papers on Malaysian History*, edited by K.G, Toregonning, pp. 256–267. Singapore: Malaya Publishing House.

Jones, Matthew. 2002. *Conflict and Confrontation in South East Asia, 1961–1965*. Cambridge: Cambridge University Press.

Kahn, Joel S. 2006. *Other Malays: Nationalism and Cosmopolitanism in the Modern Malay World*. Singapore: NUS Press.

Khasnor Johan. 1984. *The Emergence of the Modern Malay Administrative Elite*. Singapore: Oxford University Press.

Khasnor Johan. 1996. *Educating the Malay Elite, The Malay College Kuala Kangsar, 1905–1941*. Kuala Lumpur: Pustaka Antara.

Khasnor Johan. 2005. *MCKK 1905–2005: Leadership: But What's Next?* Shah Alam: Marshall Cavendish.

Khoo Boo Teik. 1995. *Paradoxes of Mahathirism: An Intellectual Biography of Mahathir Mohamad*. Kuala Lumpur: Oxford University Press.

Khoo Kay Kim. 1979a. Local Historians and the Writing of Malaysian History in the Twentieth Century. In *Perceptions of the Past in Southeast Asia*, edited by Anthony Reid and David Marr, pp. 299–311. Singapore: Heinemann Educational Books (Asia).

Khoo Kay Kim. 1979b. Ibrahim Yaakob dan KMM. *Widya* 21 (May): 34–41.

Khoo Kay Kim. 1991. *Malay Society: Transformation and Democratisation*. Subang Jaya: Pelanduk Publications.

Kratoska, Paul H., ed. 1983. *Honourable Intentions: Talks on the British Empire in South-East Asia Delivered at the Royal Colonial Institute, 1874–1928*. Singapore: Oxford University Press.

Kratoska, Paul H. 2018 [1998]. *The Japanese Occupation of Malaya and Singapore, 1941–1945: A Social and Economic History*, second edition. Singapore: NUS Press.

Liow, Joseph and Bhubhindar Singh. 2004. The Rise and Demise of Melayu Raya: Racialization, Indigenisation and Politicization of Colonial Knowledge in the Pre-War Indo-Malay World. Paper presented at the annual meeting of the International Studies Association, Montreal, Canada, 17 March 2004.

Liow Chinyong, Joseph. 2005. *The Politics of Indonesia-Malaysia Relations: One Kin, Two Nations.* London and New York: Routledge.

Liow Chinyong, Joseph. 2015 [1995]. *Dictionary of the Modern Politics of Southeast Asia*, fourth edition. London and New York: Routledge.

Loh Fook Seng, Philip. 1975. *Seeds of Separatism: Educational Policy in Malaya, 1874–1940.* Kuala Lumpur: Oxford University Press.

Lomas, M. 1948 [1940]. The Malay Women's Training College, Malacca. In *Education in Malaya: Being Articles Reprinted from "Oversea Education" (published by The Colonial Office), 1930–1942, and 1946*, pp. 123–126. Kuala Lumpur: The Government Press.

Mackie, J.A.C. 1974. *Konfrontasi: The Indonesian-Malaysian Dispute, 1963–1966.* Kuala Lumpur: Oxford University Press.

Mahathir Mohamad. 1993 [1991]. Malaysia: The Way Forward. In *Malaysia's Vision 2020: Understanding the Concept, Implications and Challenges*, edited by Ahmad Sarji Abdul Hamid, pp. 403–420. Petaling Jaya: Pelanduk Publications.

Mahathir Mohamad. 1997 [1991]. UMNO ke Arah Abad ke-21 (Ucapan di Perhimpunan Agung UMNO, Dewan Merdeka, Pusat Dagangan Dunia Putra, Kuala Lumpur, pada 8, 9 dan 10 November 1991). In *Amanat Presiden: Landasan bagi Pembangunan Banga dan Negara*, vol. 2, compiled by Wan Mohd. Mahyiddin and Haji Nik Mustaffa Yusof, pp. 506–525. Shah Alam: Penerbit Fajar Bakti.

Maier, Hendrik M.J. 1988. *In the Center of Authority: The Malay Hikayat Merong Mahawangsa.* Ithaca: Southeast Asia Program, Cornell University.

Malay College, 1905–1965. 1965. Singapore and Kuala Lumpur: The Straits Times Press.

Mandal, Sumit. 2004. Transethnic Solidarities, Racialisation and Social Equality. In *The State of Malaysia: Ethnicity, Equity and Reform*, edited by Edmund Terrence Gomez, pp. 49–78. London and New York: RoutledgeCurzon.

Marsden, William. 1986 [1811]. *The History of Sumatra*, a reprint of the third edition introduced by John Bastin. Singapore: Oxford University Press.

Matheson, Virginia. 1979. Concepts of Malay Ethos in Indigenous Malay Writings. *Journal of Southeast Asian Studies* X (2): 351–371.

Maxwell, George. 1983 [1927] Some Problems of Education and Public Health in Malaya. In *Honourable Intentions: Talks on the British Empire in South-East Asia delivered at the Royal Colonial Institute, 1874–1928*, edited by Paul H. Kratoska, pp. 401–422. Singapore: Oxford University Press.

Maznah Mohamad. 2011. Like a Shady Tree Swept by the Windstorm: Malays in Dissent. In *Melayu: The Politics, Poetics and Paradoxes of Malayness*, edited by Maznah Mohamad and Syed Muhd. Khairudin Aljunied, pp. 34–67. Singapore: NUS Press.

McIntyre, Angus. 1973. The "Greater Indonesia" Idea of Nationalism in Malaya and Indonesia. *Modern Asian Studies* 7 (1): 75–83.

MCOBA (The Malay College Old Boys Association), ed. 2004. *Malay College: Impressions.* Kuala Lumpur: Utusan Publications & Distributors.

Milner, A.C. 1992. 'Malayness': Confrontation, Innovation and Discourse. In *Looking in Odd Mirrors: The Java Sea*, edited by V.J.H. Houben, H.M.J. Maier and W. van der Molen, pp. 43–59. Leiden: Rijksuniversiteit.

Milner, Anthony. 2002 [1995]. *The Invention of Politics in Colonial Malaya*, second edition. Cambridge: Cambridge University Press.

Milner, Anthony. 2005. Historians Writing Nations: Malaysian Contests. In *Nation-Building: Five Southeast Asian Histories*, edited by Wang Gungwu, pp. 117–161. Singapore: Institute of Southeast Asian Studies.

Milner, Anthony. 2008. *The Malays*. Chichester: Wiley-Blackwell.

Milner, Anthony. 2011. Localizing the Bangsa Melayu. In *Bangsa and Umma: Development of People-grouping Concepts in Islamized Southeast Asia*, edited by Yamamoto Hiroyuki, Anthony Milner, Kawashima Midori and Arai Kazuhiro, pp. 17–36. Kyoto: Kyoto University Press.

Milner, Anthony and Helen Ting. 2014. Race and Its Competing Paradigms: A Historical Review. In *Transforming Malaysia: Dominant and Competing Paradigms*, edited by Anthony Milner, Abdul Rahman Embong and Tham Siew Yean, pp. 18–58. Singapore: Institute of Southeast Asian Studies.

Mohamed Noordin Sopiee. 1973. The Advocacy of Malaysia – before 1961. *Modern Asian Studies* 7 (4): 717–732.

Mohamed Noordin Sopiee. 1974. *From Malayan Union to Malaysia Separation: Political Unification in the Malaysia Region 1945–1965*. Kuala Lumpur: Penerbit Universiti Malaya.

Mohamed Salleh Lamry. 2006. *Gerakan Kiri Melayu dalam Perjuangan Kemerdekaan*. Bangi: Penerbit Universiti Kebangsaan Malaysia.

Mohd. Taib Othman. 1966. *The Language of Editorials in Malay Vernacular Newspapers up to 1941: A Study in the Development of the Malay Language in Meeting New Needs*. Kuala Lumpur: Dewan Bahasa dan Pustaka.

Muhammad Ghazali Shafie. 1998a. *Malay Nationalism and Globalisation*. Bangi: Penerbit Universiti Kebangsaan Malaysia.

Muhammad Ghazali Shafie. 1998b. *Ghazali Shafie's Memoir on the Formation of Malaysia*. Bangi: Penerbit Universiti Kebangsaan Malaysia.

Muhammad Ikmal Said. 1992. Ethnic Perspective of the Left in Malaysia. In *Fragmented Vision: Culture and Politics in Contemporary Malaysia*, edited by Joel S. Kahn and Francis Loh Kok Wah, pp. 254–281. Sydney: Allen and Unwin.

Muhammad Yamin. 1959. *Naskah Persiapan Undang-Undang Dasar 1945*, Vol. 1. (n.p.): Jajasan Prapantja.

Muhammad Yusuf Harun. 1982. Abdulhadi Bin Haji Hassan. In *Melaka dan Sejarahnya*, edited by Khoo Kay Kim, pp. 127–131. Melaka: Persatuan Sejarah Malaysia Cawangan Melaka.

Mustapha Hussain. 1979. Kesatuan Melayu Muda dan Perjuangannya. *Dewan Masyarakat* 17 (11) (November 1979): 36–37.

Mustapha Hussain. 1999. *Memoir Mustapha Hussain: Kebangkitan Nasionalisme Melayu Sebelum UMNO*. Kuala Lumpur: Dewan Bahasa dan Pustaka.

Nabir Haji Abdullah. 1976. *Maahad Il Ihya Assyariff Gunung Semanggol, 1934–1959*. Bangi: Jabatan Sejarah, Universiti Kebangsaan Malaysia.

Nagata, Judith A. 1974. What is a Malay?: Situational Selection of Ethnic Identity in a Plural Society. *American Ethnologist* 1(2): 331–350.

Nagata, Judith A. 1979. *Malaysian Mosaic: Perspective from a Poly-Ethnic Society*. Vancouver: University of British Columbia Press.

Nagata, Judith. 2011. Boundaries of Malayness: "We Have Made Malaysia: Now It is Time to (Re)Make the Malays but Who Interprets the History?" In *Melayu: The Politics, Poetics and Paradoxes of Malayness*, edited by Maznah Mohamad and Syed Muhd. Khairudin Aljunied, pp. 3–33. Singapore: NUS Press.

Nagatsu Kazufumi. 2001. Pirates, Sea Nomads or Protectors of Islam?: A Note on "Bajau" Identifications in the Malaysian Context. *Asian and African Area Studies* 1: 212–230.

Nair, Sheila. 1999. Colonial "Others" and Nationalist Politics in Malaysia. *Akademika* 54: 55–79.

Nasution, A.H. 1977. *Sekitar Perang Kemerdekaan Indonesia, jilid 1: Proklamasi*. Bandung: DISJARAH-AD and Penerbit Angkasa Bandung.

Nicholas, Colin. 2000. *The Orang Asli and the Contest for Resources: Indigenous Politics, Development and Identity in Peninsular Malaysia*. Kuala Lumpur: Center for Orang Asli Concerns.

Nik Anuar Nik Mahmud, Muhammad Haji Salleh and Abd. Ghapa Harun. 2011. *Biografi Tun Abdul Razak: Negarawan dan Patriot*. Bangi: Penerbit Universiti Kebangsaan Malaysia.

Nobuta Toshihiro. 2009. *Living on the Periphery: Development and Islamization among the Orang Asli in Malaysia*. Kyoto: Kyoto University Press.

Ongkili, James P. 1985. *Nation-building in Malaysia 1946–1974*. Singapore: Oxford University Press.

Ooi, Keebeng. 2003. Three-Tiered Social Darwinism in Malaysian Ethnographic History. *Southeast Asian Studies* 41 (2): 162–179.

Osborne, Milton E. 1964. *Singapore and Malaysia*. Ithaca: Southeast Asia Program, Department of Far Eastern Studies, Cornell University.

Poulgrain, Greg. 1998. *The Genesis of Konfrontasi: Malaysia, Brunei and Indonesia 1945–1965*. London: C. Hurst.

Purdom, N. 1948 [1931]. Needlework and Craft Instruction in Malay Girls' Schools. In *Education in Malaya: Being Articles Reprinted from "Oversea Education" (published by The Colonial Office), 1930–1942, and 1946*, pp. 33–37. Kuala Lumpur: The Government Press.

PUTERA-AMCJA (Pusat Tenaga Ra'ayat and All-Malaya Council of Joint Action). 1947. *The People's Constitutional Proposals for Malaya*. Kuala Lumpur: Ta Chong Press.

Puthucheary, Mavis. 1978. *The Politics of Administration: The Malaysian Experience*. Kuala Lumpur: Oxford University Press.

Quinton, Anthony. 1988. Positivism. In *The Fontana Dictionary of Modern Thought*, second edition, edited by Alan Bullock, Oliver Stallybrass and Stephen Trombley, p.669. London: Fontana Press.

Ramlah Adam. 1991. *Maktab Melayu Melaka, 1900–1922*. Kuala Lumpur: Dewan Bahasa dan Pustaka.

Ramlah Adam. 1992. *Dato' Onn Ja'afar: Pengasas Kemerdekaan*. Kuala Lumpur: Dewan Bahasa dan Pustaka.

Ramlah Adam. 1994. *Ahmad Boestamam: Satu Biografi Politik*. Kuala Lumpur: Dewan Bahasa dan Pustaka.

Ramlah Adam. 1996. *Burhanuddin Al-Helmy: Suatu Kemelut Politik*. Kuala Lumpur: Dewan Bahasa dan Pustaka.

Ramlah Adam. 1999. *Sumbanganmu Dikenang*. Kuala Lumpur: Dewan Bahasa dan Pustaka.

Ramlah Adam. 2004a. *Gerakan Radikalisme di Malaysia (1938–1965)*. Kuala Lumpur: Dewan Bahasa dan Pustaka.

Ramlah Adam. 2004b. *Biografi Politik Tunku Abdul Rahman Putra*. Kuala Lumpur: Dewan Bahasa dan Pustaka.

Ramlah Adam; Shakila Parween Yacob; Abdul Hakim Samuri; and Muslimin Fadzil. 2003. *Sejarah Tingkatan 5*. Kuala Lumpur: Dewan Bahasa dan Pustaka.

Ranjit Singh, D.S. 1998. British Proposals for a Dominion of Southeast Asia, 1943–1957. *Journal of the Malaysian Branch of the Royal Asiatic Society* 71 (1): 27–40.

Rashid Maidin. 2005. *Memoir Rashid Maidin: Daripada Perjuangan Bersenjata kepada Perdamaian*. Petaling Jaya: Strategic Information Research Development.

Ratnam, K.J. and Milne, R.S. 1967. *The Malayan Parliamentary Election of 1964*. Singapore and Kuala Lumpur: University of Malaya Press.

Reid, Anthony. 1979. The Nationalist Quest for an Indonesian Past. In *Perceptions of the Past in Southeast Asia*, edited by Anthony Reid and David Marr, pp. 281–298. Singapore: Heinemann Educational Books (Asia).

Reid, Anthony. 2004. Understanding Melayu (Malay) as a Source of Diverse Modern Identities. In *Contesting Malayness: Malay Identity Across Boundaries*, edited by Timothy P. Barnard, pp. 1–24. Singapore: Singapore University Press.

Reid, Anthony. 2009. *Imperial Alchemy: Nationalism and Political Identity in Southeast Asia*. Cambridge: Cambridge University Press.

Reid, Anthony and Marr, David, eds. 1979. *Perceptions of the Past in Southeast Asia*. Singapore: Heinemann Educational Books.

Ridely, Mark. 1988. Evolutionism. In *The Fontana Dictionary of Modern Thought*, edited by Alan Bullock and Oliver Stallybrass, pp. 292–293. London: Fontana.

Roff, William R. 1994 [1967]. *The Origins of Malay Nationalism*, second edition. Kuala Lumpur: Oxford University Press.

Roff, William R. 2009. *Studies on Islam and Society in Southeast Asia*. Singapore: NUS Press.

Roslan Saadon. 2009. *Gagasan Nasionalisme Melayu Raya: Pertumbuhan dan Perkembangan*. Shah Alam: Karisma Publications.

Rosnani Hashim. 2004 [1996]. *Educational Dualism in Malaysia: Implications for Theory and Practice*, second edition. Kuala Lumpur: The Other Press.

Rustam A. Sani. 1986 [1976]. Melayu Raya as a Malay 'Nation of Intent.' In *The Nascent Malaysian Society*, second edition, edited by H.M. Dahlan, pp. 25–38. Bangi: Penerbit Universiti Kebangsaan Malaysia.

Rustam A. Sani. 2008. *Social Roots of the Malay Left: An Analysis of the Kesatuan Melayu Muda*. Petaling Jaya: Strategic Information and Research Development Centre.

Sakai, Minako. 2009. Creating a New Centre in the Periphery of Indonesia: Sumatran Malay Identity Politics. In The Politics of the Periphery in Indonesia: Social and Geographical Perspectives, edited by Minako Sakai, Glenn Banks and John H. Walker, pp. 62–83. Singapore: NUS Press.

Sakai, Minako. 2010. Reviving Malay Connections in the Globalised Southeast Asia. In *Regional Minorities and Development in Asia*, edited by Huhua Cao and Elizabeth Morrel, pp. 121–136. London and New York: Routledge.

Salazar, Zeus A. 1998. *The Malayan Connection: Ang Pilipinas sa Dunia Melayu.* Quezon City: Palimbagan ng Lahi.

Sekretariat Dunia Melayu Dunia Islam. n.d. *Charter of the Malay and Islamic World Secretariat.* Melaka: Sekretariat Dunia Melayu Dunia Islam.

Selvaratnam, Viswanathan. 1989. Change amidst Continuity: University Development in Malaysia. In *From Dependence to Autonomy: The Development of Asian Universities*, edited by Philip G. Altbach and Viswanathan Selvaratnam, pp. 187–205. Dordrecht: Kluwer Academic Press.

Shaharom Husain. 1996. *Memoir Shaharom Husain: Selingkar Kenangan Abadi.* Bangi: Penerbit Universiti Kebangsaan Malaysia.

Shamsiah Fakeh. 2004. *Memoir Shamsiah Fakeh: Dari AWAS ke Rejimen Ke-10.* Bangi: Penerbit Universiti Kebangsaan Malaysia.

Shamsul A.B. 1996a. Debating about Identity in Malaysia: A Discourse Analysis. In *Mediating Identities in a Changing Malaysia*, edited by Zawawi Ibrahim, pp. 8–31, Special Issue of *Southeast Asian Studies* 34 (3).

Shamsul A.B. 1996b. The Construction and Transformation of a Social Identity: Malayness and Bumiputeraness Re-examined. *Journal of Asian and African Studies* 52: 15–33.

Shamsul A.B. 1996c. Nations-of-Intent in Malaysia. In *Asian Forms of the Nation*, edited by Stein Tonnesson and Hans Antlov, pp. 323–347. London: Curzon Press.

Shamsul A.B. 1997. The Economic Dimension of Malay Nationalism: The Socio-Historical Roots of the New Economic Policy and Its Contemporary Implications. *The Developing Economies* 35 (3): 240–261.

Shamsul A.B. 1999. Identity Contestation in Malaysia: A Comparative Commentary on "Malayness" and "Chineseness". *Akademika* 55: 16–37.

Shamsul A.B. 2003. The Malay World: The Concept of Malay Studies and National Identity Formation. In *Malaysia: Islam, Society and Politics*, edited by Virginia Hooker and Norani Othman, pp. 101–125. Singapore: Institute of Southeast Asian Studies.

Shamsul A.B. 2004. A History of an Identity, an Identity of a History: The Idea and Practice of "Malayness" in Malaysia Reconsidered. In *Contesting Malayness: Malay Identity Across Boundaries*, edited by Timothy P. Barnard, pp. 135–148. Singapore: Singapore University Press.

Sheppard, Mubin. 1969. Introduction. In *Start from Alif: Count from One, An Autobiographical Memoire*, written by Richard Winstedt, pp. vii–xiii. Kuala Lumpur: Oxford University Press.

Sheppard, Mubin. 1995. *Tunku: His Life and Times: The Authorized Biography of Tunku Abdul Rahman Putra Al-Haj.* Petaling Jaya: Pelanduk Publications (M).

Simandjuntak, B. 1969. *Malayan Federalism, 1945–1969: A Study of Federal Problems in a Plural Society.* Kuala Lumpur: Oxford University Press.

Simpson, J.A.; and Weiner, E.S.C. 1989. *The Oxford English Dictionary*, second edition, vol. IX. Oxford: Clarendon Press.

Smith, Anthony D. 1986. *The Ethnic Origins of Nations.* Oxford: Blackwell.

Smith, Anthony D. 2000. *The Nation in History: Historiographical Debates about Ethnicity and Nationalism.* Cambridge: Polity Press.

Soda Naoki. 2000. *Melayu Raya and Malaysia: Exploring Greater Malay Concepts in Malaya.* Tokyo: Setsutaro Kobayashi Memorial Fund, Fuji Xerox.

Soda Naoki. 2002. Indigenizing Colonial Knowledge: The Formation of Malay Identity in British Malaya. *IIAS Newsletter* 29: 28.

Soenarno, Radin. 1960. Malay Nationalism, 1896–1941. *Journal of Southeast Asian History* 1: 1–28.

Soh, Byungkuk. 1993. From Parochial to National Outlook: Malay Society in Transition, 1920–1948. Ph.D. dissertation, Ohio University.

Soh, Byungkuk. 2005. Ideals without Heat: Indonesia Raya and the Struggle for Independence in Malaya, 1920–1948. *Wacana* 7(1): 1–30.

Stevenson, Rex. 1975. *Cultivators and Administrators: British Educational Policy towards the Malays, 1875–1906*. Kuala Lumpur: Oxford University Press.

Stocking, George W., Jr. 1982 [1968]. *Race, Culture, and Evolution: Essays in the History of Anthropology*. Chicago: University of Chicago Press.

Stockwell, A.J. 1976. The Historiography of Malaysia: Recent Writings in English on the History of the Area since 1874. *The Journal of Imperial and Commonwealth History* 5(1): 82–110.

Stockwell, A.J. 1979. *British Policy and Malay Politics during the Malayan Union Experiment, 1942–1948*. Kuala Lumpur: The Malaysian Branch of the Royal Asiatic Society.

Stockwell, A.J. 1982. The White Man's Burden and Brown Humanity: Colonialism and Ethnicity in British Malaya. *Southeast Asian Journal of Social Sciences* 10 (1): 44–68.

Stockwell, A.J. 1998. Malaysia: The Making of a Neo-Colony? *The Journal of Imperial and Commonwealth History* 26(2): 138–156.

Stockwell, A.J., ed. 1995. *British Documents on the End of Empire, Series B. Volume 3: Malaya, Part 1: The Malayan Union Experiment 1942–1948*. London: Her Majesty's Stationery Office (HMSO).

Swettenham, F.A. 1983 [1896]. British Rule in Malaya. In *Honourable Intentions: Talks on the British Empire in South-East Asia delivered at the Royal Colonial Institute, 1874–1928*, edited by Paul H. Kratoska, pp. 170–211. Singapore: Oxford University Press.

Tan Liok Ee. 1988. *The Rhetoric of Bangsa and Minzu: Community and Nation in Tension, The Malay Peninsula, 1900–1955*, Working Paper No. 52. Clayton: Center of Southeast Asian Studies, Monash University.

Tan Tai Yong. 2008. *Creating "Greater Malaysia": Decolonization and the Politics of Merger*. Singapore: Institute of Southeast Asian Studies.

Taylor, M.C. 1948 [1939]. Domestic Science in Malay Girls' Schools in Perak. In *Education in Malaya: Being Articles Reprinted from "Oversea Education" (published by The Colonial Office), 1930–1942, and 1946*, pp. 105–109. Kuala Lumpur: The Government Press.

Thongchai Winichakul. 1994. *Siam Mapped: A History of the Geo-Body of a Nation*. Honolulu: University of Hawaii Press.

Ting, Helen. 2009. Malaysian History Textbook and the Discourse of *Ketuanan Melayu*. In *Race and Multiculturalism in Malaysia and Singapore*, edited by Daniel Goh, Philip Holden, Matilda Gabrielpillai and Khoo Gaik Cheng, pp. 36–52. London and New York: Routledge.

Ting, Helen. 2014a. The Battle over the Memory of the Nation: Whose National History? In *Controversial History Education in Asian Contexts*, edited by

Mark Baildon, Loh Kah Seng, Ivy Maria Lim, Gül İnanç and Junaidah Jaffar, pp. 41–57. London and New York: Routledge.

Ting, Helen. 2014b. Race Paradigm and Nation-Building in Malaysia. In *Transforming Malaysia: Dominant and Competing Paradigms*, edited by Anthony Milner, Abdul Rahman Embong and Tham Siew Yean, pp. 82–110. Singapore: Institute of Southeast Asian Studies.

Tomizawa Hisao. 2010. Old and New Aspects of Malayness in the Contemporary Dunia Melayu Movement. In *Tinta di Dada Naskhah: Melakar Jasa Dato' Dr. Abu Hassan Sham*, edited by Hashim Ismail, pp. 29–44. Kuala Lumpur: Jabatan Penerbitan Akademi Pengajian Melayu, Universiti Malaya.

Tsuboi Yuji. 2018. Alternative Vision of Malayan Decolonization from the Perspective of Muslim Intellectuals in Singapore. In *Islam and Cultural Diversity in Southeast Asia, Vol. 2: Perspectives from Indonesia, Malaysia, the Philippines, Thailand, and Cambodia*, edited by Tokoro Ikuya and Tomizawa Hisao, pp. 147–169. Fuchu: Research Institute for Languages and Cultures of Asia and Africa, Tokyo University of Foreign Studies.

Tunku Abdul Rahman Putra. 1987 [1986]. *Political Awakening*. Petaling Jaya: Pelanduk Publications.

Tunku Abdul Rahman Putra. 1997 [1955]. Menubuhkan Kerajaan Sendiri (Ucapan di Majlis Mesyuarat Agung UMNO di Bangunan Ibu Pejabat UMNO, Kuala Lumpur, pada 25 dan 26 Disember 1955). In *Amanat Presiden: Landasan bagi Pembangunan Banga dan Negara*, vol. 1, compiled by Wan Mohd. Mahyiddin and Haji Nik Mustaffa Yusof, pp. 252–266. Shah Alam: Penerbit Fajar Bakti.

Tunku Abdul Rahman Putra. 1997 [1961]. Rancangan Penubuhan Malaysia (Ucapan di Perhimpunan Agung Khas UMNO di Dewan Perbandaran, Kuala Lumpur, pada 4 November 1961). In *Amanat Presiden: Landasan bagi Pembangunan Banga dan Negara*, vol. 1, compiled by Wan Mohd. Mahyiddin and Haji Nik Mustaffa Yusof, pp. 394–401. Shah Alam: Penerbit Fajar Bakti.

Ungku Maimunah Mohd. Tahir. 1987. *Modern Malay Literary Culture: A Historical Perspective*. Singapore: Institute of Southeast Asian Studies.

UPSI (Universiti Pendidikan Sultan Idris). 2000. *SITC-UPSI: Pelopor Pendidikan Bangsa*. Petaling Jaya: Addison Wesley Longman Malaysia.

Vasil, R.K. 1980. *Ethnic Politics in Malaysia*. New Delhi: Radiant Publishers.

Vickers, Adrian. 2004. "Malay Identity": Modernity, Invented Tradition and Forms of Knowledge. In *Contesting Malayness: Malay Identity Across Boundaries*, edited by Timothy P. Barnard, pp. 25–55. Singapore: Singapore University Press.

Wade, Geoff. 2013. Operation Coldstore: A Key Event in the Creation of Modern Singapore. In *The 1963 Operation Coldstore in Singapore: Commemorating 50 Years*, edited by Poh Soo Kai, Tan Kok Fang and Hong Lysa, pp. 15–72. Petaling Jaya: Strategic Information and Research Development Centre.

Walford, Geoffrey. 1986. *Life in Public Schools*. London: Methuen.

Walker, R.P.S. 1948 [1940]. Arts and Crafts at a Training College in British Malaya. In *Education in Malaya: Being Articles Reprinted from "Oversea Education" (published by The Colonial Office), 1930–1942, and 1946*, pp. 127–130. Kuala Lumpur: The Government Press.

Wang Gungwu. 2005. Contemporary and National History: A Double Challenge. In

Nation-Building: Five Southeast Asian Histories, edited by Wang Gungwu, pp. 1–19. Singapore: Institute of Southeast Asian Studies.

Watson, C.W. 1996. The Construction of the Post-Colonial Subject in Malaysia. In *Asian Forms of the Nation*, edited by Stein Tonnesson and Hans Antlov, pp. 297–322. Richmond, Surrey: Curzon Press.

Wilkinson, R.J. 1903. *A Malay-English Dictionary.* Singapore: Kelly & Walsh.

Wilkinson, R.J. 1925 [1908]. Life and Customs, Part I: The Incidents of Malay Life. *Papers on Malay Subjects*, First Series. Kuala Lumpur: Government Press.

Wilkinson, R.J. 1932. Some Malay Studies. *Journal of the Malayan Branch of the Royal Asiatic Society* X (I): 67–137.

Wilkinson, R.J. 1971 [1923]. A History of the Peninsular Malays, with Chapters on Perak and Selangor. In *Papers on Malay Subjects*, edited by R. J. Wilkinson, selected and introduced by P. L. Burns, pp. 13–151. Kuala Lumpur: Oxford University Press.

Wilkinson, R.J. 1975 [1923]. *A History of the Peninsular Malays, with chapters on Perak & Selangor.* New York: AMS Press.

Willis, Paul. 1977. *Learning to Labour: How Working Class Kids Get Working Class Jobs.* Farnborough: Saxon House.

Winstedt, R.O. 1918. *Ilmu Alam Melayu, iaitu Sa-buah Kitab Pemimpin bagi Segala Guru-Guru Melayu.* Singapore: Methodist Publishing House.

Winstedt, R.O. 1923a. *Education in Malaya.* Singapore: Fraser and Neave.

Winstedt, R.O. 1923b. *Malaya: The Straits Settlements and the Federated and Unfederated Malay States.* London: Constable.

Winstedt, R.O. 1925. *Shaman Saiva and Sufi: A Study of the Evolution of Malay Magic.* London: Constable.

Winstedt, R.O. 1926 [1918] *Ilmu Alam Melayu, iaitu Sa-buah Kitab Pemimpin bagi Segala Guru-Guru Melayu*, third and revised edition. Singapore: Fraser & Neave.

Winstedt, R.O. 1927 [1918]. *Kitab Tawarikh Melayu*, fourth edition. Singapore: Fraser & Neave.

Winstedt, R.O. 1931. The Educational System of Malaya. In *Educational Year Book 1931*: 79–140.

Winstedt, R.O. 1935. A History of Malaya. *Journal of the Malayan Branch of the Royal Asiatic Society* XIII (I).

Winstedt, R.O. 1940. A History of Malay Literature. *Journal of the Malayan Branch of the Royal Asiatic Society* XVII (III): 1–141.

Winstedt, R.O. 1947. Obituary: Richard James Wilkinson, C. M. G. (1867–5 December 1941). *Journal of the Malayan Branch of the Royal Asiatic Society* XX (I): 143–144.

Winstedt, R.O. 1968. *A History of Malaya*, third edition revised. Kuala Lumpur: Marican & Sons.

Winstedt, R.O. 1969. *Start from Alif: Count from One, An Autobiographical Memoire.* Kuala Lumpur: Oxford University Press.

Wong Hoy Kee, Francis and Ee Tiang Hong. 1975 [1971] *Education in Malaysia*, second edition. Kuala Lumpur: Heinemann Educational Books (Asia).

Yazid Ahmad. 1948 [1931]. The Work of the Translation Bureau. In *Education in Malaya: Being Articles Reprinted from "Oversea Education" (published by*

The Colonial Office), 1930–1942, and 1946, pp. 31–32. Kuala Lumpur: The Government Press.

Yazid Ahmad. 1948 [1935]. Village School Gardens in Malaya. In *Education in Malaya: Being Articles Reprinted from "Oversea Education" (published by The Colonial Office), 1930–1942, and 1946*, pp. 53–55. Kuala Lumpur: The Government Press.

Yeo Kim Wah. 1982. *The Politics of Decentralization: Colonial Controversy in Malaya*. Kuala Lumpur: Oxford University Press.

Yoshino, Kosaku. 1992. *Cultural Nationalism in Contemporary Japan: A Sociological Enquiry*. London and New York: Routledge.

Zainal Abidin Ahmad. 1940. Modern Developments. *Journal of the Malayan Branch of the Royal Asiatic Society* XVII (III): 142–162.

Zainal Abidin Ahmad. 1941a. Recent Malay Literature. *Journal of the Malayan Branch of the Royal Asiatic Society* 19 (1): 1–20.

Zainal Abidin Ahmad. 1941b. Malay Journalism in Malaya. *Journal of the Malayan Branch of the Royal Asiatic Society* 19 (2): 244–250.

Zainuddin Abu. 1956. Sadikit Kenangan Untok Albam. In *Albam Kenangan 1955–56, Sultan Idris Training College*, 36–37. Tanjung Malim: Sultan Idris Training College.

Zulkipli Mahmud. 1979. *Warta Malaya: Penyambung Lidah Bangsa Melayu 1930–1941*. Bangi: Jabatan Sejarah, Universiti Kebangsaan Malaysia.

Japanese Sources

Boeicho Boeikenshujo Senshishitsu, ed. 1976. *Nansei Homen Rikugun Sakusen; Mare Ran'in no Boei* [Military Operations in the Southwest Region: The Defense of Malaya and the Netherlands East Indies]. Tokyo: Asagumo Shimbun Sha.

Boeicho Boeikenkyujo Senshibu, ed. 1985. *Shiryoshu Nanpo no Gunsei* [A Collection of Historical Records on Military Administration in the South Area]. Tokyo: Asagumo Shimbun Sha.

Fujiwara Iwaichi. 1966. *F Kikan* [F Agency]. Tokyo: Hara Shobo.

Hara Fujio. 1997. Kankyakusareta Daiikkai Marejin Keizai Kaigi [The First Malay Economic Conference of 1947]. *Kaigai Jijo* [Journal of World Affairs] 45 (1): 64–71.

Hara Fujio. 2009. *Mikan ni Owatta Kokusaikyoryoku: Maraya Kyosanto to Kyodaito*. [An Unfinished International Cooperation: Malayan Communist Party and Its Brother Parties]. Tokyo: Fukyo Sha.

Itagaki Yoichi 1988 [1968]. *Ajia tono Taiwa* [Dialogue with Asia], second edition. Tokyo: Ronso Sha.

Kato Tsuyoshi. 2017. "Kokka Eiyu" Izen: "Sokoku" no Soshutsu to Nazuke wo Megutte [Before 'National Heroes': Invention and Naming of 'Motherland']. In *"Kokka Eiyu" ga Utsusu Indonesia* [Nation and Heroes: The Dynamism of Modern Indonesian Society], edited by Yamaguchi Hiroko, Kaneko Masanori and Tsuda Koji, pp. 260–317, Matsumoto: Mokusei Sha.

Nagai Shin'ichi. 1978. *Gendai Mareshia Seiji Kenkyu* [Modern Malaysian Politics]. Tokyo: Institute of Developing Economies.

Oguma Eiji. 1995. *Tan'itsu Minzoku Shinwa no Kigen: "Nihonjin" no Jigazo no Keifu*

[The Origin of the Myth of Ethnic Homogeneity: The Genealogy of "Japanese" Self–Images]. Tokyo: Shin'yo Sha.

Suzuki Yoichi. 1998. Mareshia Koso no Kigen [The Origins of the Malaysia Plan]. *Jochi Ajia Gaku* [The Journal of Sophia Asian Studies] 16: 151–169.

Suzuki Yoichi. 2001. Gureta Mareshia, 1961–1967: Teikoku no Tasogare to Tonan Ajia Jin [Greater Malaysia: The End of Empire and Southeast Asians]. *Kokusai Seiji* [International Relations] 126: 132–149.

Suzuki Yoichi. 2017. Mareshia no Sosetsu ni tsuite: Hanto Boruneo Kyoryoku Kankei Keisei no Katei (1) [The Founding of Malaysia: Development of Co–operative Relationship between the Peninsular and Borneo Territories (1)]. *Shimonoseki Shiritsu Daigaku Ronshu* [Shimonoseki City University Review] 61(2): 37–81.

Suzuki Yoichi. 2018. Mareshia no Sosetsu ni tsuite: Hanto Boruneo Kyoryoku Kankei Keisei no Katei (2) [The Founding of Malaysia: Development of Co–operative Relationship between the Peninsular and Borneo Territories (2)]. *Shimonoseki Shiritsu Daigaku Ronshu* [Shimonoseki City University Review] 61(3): 125–180.

Tsuboi Yuji. 2004. Eiryoki Maraya ni okeru "Marejin" Wakugumi no Keisei to Imin no Ichizuke: Surangorushu no Punfuru wo Chushin ni [The Place of Immigrants in the Formation of the "Malay" Framework in British Malaya: The Case of Local Chiefs (*Penghulus*) in Selangor]. *Tonan Ajia: Rekishi to Bunka* [Southeast Asia: History and Culture] 33: 3–25.

Tsuboi Yuji. 2016. 1930 Nendai Shoto no Eiryo Maraya ni okeru Marejinsei wo meguru Ronso: Jawi Shinbun Majurisu no Bunseki kara [Controversies around Malayness in British Malaya during the 1930s: An Analysis of *Jawi* Newspaper *Majlis*]. *Tonan Ajia: Rekishi to Bunka* [Southeast Asia: History and Culture] 45: 5–24.

Tsurumi Yoshiyuki. 1981. *Marakka Monogatari* [A Story of Melaka]. Tokyo: Jiji Tsushin Sha.

Yamamoto Hiroyuki. 2006. *Datsushokuminchika to Nashonarizumu: Eiryo Kita Boruneo ni okeru Minzoku Keisei* [Decolonization and Nationalism: The Creation of Nations in British North Borneo]. Tokyo: University of Tokyo Press.

Index